Praise for *Complete Care*

"Guaranteed to help your beloved pet live a happier, healthier, fuller life. While this comprehensive and groundbreaking book presents cutting edge medical information, Shojai makes sure that it's proven and practical. Captivating true stories of 'successful agers' will motivate you to make sure you give your pets the best care possible."

—Dr. Marty Becker, resident veterinarian on *Good Morning America* and author of *The Healing Power of Pets*

"What a read! *Complete Care for Your Aging Cat* provides a practical, easy-to-read guide about health care for the aging cat. If you have an aging cat, this is a must-have book. It provides simple question-and-answer treatment of essentials of aging cats."

—Johnny D. Hoskins, DVM, Ph.D., and internist for older dogs and cats

Praise for Amy D. Shojai's *Complete Kitten Care*

"What baby expert Dr. Benjamin Spock did for people, kitten expert Amy Shojai has done for cats. . . . Everything you need to know to begin a blissful life with your kitty."

—Ed Sayres, president, San Francisco SPCA

"When you purchase a kitten, there should be four requirements by law: food, water dish, litter box, and this book."

—Steve Dale, *Pet Central* radio host and syndicated columnist

"Finally there's an informative, fun-filled guide to help us raise the best cats possible . . . filled with practical solutions, delightful stories, and the latest in kitten-care research."

—Bob Walker and Frances Mooney, authors of *The Cats' House* and *Cats into Everything*

"Covers kitten selection and care issues from A to Z . . . [a] thorough guide to getting your new baby off on the right paw."

—Carole Nelson Douglas, author of the Midnight Louie mysteries

"Another great book from Amy Shojai. . . . *Complete Kitten Care* should be as important to the owner as kitten food is to the kitten."

—Bob Vella, host of nationally syndicated *Pet Talk America* and author of *300 Incredible Things for Pet Lovers on the Internet*

continued . . .

"A wealth of information for first-time kitten owners. Amy Shojai shows you how to enjoy kittenhood."

> —Pam Johnson-Bennett, feline behaviorist and author of
> *Think Like a Cat* and *Psycho Kitty?*

"*Complete Kitten Care* will give you all the information you need to successfully grow your young feline. Informative and fun to read."

> —John C. Wright, Ph.D., certified applied animal behaviorist
> and author of *Is Your Cat Crazy?*

"A must-have for anyone considering kittenhood. . . . This book covers it all, from selecting a compatible kitten to handling emergencies, in a comprehensive and understandable manner."

> —H. Ellen Whiteley, DVM, author of
> *Understanding and Training Your Cat or Kitten*

"Thorough, entertaining and authoritative . . . a primer on the feline mystique, one that owners are sure to turn to again as their kitten grows into cathood."

> —Kim Thornton, president, Cat Writers' Association

"Amy Shojai has once again given the cat-loving public a concise, easy-to-understand book. I wish it could accompany every kitten going to a new home."

> —Kitty Angell, secretary, Cat Fanciers' Association Inc.

"Amy Shojai, the doyenne of pet care books, has come up with another winner. There's something here for everyone, whether you're a newbie at kitten care or an old pro. This book is an extremely comprehensive resource that will ensure selection of your perfect kitten and guide you in helping him become a happy, healthy, lifelong companion."

> —Sally Bahner, freelance writer and feline expert

Praise for Amy D. Shojai's *Pet Care in the New Century*

"Thoughtful, groundbreaking, and often inspirational . . . an important work that everyone who cares about pets and the future of veterinary medicine must read."

—Gina Spadafori, author of *Dogs for Dummies*

"A worthwhile addition to the library of dog and cat owners."
—*Bellwether, University of Pennsylvania Journal of Veterinary Medicine*

"Wow! After thirty-one years of practice, I am amazed that a person can create a book that covers all aspects of modern veterinary care. This book will prove to be an invaluable resource to companion animal lovers, students and the profession. I am in awe that Ms. Shojai has been able to pull so many people together in this work."

—Robert A. Taylor, DVM, seen on TV's *Emergency Vets*

"Amy Shojai delivers cutting-edge medicine with more flair than Emeril Lagasse, presenting the amazing array of astonishing advances in veterinary medicine. If you have a pet with heart disease, cancer, kidney failure—or any other serious medical condition—this easy to comprehend book is a credible place to start for your research. Shojai continues to rank among the most authoritative and thorough pet reporters."

—Steve Dale, syndicated newspaper columnist of *My Pet World*,
    and host of the radio programs *Animal Planet Radio* and *Pet Central*

Other NAL books by Amy D. Shojai

COMPLETE CARE FOR YOUR AGING DOG

COMPLETE KITTEN CARE

PET CARE IN THE NEW CENTURY:
Cutting-Edge Medicine for Dogs and Cats

COMPLETE CARE FOR

Your Aging Cat

AMY D. SHOJAI

NEW AMERICAN LIBRARY

New American Library
Published by New American Library, a division of
Penguin Group (USA) Inc., 375 Hudson Street, New York, New York 10014, U.S.A.
Penguin Books Ltd, 80 Strand, London WC2R 0RL, England
Penguin Books Australia Ltd, 250 Camberwell Road, Camberwell, Victoria 3124, Australia
Penguin Books Canada Ltd, 10 Alcorn Avenue, Toronto, Ontario, Canada M4V 3B2
Penguin Books (N.Z.) Ltd, Cnr Rosedale and Airborne Rds, Albany Auckland 1310, New Zealand

Penguin Books Ltd, Registered Offices: 80 Strand, London WC2R 0RL, England

First published by New American Library, a division of Penguin Group (USA) Inc.

First Printing, July 2003
1   3   5   7   9   10   8   6   4   2

(NAL) REGISTERED TRADEMARK—MARCA REGISTRADA

LIBRARY OF CONGRESS CATALOGING-IN-PUBLICATION DATA:

Shojai, Amy, 1956–
    Complete care for your aging cat / Amy D. Shojai.
        p.   cm.
    Includes bibliographical references (p.).
    ISBN 0-451-20788-2 (alk. paper)
    1. Cats.   2. Cats—Aging.   3. Cats—Diseases.   4. Veterinary geriatrics.
    I. Title.

SF447 .S47 2003
636.8'089897—dc21

                                                                    2002040988

Set in New Caledonia
Designed by Eve L. Kirch

Printed in the United States of America

For Bobbie Grant—

Missing you.

ACKNOWLEDGMENTS

Many individuals helped make this book a reality by sharing their expertise, help, and inspirational pet stories. My family, especially my husband, Mahmoud, and many wonderful friends remind me daily of what's truly important. You all know who you are—and I can't thank y'all enough.

My colleagues from the Dog Writers Association of America, Cat Writers' Association, and other "pet fanciers" never fail to inspire and impress me with their professionalism and support. I'd especially like to thank Deb Eldridge, Karen Henry, Lori May, Lynn Miller, Stacy Pober, Dusty Rainbolt, and Michelle West for sharing a few of their expert sources, especially for the E-lists and on-line health care contacts. Interestingly, this book was born at The Writer's BBS International Writers Community (http://www.writersbbs.com) when answering a question about book proposals gave me the idea. It seems that the Furry Muse strikes with inspiration in many places.

The many "Golden Moments" add so much to the book. Thank you to Lynn Alfino, Karen Allison, Wendy Braun, Barb Crandall, Andrea Dorn, Bonnie Cheak, Marc Gorelnik, Karen Holden, Chris Jevitz, Deborah Harding, Elizabeth Jones, Sandi Maltese, Judy Miley, Linda Moore, Linda Parker, Jennifer Schilling, Linda Weber, Michelle West, and Yasmine Galenorn for sharing these lovely stories about your special cats. I am touched by your generosity.

Heartfelt appreciation goes to the many veterinarians and pet professionals who allowed me to report their groundbreaking therapies for aging cats. I must also thank the countless veterinary schools and specialty colleges who put me in touch with these experts and pet owners, most particularly the American Veterinary Medical Association; Tania Banak of the University of Wisconsin—Madison; Chris Beuoy of the University of Illinois; Cheryl May of Kansas State University; Cynthia K. Ebbers of the American College of Veterinary Internal Medicine; Pat Edwards of Louisiana State University; Lynn Narlesky of the University of California—Davis; Lisa Sigler and Chuck Montera of the American College of Veterinary Surgeons; and Derek Woodbury of the American Animal Hospital Association. The wide range of experts you suggested helped give this book wonderful credibility—I am in your debt.

My appreciation goes to my editor, Ellen Edwards, who makes me look good. Meredith Bernstein, my agent, makes my pet-writing dream possible. I can't thank them enough.

Finally, this book wouldn't be possible without all the special cats that share our hearts—and the loving owners dedicated to providing the best care possible for their aging furry family members. Without you, this book would never have been written.

CONTENTS

PART TWO: A-TO-Z HEALTH CONCERNS

PART THREE: ADDITIONAL RESOURCES

The last decade has seen an evolution in the way people treat their cats. We have become a nation of cat lovers—there are more than 75 million cats kept in 35 percent of U.S. households, a number expected to rise to 84 million by the year 2005. No longer are cats thought of as mere pets. Seventy percent of owners consider their pets to be part of their family. Consequently, the health care extended to furry family members has been greatly expanded.

A lifetime of better care means cats today live longer, healthier lives than ever before. In the past fifty years the average life span of cats has tripled, and many now live into their late teens or early twenties. Susan Little, DVM, a feline specialist at Bytown Cat Hospital in Ottawa, Canada, says, "Having better nutrition and better health care for cats when they're younger means you see a lot more older cats."

Today, 40 percent of all pet owners have an animal aged seven or older. What has prompted this shift to an aged pet population? For one thing, cats used to spend most of their time outside with little or no supervision. Consequently, they became victims of extremes of temperature, malice from disgruntled neighbors or other pets, exposure to disease, and accidental injuries that cut their lives short.

For example, cats in the past were typically infested with a variety of disease-causing parasites, which also made them more susceptible to other illnesses and less able to recover. They ate a mixed diet of table scraps, commercial canned food, and whatever wildlife they could catch.

Viral diseases such as panleukopenia (cat distemper) and upper respiratory infections killed 50 percent or more of kittens before their first birthday. Repeated pregnancies without proper nutritional support also caused early death to the mother cats, and produced offspring that often were unable to survive past kittenhood. Roaming and squabbling over breeding issues resulted in debilitating fight injuries among adults, and if a cat's behavior became a problem, he was put to death. Being hit by a car was also a top cause of early feline death. Even when cats survived, owners often were unable or unwilling to treat the injuries, in part because cats were considered to be replaceable. Although a vaccine for cat distemper was available in 1965, veterinarians saw fewer than 25 percent of pet cats even once a year and most cats weren't protected. Many cats died of feline leukemia virus (FeLV), which was first identified in 1967, or from feline infectious peritonitis (FIP). There were no treatments or preventive medicine available. People simply put the injured or sick cat to sleep, then got another pet and didn't think much about it.

Until the last decade, few cats lived long enough to suffer from "old cat" conditions such as arthritis or hyperthyroidism. Those that did were rarely treated, either because owners weren't interested, or the veterinary community hadn't yet developed the ability to diagnose and treat such conditions on a routine basis.

Today, cats are living longer primarily because owners are more knowledgeable and take better care of them, says Steven L. Marks, BVSc, a surgeon and internist at Louisiana State University. Most pet cats live most of the time inside the house with their human family. Many cats are exclusively indoor pets. And if a behavior problem develops, instead of replacing the cat, owners seek help to correct the problem.

Cats are also living longer because better veterinary treatments are now available, and are routinely sought by owners. Cats regularly receive preventive medications to guard against deadly pests such as heartworms, intestinal parasites, ticks, and fleas. Palatable and nutritious cat foods support the animal's ability to develop healthy bones, muscles, and immune system during all life stages—kitten growth, reproduction, adult maintenance, and senior years. Regular cat foods are now designed to prevent the most common type of urinary stone, and also contain the proper amounts of essential nutrients, such as taurine, which has virtually eliminated a type of heart disease and blindness that used to affect cats.

Advances in preventive medicine saved the lives of countless felines when highly effective vaccinations for upper respiratory diseases were developed in the mid-1970s. The 1980s saw the introduction of better tests and vaccines for FeLV and FIP. Once feline immunodeficiency virus (FIV) was identified in 1987, accurate tests helped prevent the spread of the deadly virus. The first preventive FIV vaccine, released in 2002, shows great promise for saving even more cat lives.

Modern breeders study the science and genetics of reproduction to ensure that they produce healthy pedigreed animals that live longer. Spaying and neutering of pet cats at an early age has become the norm. This eliminates potential behavior problems as well as health issues such as breast cancer, and helps to increase the life span of cats.

Finally, cats are living longer because many pet owners choose to treat chronic conditions such as diabetes and hyperthyroidism, and are able and willing to offer a wide range of treatment and home care to keep aging cats healthy, happy, and active. Rather than car accidents or viruses that cut lives short, modern cats more typically succumb to diseases such as cancer, heart failure, or kidney failure that tend to strike after age ten. Modern treatments help maintain the cat's quality of life, and this better care translates into extra years of enjoyment that people can share with their special cats.

Extra years together mean the loving bond becomes even stronger. Older cats offer the benefits of steadiness, known behaviors and temperament, calm demeanor, attributes that kittens take years to develop. For instance, children may grow up with a special cat who serves as a playmate; then as the cat ages, he evolves into a best friend and confidant during the child's turbulent teenage years. A cat can be the comforting constant in families split apart by divorce, offering stress relief to both the adults and children involved.

A cat often accompanies his youthful owner to college, is a study buddy and party friend, and then travels down the aisle with him (sometimes literally!) when the owner begins his new family. A graying older cat often "adopts" human babies as her own, and then serves as playmate or a furry security blanket to the infant. Aging cats can also give a new purpose and fill the void left in the household when children leave for college, or when a loved one's death leaves the surviving spouse bereft.

USING THIS BOOK

Your veterinarian is an outstanding source of information about your aging cat's needs. Many times, though, he or she will have only a limited amount of time available during visits to answer your questions. That's why today's cat owners educate themselves about feline needs and arrive at the veterinary office armed with information gathered from research on the Internet, other pet owners, magazines, and books—such as *Complete Care for Your Aging Cat.*

You are reading these pages because you cherish the relationship you share with your older cat—whether he's an active seven-year-old or a mellow seventeen-year-old feline. *Complete Care for Your Aging Cat* offers not only great information about what physical and emotional changes may happen as your cat becomes a senior citizen, and how veterinary care can help; it also provides practical solutions to common problems, contact information for helpful products, educational and emotional support resources, and countless cost-saving home treatments.

Owners of aging cats typically are willing to provide the extra care that keeps pets happy and comfortable. Medical help is a big part of that. Because many people are interested in alternative care in their own lives, a discussion of the pros and cons of "holistic" and conventional "allopathic" medicine for cats is covered in the book. Both approaches offer great benefits for senior cats, and combination therapies—called complementary medicine—may provide the greatest help.

On the conventional side, veterinary specialists such as surgeons and oncologists usually cost more, but they offer cutting-edge care that many cat owners are willing to fund in order to keep their cats feeling good. In fact, the 2000–2001 survey by the American Animal Hospital Association (AAHA) indicates 74 percent of pet owners would go into debt for their pet's well-being. The cost of treatment is always a concern, though, so I've included sections titled "Bottom Line," which estimate how much a given diagnosis and therapy might cost.

More and more pet owners purchase health insurance for their cats because it can make treatments and care for chronic illnesses—even cutting-edge and alternative therapies—quite affordable for the average owner. A checklist for evaluating pet insurance is included to help you make informed decisions. Another potential cost-saving measure is home nursing care, which also can keep your cat happier and more comfortable during convalescence. The most common nursing techniques are described to help you decide which might be a good option for your situation.

Because of a lifetime of good care, many aging cats stay healthy throughout their golden years and won't require anything but routine veterinary care. That makes it even more important for owners to know how to be good partners in their cat's good health. After all, you live with your cat all year long, you know him best, and you will be the first to recognize a problem and get help if something goes amiss.

Complete Care for Your Aging Cat offers practical ways to ensure a high level of enjoyment and happiness for both you and your cat, as he continues to age. It's important to understand how bones and muscles change with age, and that aging eyes and ears can influence behavior, for example. Senior cats often need help grooming themselves, and become less willing to walk up and down stairs. Providing a ramp, some comb time, and an extra litter box keeps everyone happy and prevents "accidents" that upset human and cat alike. Many owners of aging cats willingly rearrange their schedules to accommodate their pet—coming home for lunch to give a pill or special meal, for example. After all, it's what we do for our friends.

There are so many easy, simple, and inexpensive ways for you to keep an aging cat happy and healthy! This book provides guidelines to create your own "health report card" to keep track of normal versus warning signs, and learn when you can treat problems at home and when a veterinary visit is needed. It also includes all the latest research about how pet owners can maintain old-cat physical health by choosing the right nutrition, providing safe and effective exercise, using easy grooming tips, and making positive changes to the cat's home environment. Old cats may lose their sense of smell so that food is less appealing. Zapping the food in the microwave for 10 seconds may be all that's necessary to stimulate their flagging appetite.

As a cat ages, his social standing among the other pets in the household may change. That can be due to health issues, changes in his activity level, or reduced ability to hear and see. You can help him adjust to his new position and any physical limitations by using many of the tips offered in this book. Keeping the kitty soul healthy is equally important to quality of life, so you'll get ideas of ways to enrich your cat's emotional and mental health.

Throughout the book you'll find boxes with quick, helpful information to owners of aging cats. For example, "Comfort Zone" offers product suggestions that are particularly applicable to the well-being of senior cats. Look especially for "Golden Moments," heartwarming stories of real cats and their people who are continuing to enjoy life while dealing with old-pet concerns. Read how Zepp got a new kidney, Casey beat cancer, Rudy still "sees" what's important, and how Midgie's legacy of love lives on. If you're like me, you'll become a bit misty-eyed reading these inspirational stories that honor the love we share for our own cats.

A frank discussion of quality-of-life issues—your own and the cat's—is also covered. Every pet partnership is different, and you have to be sensitive to your family and to your cat as to when is the best time to end his life. Grief is a normal part of losing a special cat. I've suggested ways to validate grief, help yourself and your children through this process, and honor the memory of a special pet.

Don't forget to take a look at the resources in the appendices, which include veterinary associations, subscription E-mail lists related to specific senior-cat concerns, and contact information for the products mentioned earlier in the book. There's also a list of must-have home remedies, a glossary of terms, and information about the experts who were interviewed for this book. The credentials of the experts quoted in each chapter are mentioned there only briefly. Unless otherwise noted, all the "Dr." designations in the book refer to veterinarians. You or your veterinarian can contact these experts through the university or clinic with which they're associated to see if your cat might benefit from their help.

I hope you'll find this book to be a valuable resource for senior feline care that will benefit you, your cat, and your veterinarian. More than anything, *Complete Care for Your Aging Cat* is a celebration of the lifetime of love we share with our special pets. Today, pet owners have more and better options than ever before to ensure that they enjoy their cat's glorious golden years.

PART ONE

How Cats Age

CHAPTER 1

Defining "Old"

What is considered "old" for a cat? The question is complicated by the impact of genetics, environment, and individual characteristics. Consider human beings: one person may act, look, and feel "old" at sixty-five, while another sixty-five-year-old remains an active athlete with a youthful attitude and appearance. The same is true for cats.

"I think that actually varies a lot, and it's getting older every year," says Rhonda L. Schulman, DVM, an internist at the University of Illinois. "It used to be that eight was the major cutoff for the cat that was geriatric. Now we're moving to the point that's a prolonged middle age." The oldest cat on record was Granpaws Rex, a Sphynx cat who lived to the age of thirty-four.

A good definition of old age for an animal is the last 25 percent of his life span, says Sarah K. Abood, DVM, a clinical nutritionist at Michigan State University. However, since we can't predict what an individual cat's life span will be, the beginning of old age is a bit arbitrary. Certain families of cats may be longer lived than others, in the same way that some human families enjoy a much greater longevity than others. The life span of your cat's parents and grandparents is a good predictor of how long you can expect your cat to live. People who share their lives with pedigreed cats may be able to access this information through the cat's breeder.

The longevity of cats whose heritage is unknown is much more difficult to predict. Even when felines are "part" Siamese or Persian, for example, these felines may inherit the very worst, or the very best, of the parents.

The majority of pet cats are Domestic Shorthair or Domestic Longhair kitties of mixed ancestry, and the products of unplanned breeding. That by itself points to a poorer-than-average level of health for the parents, which in turn would be passed on to the kittens. Siblings within the same litter may have different fathers, and can vary greatly in looks, behavior, and health. When all is said and done, one should expect the random-bred cat-next-door kitty to be neither more nor less healthy than its pedigreed ancestors—as long as they all receive the same level of care and attention.

"If you get a kitten, it is very likely you will have this cat for the next fifteen to twenty years," says Dr. Abood. That means the last 25 percent of his life span would be after twelve to fifteen years. To simplify matters, most veterinarians consider cats to be "senior citizens" starting at about seven to eight years old, and geriatric at fourteen to fifteen.

Here's some perspective comparing cat age to human age. "The World Health Organization says that middle-aged folks are forty-five to fifty-nine years of age and elderly is sixty to seventy-four. They considered *aged* as being over seventy-five," says Debbie Davenport, DVM, an internist with Hill's Pet Nutrition. "If you look at cats of seven years of age as being *senior*, a parallel in human years would be about fifty-one years," she says. A geriatric cat at ten to twelve years of age would be equivalent to a seventy-year-old human.

Veterinarians used to concentrate their efforts on caring for young animals. When pets began to develop age-related problems, the tendency among American owners was to just get another pet. That has changed, and today people cherish their aged furry companions and want to help them live as long as possible.

Modern cats age seven and older can still live full, happy and healthy lives. Age is not a disease. Age is just age, says Sheila McCullough, DVM, an internist at University of Illinois. "There are a lot of things that come with age that can be managed successfully, or the progression delayed. Renal failure cats are classic examples." It's not unusual for cats suffering kidney failure to be diagnosed in their late teens or even early twenties. "I had a woman with a twenty-three-year-old cat who asked should she change the diet. I said, don't mess with success!" says Dr. McCullough. These days veterinarians often see still-healthy and vital cats of a great age. "I think if the cat lives to twenty-five years, I shouldn't be doing anything but saying hello," says Steven L. Marks, BVSc, an internist and surgeon at Louisiana State University. "If you've ever had a pet live that long, you want them *all* to live that long."

BENEFITS OF SENIOR PETS

There's nothing more endearing than a kitten. But they can also be non-stop dynamos, frustrating to predict and a magnet for trouble. Although kittens can be wonderful fun, nothing matches the deep bond you have developed with your old cat buddies over a period of years.

Mature cats have many advantages over kittens. Probably the biggest advantage is that together you have created a partnership, and already know each other and have adjusted to individual needs and foibles. All the hard work is done. She's been trained to scratch the scratching post and use the litter box. You trust her not to swing from the drapes or empty the potted palm while you're away. She's learned to wake you promptly at 6:45 for work, and meets you at the door each evening. She no longer climbs the Christmas tree or unrolls the toilet paper, and rearranges your sock drawer only if you're gone overnight and she's lonely. She stopped hiding the kids' stuffed animals, and settles for the toy squeaky mouse she's carried around like a teddy bear since you brought her home ten years ago. She reminds you when it's time for a pill and afternoon nap—for both of you. And she acts as if the new grandbaby is her own kitten, and showers the infant with attention, gentle play, and protective care—dropping favorite cat toys in the crib, and even putting up with toddler tail tugs with a patient feline purr. Countless children have learned to walk while reaching for the tempting tail of a feline friend.

In fact, one of the best ways to introduce young children to the positive aspects of cats is with a calm, patient adult animal. Parents already have their hands full dealing with infants and toddlers, and don't need the added stress of an in-your-face kitten. Children can share birthdays with the aging cat and still be relatively young when she enters her golden years.

It's not unusual for a young person to say that one special cat has *always* been a part of their life—and in times of family crises or emotional upset, the cat can ease the tension and help heal the pain simply by being there to pet and talk to. A broken heart, disagreements with siblings or parents, even physical or emotional trauma can all be helped by the mere presence of a cat that the child loves.

An older cat can be a stabilizing influence on children, teach them responsibility and empathy for other living creatures, and even help them make friends with their peers. For example, a child who is shy with other children because of a perceived disability often comes out of her shell when accompanied by a furry friend—the cat remains the focus of interaction rather than the child's "different" look or behavior. Older cats often are ideal for such relationships, because they aren't as active as younger cats, may be more patient, and have learned what to expect. There's a benefit to the old cat, too—playing and interacting with children keeps the kitty brain and body active and youthful.

The advantages of loving an older cat are not limited to children. Studies have shown that contact with cats offers great physical and emotional health benefits to people of all ages, from children and adolescents to adults and senior citizens.

Couples whose children have left for college and are recent empty nesters can receive great comfort from the presence of a furry companion. People of any age who lose a spouse to divorce or death—but particularly older owners—benefit greatly from a cat's nonjudgmental love. Petting a cat lowers the blood pressure, and caring for a cat gives owners a purpose to concentrate on beyond any hurt or pain they are suffering. Playing with and grooming the cat, shopping for litter and food, and giving medicine to an old kitty friend keeps people connected to the world and other people around them.

Old cats are often the companions of aging owners because that old pet has the same problems they do, says William Tranquilli, DVM, a professor and pain specialist at the University of Illinois. "They don't necessarily want a young pet; they want to do what they can to help their old buddy." They're willing to spend the money and often have more time to treat chronic disease to try to make the old animal more comfortable. And because the pets that we love are good for human health, just having a cat around can reduce the trips owners take to their own doctors. Some physicians recommend that heart attack survivors keep a pet, because it increases their rate of survival.

People whose human family members live far away become even more emotionally dependent on the cat. "I've met many elderly people whose cat has become the most important thing in their life. It's a family member, and it may be the only remaining family member," says Dr. Little. Of those pet owners who have a will, 27 percent have included provisions for their pets. Prolonging the cat's life touches on a host of social and emotional issues.

Cats who have spent a decade or more with us have learned what we like and expect—and we've learned to anticipate the senior cat's needs, likes, and dislikes. Over the span of years, we build and then enjoy a comfortable companionship together. Our aging pets share with us our life experiences, successes and failures, and joys and sorrows, and they represent milestones in our lives, says Signe Beebe, DVM, a veterinary acupuncturist and herbologist practicing in Sacramento. They may have celebrated with us when we graduated school, married, and had children or grandchildren—or comforted us when we divorced, retired, or lost a spouse. They have been there for us through everything. The more time we spend together, the greater our affection grows. Our compassion, love, and empathy for each other reach a depth that has no parallel in human existence.

"We share our secret souls with our pets in ways we wouldn't dare with another human being," says Dr. Wallace Sife, a psychologist and president of the Association for Pet Loss and Bereavement. "We're human beings, and love is love. Love for a pet is no different than love for another human being."

WHAT TO EXPECT

Pet owners relish spending time with their older cats. As the cat ages, chances are she'll need more medical care. The most common health problems of senior cats mirror those of aging humans. They include kidney disease, cancer, diabetes, hyperthyroidism, heart disease, arthritis, obesity, and dental disease. Cats are also prone to sensory loss—eyesight, hearing, and scent sense fade with age. A certain percentage of aging cats also develop behavioral changes that mimic those of human Alzheimer's patients, says Dr. Little.

"People need to recognize that older animals get diseases more frequently, and most of these diseases are progressive," says Dr. Marks. Problems such as kidney failure or hyperthyroid disease will not go away, but pets *can* live with these conditions and enjoy a happy life for months to years after the diagnosis. "I think one of the strategies associated with the senior pet is making the owners aware of what realistic goals are for these particular diseases," says Bill Fortney, DVM, director of community practice at Kansas State University. "In diseases of the young and middle-aged, we often think in terms of *cure*. But with arthritis, kidney failure, and cancer we look at control, management, and setting realistic quality-of-life goals for the pet."

A large majority of cats remain relatively healthy throughout their golden years and won't require more than routine medical care. "There are symptoms of aging that don't seem to impact the quality of life," says Dr. Fortney. "For example, a cat has a graying muzzle, a little bit of muscle wasting, and their eyes are a bit clouded over," he says. Elderly cats don't care about gray hair, and they often develop a bluish or hazy-milky pupil called nuclear sclerosis, which is a normal aging change that won't bother them.

Even when they don't have special health care problems, though, all senior cats require more emotional support and nutritional help than younger pets. As the most important person in your cat's life, it's up to you to help her make the transition into a graceful old age. Some changes will be minor and probably won't cause much of a change to your routine. Others may require bigger commitments on your part to help keep the cat happy and comfortable, as well as reduce the potential for aggravating age-related problems.

For example, you'll need to provide a new diet designed specifically for the needs of an older cat. If you have a food-motivated cat who inhales anything you put in the bowl, the diet change won't be a hardship for either one of you. Cats with more discriminating palates, though, may take some adjustment to accept a new diet, particularly since their sense of smell and taste might interfere with how much they like it. You may need to adjust your schedule to increase meals from once or twice a day to three or four times to ensure she gets enough nutrition. Cats with dental problems or missing teeth, common in older cats, often do better on a soft diet rather than dry kibbles.

Similarly, some cats will require more frequent bathroom breaks. That probably won't be a problem if she has a pet door, or spends much of her day in the yard. Otherwise, though, adding another litter box or two—one upstairs and one downstairs, or on both ends of the house—may save your carpet and your relationship.

Older cats often sleep much more during the day, and less at night, and may disrupt your own rest. Something as simple as confining her to a bedroom with all the necessary kitty accoutrements allows you both the luxury of sleeping through the night. Of course, it doesn't bother some folks to be paw-tapped awake at 3:00 A.M. for a game of chase-the-feather, particularly if you're getting up anyway for your own late-night potty break.

Aging cats tend to lose stamina for the long play periods they enjoyed during their youth. Be aware that if she follows you to the basement to help with the laundry, she may beg you to carry her back upstairs. Older cats often have trouble navigating stairs, reaching a favorite window perch, or leaping onto a favorite sofa or the bed. Such cats require a helpful boost up and down. You may need to find a more convenient place for her bed—one that's not elevated, for example, and is toasty warm from the morning sun. That can help relieve stiff joints.

If she's put on the pounds, as many cats do when they get older, she shouldn't be left outside for long during hot weather. Overweight aging cats overheat much more quickly and can have problems breathing and

Sammy is now twelve years old, and still manages to reach his favorite lookout. When leaps become painful, placing a step stool near the cat's preferred perches is a simple way to accommodate his needs. *(Photo Credit: Bonnie Cheak)*

even die from temperature extremes. Cold weather poses the opposite problem when the skin and fur thins, and aging cats become heat magnets during the winter months. Cats don't tend to tolerate wearing clothing as well as dogs do, but some shivery cats may benefit from a sweater during cold weather.

Cats who spent lots of time outside during their youth tend to do much better as indoor pets, and even prefer an indoor lifestyle once they reach old age. For example, arthritis can make it difficult for them to climb to safety out of the reach of stray dogs, or unable to dodge across the street in time to beat oncoming traffic. A warm blanket or lap to snuggle in is preferable to lounging on the hood of a car, particularly when they aren't as able to leap to get out of the way when the motor starts.

Although senior cats are the same constant friend we've always known, they tend to become less patient as they get older. She'll rely more on routine, want her dinner *right now*, and demand attention *this instant*. She may continue to enjoy interaction with the other pets and children, but aging cats tend to reach their tolerance level more quickly. Every cat is different, and adding a younger pet (or a new baby) to the household gives some cats a jolt of energy like the fountain of youth. But others turn into catty curmudgeons if faced with any change in routine. Stress of any kind can prompt behavior problems, such as scratching the wrong object or urinating outside the box. She's not being vindictive or mean. She's either telling you she has a physical problem, or she's using these familiar self-scents to calm her nerves and make herself feel better about the upsetting situation.

For instance, she may go into mourning, and cry and wander around the house looking for her favorite teenager who's left for college, or a beloved companion cat that's died. Shutting her out of the new baby's room could put her tail in a twist. At any age, and particularly as she grows older, the senior citizen needs to feel she's still an important part of the family and be included as much as possible. Instead of shutting the door to the nursery, put up a baby gate so she can watch and sniff and hear the new family member, and she'll take a much more positive interest.

Loss of hearing means that previously attentive cats seem to ignore you. She may also startle more easily, so you'll need to explain to visitors and family members not to sneak up on her, or she might hiss or bite out of fear without meaning to. Some hearing-impaired cats begin meowing a lot more—they can't hear themselves, or you, and so use their "alarm cry" to get attention. You'll also learn to stomp a foot, wave your hand, or use other visual signals to gain her attention. Cats readily learn hand signals in lieu of voice directions, and adjust so quickly to dimming senses that you may not know anything is different at all. For instance, instead of hearing, "Here, kitty, kitty" at mealtime, cats quickly learn that switching the kitchen light on and off at the appropriate time means dinner is served, and come running.

If your cat loses her vision, you'll need to cat-proof the house to protect her from injury. Products designed for child safety can be adapted for use with elderly cats. For example, a baby gate across the stairs will keep her from falling. Baby gates also work well to confine cats into safe—or easily cleaned—

areas of the home. "Safety Turtle" for pets (www.poolcenter.com) protects her from drowning should she fall into the hot tub, for example. The Turtle band is attached to the cat's collar, the remote plugged into an outlet, and the alarm will sound if the Turtle band becomes submerged in water.

Some boarding facilities make special arrangements for the needs of an older cat. Hotels may welcome kitty as a guest if arrangements are made in advance. However, because aging cats become so attuned to routine and familiarity, they often do better staying home with a visiting pet sitter when you go out of town rather than being boarded in a noisy, strange kennel or left in a strange hotel room.

If a cat requires special medications, you'll need to make arrangements with a person able to administer the treatment. Ask if one of the technicians at your veterinary clinic is available. Other times, owners make the choice to postpone or forgo some trips in order to ensure the needs of their cat—both physical and emotional—are met.

Golden Moments: Making Allowances

When Deborah Harding walked past the pet store nearly two decades ago, she lost her heart to the smallest kitten, a little gray-and-white beauty. "She stood up on her hind legs looking at me, and she was coming home," says Deborah. Kyrie always talks, and meows back when you speak to her. "She loves to sit in your lap. In fact, if you can get her off of you, you're doing really well!"

Kyrie used to be quite playful, but that's nearly stopped in the past year or so. "All she wants to do is sit on your lap. Every once in a while she'll get this burst of energy and she'll chase your fingers," says Deborah. "Other than that, she doesn't really play with her toys as much anymore."

Kyrie had a bad time last year when her nineteen-year-old cat buddy, Nimue, died. Deborah's children, then aged twelve and fourteen, had never known the house without the two cats. "The cats were here first. Nimue was huge, thirty pounds, and the girls used to lie with their heads on her. They were extremely close," says Deborah.

Kyrie knew her friend was sick and would groom her. The two cats were the same age, and had grown up together, and got along famously. Kyrie went into mourning after her friend died, and for a while she refused to go downstairs, because that had been Nimue's domain. Deborah took food to her so that she'd eat. It took about two months before Kyrie ventured back downstairs, and even then she avoided the now-empty cat bed "shrine" beneath Deborah's desk as though her friend still owned the property.

But at the end of three months, with pampering from Deborah and the rest of the family, Kyrie seemed to feel more herself. Despite her advanced age, Deborah says she's doing quite well these days, and sees the veterinarian regularly.

"At one time, she was getting a little chubby," she says. Lately she started losing weight. Deborah figured out Kyrie could no longer eat the hard cat food. "We started giving her the soft cat food and she's starting to pick up some weight again," says Deborah.

"I've also had to switch to having two litter boxes," says Deborah. The family lives on three floors. Kyrie never goes to the bedrooms on the third floor, but does travel between the middle floor and the basement. "When you get older, just like all of us, you can't always make it." The family continues to make allowances for the aging cat, to keep her as comfortable and happy as possible.

INSURANCE AND CARE PLANS

Although the cost for medical care for cats is much less than comparable human treatments, paying for chronic care can be a financial burden for dedicated owners. In most cases, veterinarians are sympathetic and open to arranging payment plans when the cost exceeds your ability to pay.

The bills for chronic care can really mount up. Health care programs for animals and insurance provides older pets a better opportunity to get the service they need, by offering a way to pay a portion of the cost.

Founded in 1980 with the support of 750 independent veterinarians, Veterinary Pet Insurance (VPI) is the oldest and (currently) largest health insurance provider for dogs and cats. A number of regional pet insurance companies have since become available, but VPI is currently the only national provider of pet health insurance in the United States. "Likewise there is only one national provider in Canada, Pet Plan Insurance," says Randy Valpy, vice president and general manager of Pet Plan Insurance. "Both of our firms believe that the number of insured pets will grow fivefold during the next five years."

Today, the nation's estimated 23,000 veterinary hospitals each serve an average of twenty-five pet insurance policyholders, and that number continues to grow. "At VPI, we've grown 58 percent in the past five years," says Jack Stephens, DVM, founder of the company. He predicts that more pet owners will turn to insurance to take advantage of veterinary care that continues to rise in sophistication and cost. "We have and always will strive to make the miracles of veterinary medicine affordable," says Dr. Stephens.

Pet insurance typically works by reimbursing the cat owner for a predetermined amount that has been allotted for the specific veterinary service after it's been performed. For example, you would pay your veterinarian in full, then submit the receipts to the insurance company in order to receive payment back according to the amount designated by your cat's particular coverage schedule. "We don't tell the veterinarian what to charge," says Dr. Stephens. "But we do have a fee schedule so it controls our cost." VPI allows pet owners to choose their veterinarian.

Health programs like Pet Assure are not true insurance companies. They simply offer a percentage discount on any veterinary care across the board, regardless of health status, age, or preexisting condition. The Pet Assure service is limited to only those veterinarians enrolled in the program. Similarly, VetSmart Clinics (located across the country in many PETsMART stores) offer Banfield's Optimum Wellness Plans that discount many preventive care services by about 50 percent, with memberships that can be paid on a monthly basis. CareCredit, based in Anaheim, California, offers the clients of participating veterinarians the option of paying for expensive services on a monthly installment basis.

The amount covered varies from company to company, from plan to plan, and from city to city. As with human insurance, preexisting conditions may be disallowed, so you must buy the insurance before the cat develops the problem. Age also influences the cost.

VPI does not have a senior pet policy, says Elizabeth Hodgkins, DVM, medical director and vice president of claims for VPI. "We will insure any pet, regardless of age. But premiums go up as the animal ages." For example, for about the same kind of coverage, a cat that is one year old might cost $234 a year, while a cat that's twelve costs $492. "That's very similar to life insurance for people, where you pay a whole lot more if you're fifty than if you're twenty," says Dr. Hodgkins.

A new program from PetCare Insurance recently introduced through Reader's Digest offers QuickCare Senior coverage. It's tailored for accidents and illnesses common to older cats, including coverage for cancer, stroke, seizures, and heart problems, with no upper age limit for enrollment. In addition to Reader's Digest, PetCare Insurance has strategic partnerships with Petco and Petfinder.com that allows them to offer special policies for specific situations. For example, QuickCare for Indoor Cats provides protection for illnesses or accidents specific to an indoor lifestyle. ShelterCare is designed to meet the needs of pets recently adopted from an animal shelter or rescue group, and the first two months are free when your cat is adopted through a Petfinder.com–affiliated shelter. However, PetCare Insurance is not available in all states.

Companies also define the age breaks differently. For example, Pets-Health Care Plan based in Ohio defines eligible cats as being between the age of eight weeks and prior to turning eleven, with additional premiums that apply to cats over that age; once the cat is enrolled, coverage can continue for the lifetime of your pet. This coverage is available in most, but not all states. For PetPlan Insurance, you can start the insurance anytime from eight weeks to the cat's tenth birthday, and the premiums stay the same as the cat ages, but the deductible increases for cats at ten years of age for the basic plan. VPI defines age brackets for general premium increases as eight weeks to one year; one to four years; five to seven years; eight to nine years; and ten and over, with an increase each year thereafter.

It's important to purchase insurance as early as possible, before health problems develop. Not every preexisting condition disqualifies the cat from coverage—if he's fully recovered from being hit by a car, for example, that wouldn't preclude coverage. "But some pets become uninsurable as they get older," warns Dr. Hodgkins. "We will not insure pets that have already had cancer. If your pet has had a condition that is potentially life threatening and a recurrent problem, then it would become uninsurable."

In fact, some companies offer special coverage for catastrophic illness at a very low rate, if you purchase it when the cat is young and still healthy. VPI's "cancer rider" doubles the benefits for any diagnosis and treatment of cancer, and costs about $34 per year for a one-year-old cat compared to $139 per year for a twelve-year-old cat. The premium cost is locked in when it is purchased before the pet is two years old. "It's pennies a day," says Dr. Hodgkins. "You're going to spend way more on your Starbucks coffee than on the policy plus the cancer endorsement."

While VPI coverage is available nationwide, PetPlan Insurance is available only in Canada, and some carriers such as PetsHealth Care Plan are available only in certain states. Certain plans participate only with listed network veterinarians (similar to some human HMOs); others allow a choice of any practitioner. Additional differences may include variations in the cost of the deductible or higher premiums for certain metropolitan areas that have higher typical veterinary fees.

Most basic plans will cover only accident and illness, and routine care such as vaccinations, spay/neuter surgeries, teeth cleaning, and flea treatments generally require additional coverage. For example, VPI coverage addresses more than 6,400 health conditions, including diagnosis and treatment for liver, heart, and kidney disease, cataracts, diabetes, and cancer, which are most common in aging cats.

Alternative medical care—chiropractic and acupuncture, for example—also may be covered as long as it is prescribed and performed by a veterinarian. Even experimental therapies such as kidney transplants, innovative cancer therapies, hearing aids, and the like may be covered when recommended by the veterinarian.

"We encourage specialists because we think specialists give the best treatment more quickly, which ultimately saves money in the end, and saves the animal," says Dr. Hodgkins. To encourage referrals to specialists, VPI policies start the benefit schedules over again when your cat is referred to a specialist. For example, if your veterinarian has performed $700 worth of the $800 treatment allotment, when you go to the specialist, you have that $800 available again.

In Canada the percentage of insured pets is only about 0.5 percent. "In Europe the acceptance of pet health insurance is far more common," says Valpy. "In the U.K. over 15 percent of all pets are insured, and in Sweden over 41 percent of all pets are insured."

The numbers of insured pets in the United States barely doubles that of Canada. "We currently estimate that the entire pet health insurance industry is a little bit less than one percent of all pets owned in the U.S.," says Dr. Hodgkins. "Of that, not more than a third are seniors." That's unfortunate, she says, because older cats stand to benefit the most from pet insurance. "You can have automobile insurance for forty years and never have an accident," says Dr. Hodgkins. "But sadly, your pet will ultimately sicken and die. Pet health insurance is something that even if it takes ten or fifteen years for you to use it, you will."

Owners of aging cats must make health care decisions that often are based on financial limitations. "There is nothing more frustrating for a veterinarian than knowing you can heal a sick patient, but the owner lacks financial resources and instructs you to put the pet down," says Dr. Stephens. Pet insurance may be an option that helps remove some of the burden and reduce what Dr. Stephens characterizes as "economic euthanasia."

Ask your veterinarian for a recommendation about pet insurance. You can also search the Internet. A brief list of contact information for representative companies is provided in Appendix A. Be aware that this industry is so new that companies may come and go, contact information may become outdated, and coverage could change.

"Get the insurance as soon as you can," advises Dr. Hodgkins. "Many older animals become ineligible because of the development of these diseases, and they're the same diseases that we'd happily pay for if they'd purchased the insurance before."

SHOPPING FOR INSURANCE

A number of companies with different plans are available, and the ideal time to purchase coverage is when your older cat is still healthy. Ask these questions to help make the best choice for your individual situation:

1. Is your insurance offered in my state?
2. Are multiple plans available? Most companies have more than one level of coverage.
3. What are the eligibility requirements? Ask about cat age, preexisting conditions, and if veterinary records are needed in order to qualify (for cats considered geriatric, records may be necessary).
4. When does coverage begin? There may be a thirty-day or longer "wait" period before illness coverage goes into effect. Also ask about any trial periods—some companies will refund your premium within a certain period if you're not satisfied.
5. How much is the annual premium? Ask about fee schedule coverage allowances for some of the most common senior pet conditions.
6. How much is the deductible? Is the deductible calculated on a per-year basis or a per-incident basis?
7. Is there a price break to insure multiple pets?
8. Do you have any special "riders" for veterinary specialists, cancer coverage, or other "senior pet" issues?
9. Is there a "maximum" benefit dollar amount? Is it calculated per year? Per diagnosis? Per lifetime?
10. Which breeds, if any, cost more to be covered? Are any breeds uninsurable?

QUALITY OF LIFE

We adopt our cats with the bittersweet knowledge that they will not live as long as we'd like. People who deeply love their cats are committed to keeping them both healthy and happy during the golden years. With the advent of cutting-edge veterinary care, our pet's lives can be extended longer than ever before.

However, a longer life isn't always a better life. "The quality of the patient's life is really our main concern in veterinary medicine," says Laura Garret, DVM, an oncologist at Kansas State University.

What is quality of life? The term refers to the degree of comfort and enjoyment the pet experiences in day-to-day activities. Measuring quality of life can be difficult and depends a great deal on the individual animal, the owner, and the relationship they share. You know your cat best—you know what makes her happy, and how she acts when she feels good. So one of the best ways to judge a cat's quality of life is to compare her attitude, activity level, and behaviors to the way she once was.

For instance, do Fluffy's painful hips make him hide under the bed and refuse to move, when he used to race to the bowl at the sound of the can opener? Domino now hides when medication time rolls around, when she used to leap into your lap at any excuse. Garfield was always a picky eater, and now you can't keep the bowl filled. Bosco always begs to drink from the faucet each morning, or collects his mouse toys and drops them all over the bed as you sleep. Then one day he's not meowing for breakfast. And the next week, he has no interest in playing flashlight tag. Quality of life means your senior pet feels good, stays connected with you, and enjoys his remaining time in familiar, safe, loving surroundings.

The right treatment can make an incredible difference. Because chronic problems such as hyperthyroidism or vision loss develop so gradually, pet owners often don't recognize the change until symptoms become severe. At that point, Fluffy's new behaviors may be attributed to "old age" when in fact treatment can turn back the clock and return him to the normal activities of a younger pet. Arthritis medicine may not have him swinging from the drapes, but it can put him back on his feet and out from under the bed for petting and play sessions with his favorite people.

Remember, old age is *not* a disease. Don't assume you must accept these changes just because your cat has reached seven years old or older.

TREATMENT ADVICE

Setting realistic goals is vital. Your veterinarian can help you decide on the best choices for your cat's health situation, your own emotional and financial circumstances, and your "comfort level" regarding home care. While a cure isn't always possible, health conditions of aging cats can often be controlled to ensure a good quality of life.

Kidney disease does not mean your cat is going to die tomorrow, says Dr. Marks. "With proper care, we can keep these pets going," he says, but realistically, it's impossible to predict how long treatment will help. That depends on the individual cat and the owner's commitment. "You have to look at it and say, this is a ten-year-old pet that has a disease; let's see what we can do."

Many times, senior cats are healthy but lose their sight or hearing, or develop a challenge that requires only a few environmental accommodations to keep them safe and comfortable. But for cats with a life-threatening problem, other questions must be answered. How will treatment affect his condition? Is a cure possible? If not, will a given treatment stop or slow the progression of the condition, and for how long? Will it improve the way he feels, or make him feel worse? Is it worthwhile to make him feel worse for a short time if he'll live longer? Based on these answers, owners can then decide what care path is best for their cat.

People usually are much more capable of handling home care than they think. The turning point may come, for example, when you realize giving fluid therapy several times a week can save the cat's life. Initially, learning that your cat has cancer can be devastating news. Yet your veterinarian can help explain what to expect in the way of prognosis, treatment, and side effects, if any. A cat with painful cancer will, in fact, welcome amputation that takes the pain away, and she won't worry that she "looks funny" to the other cats. In almost every situation, the outcome is better than we fear.

You should talk with your veterinarian and other family members not only to make informed decisions, but also to reduce any guilty feelings down the road. "Some people are really haunted by those kinds of decisions," says Barbara Kitchell, DVM, an oncologist at the University of Illinois. "Veterinarians offer a counseling service based on therapeutic decisions to help decide, What am I comfortable with, and How do I get comfortable with the decision and not have the guilt? There's always guilt."

The veterinarian should always explain to you the pros and cons of pursuing treatment. "Then you have to decide for yourself," says Dr. Kitchell. Changes can be made, or treatment stopped altogether, anytime during the therapy. "It's not like human medicine, where you keep people alive on a ventilator. We don't do that in veterinary medicine," she says. "It's not *life* above all things; it's *quality* of life above all things."

Certain therapies are more expensive than others, and not everyone can afford them. "Cancer therapy is very expensive. I have patients who spend $7,000 in a year, and that's your fun money, your vacation is gone," says Dr. Kitchell.

However, even when the optimum therapy is cost-prohibitive, more economical options may be available. "There's a menu of options you can select for that individual client's needs," says Dr. Kitchell. Each animal is so different that it's impossible to predict which choice will have the best results. Nor can anyone predict how much time a given therapy will give.

"I get a lot of joy out of being able to help that animal do really well throughout the rest of its geriatric life," says Dr. Beebe. She says that Traditional Chinese Medicine (TCM), which includes acupuncture and herbs, offers wonderful advantages for treatment of chronic diseases because there are so few side effects. "The animal does so well that lots of people tell me it's hard to believe they're that old or that they have cancer or kidney failure," she says. When holistic treatment is combined with mainstream Western medicine, she says the cat is more likely to remain vital and enjoy life up until the very end—rather than experiencing a traumatic decline with intermittent hospitalizations. "My clients want to try everything they can to have a good quality of life for their animal. And when they can no longer have that good quality of life, then it's time for that animal to pass on."

A whole host of emotional issues confronts the owner who chooses euthanasia of an aged cat, says Dr. Little. "Sometimes they're living alone, their spouse may have died, their kids may be in another city, and they stay in an apartment with an elderly cat. And then the cat dies. And they're alone. That's a huge social issue."

We know that our cats won't live forever. But we can take comfort in also knowing our cats don't fear death, and don't worry about tomorrow. Cats live in the "now." And that frees them to greet you each day with joyful, purring abandon.

Witnessing that freedom teaches us great lessons. "If you choose to treat an animal for cancer, you see them die with a lot of dignity and tremendous grace," says Dr. Kitchell. "Death is a process. And you see an animal go through that process. They say, 'I love you. But it's time for me to go.' You see them get themselves ready," she says. "It's so beautiful to watch, and it's so beautiful to be with them, and there's so much peace at the end that it's a lovely thing."

Four out of ten dogs and cats are aged seven years and older. This aging population constitutes more than 50 percent of patients seen by veterinarians—44.8 million pets, according to the American Veterinary Medical Association and others. The numbers will climb as loving cat owners continue to provide the best care possible for their aging companions.

Golden Moments: Loving Hershey

Linda Parker of Pittsburgh went looking for a kitten at the local pound. "At the time we were very poor, living on one income, and my first husband was going through college," she says. She thought a cat would be less expensive than a dog, and also they wouldn't need a kennel if they went away on weekends. "We got Hershey. She's a chocolate-brown Burmese and she's gorgeous." All the other kittens seemed ordinary next to Hershey. "I felt pretty fortunate to find her. We brought her home, and still haven't gotten used to her incessant talking sixteen years later," says Linda. "She needs to be talking. If she's awake, you know it because she's talking to you."

When Hershey was adopted at six months of age, Linda had a one-year-old baby. "I've since had three more children, other pets, and she's been

At sixteen, Hershey is still healthy and happy and an important member of the family. *(Photo Credit: Linda Parker)*

through two husbands, five moves, and various and sundry things, and doesn't seem daunted by it."

Hershey has always been a lap cat, and wants to be near people, or at least in the same room. She recently celebrated her sixteenth birthday, and has never had any health problems. Hershey isn't picky about her food, but does insist on cool (not warm) water, with no floating hairs, if you please. She even has a special meow demand when the water has run out. "She's very purposeful about that," says Linda.

Hershey visits the veterinarian once a year for routine vaccinations, and Linda says they're always amazed by her age. She did not have any gray hair until recently, and now has only a few on her face and a couple wispy ones where her collar would be. "She still jumps up on anything she wishes, no matter how high it is," says Linda. "I haven't noticed any increased sleeping or anything. She does do a little more random meowing."

Her "talking" has always been part of a conversation with someone. "She always wanted the last word. If you wanted her to stop, you had to stop talking to her." Now, every once in a while, Hershey will meow in rooms when nobody's there. "It's not as important to her to have an audience for her meowing now," she says. "But it gets a little annoying because she'll always find a room that echoes."

Linda takes for granted that Hershey is so healthy. She tries not to think about ever losing the cat. "Part of me says when Hershey goes, I don't know if I want another cat. I can't imagine getting one and being disappointed it's not Hershey," she says.

"She has seniority over three of my children. I don't even think of her as a pet, really. She's just here. She's obviously one of the members of the family."

CHAPTER 2

The Aging Process

Cats grow very quickly during their first twelve to eighteen months of life. Their bodies build new tissue and repair injuries at a rapid rate. That fast growth slows once adulthood is reached. Yet even when the cat has stopped growing, nothing is static at the microscopic level. Cells are continuously created, function a short time, then die and are replaced naturally. Organs such as the liver have built-in redundancies and reserves that allow the healthy cat to adapt to both internal physical stresses as well as those from her environment.

The older the cat gets, the less her body is able to replace cells that die. This interferes with the ability of the cat to maintain health or recover from illness. Normal reserves are depleted when cell turnover slows down or stops altogether.

The aging cat's old organs can't keep up as well with normal demands. Because these systems are interrelated, a deficit in one part of the body can cause problems elsewhere. For instance, an aging heart has a harder time pumping blood, and blood vessels begin to lose elasticity, and the combination contributes to high blood pressure. This, along with reduced oxygen getting to the brain, may add to behavioral changes often attributed to senility.

The aging process is not fully understood. One theory suggests that cells can replicate—reproduce themselves—only a certain number of times. This *genetic aging* is dictated by the cat's breed and inherited tendencies from her family. Just as in people, members of certain families tend to live longer than others. Siamese cats often enjoy a very long life span, whereas Persians seem to have a shorter life span than some other cat breeds.

Many experts believe oxidation influences the speed at which cells age. Oxidation is a normal part of living. The cells of the body swim in oxygen, which is necessary for many normal functions. But prolonged exposure to oxidation causes cats to age prematurely and develop disease, in the same way that metal oxidizes or rusts when exposed to air.

How does oxidation occur in cells? Their energy is produced through respiration by mitochondria, tiny structures inside each cell that are rich in fats, proteins, and enzymes. This energy-generating process also creates highly unstable and reactive atoms and molecules called free radicals. Oxidation in living tissue results when free radicals try to combine with normal atoms and molecules of the cells. This damages the cell walls and DNA, causing disease and accelerated aging.

Aged cells are less efficient. Old mitochondria are less efficient and produce less energy but generate more toxic free radicals, says Dr. Blake Hawley, a veterinarian with Hill's Pet Nutrition. "The nervous system tissue is especially vulnerable to attack by free radicals. It's really important that as the cell ages, we find ways to absorb or attack those free radicals that are produced."

Other influences outside of genetics also speed up the aging process. For example, diseases caused by feline leukemia virus and feline immunodeficiency virus suppress the immune system and make cats prone to other diseases, including certain kinds of cancer and fungal infections such as ringworm. Exposure to sunlight and toxins in the air, water, or food are environmental influences that impact aging. Injuries, such as a fracture, speed up the age-related joint degeneration known as arthritis. Improper nutrition can interfere with cell regeneration. Emotional stress suppresses the immune system and allows damage from parasite or viral infections, which can irreparably damage the body and contribute to early aging.

HOW AGE AFFECTS THE BODY

Most cats begin to slow down a bit by the time they reach seven to ten years. These changes are very gradual though, and often we don't notice any significant changes. For instance, a cat may begin seeking out warm spots that help creaky joints feel better, or sleeping an extra hour or so each day. Even the veterinarian may not detect aging changes without special tests, until they become obvious, at which point the damage may be irreversible.

Understanding how age affects the different body systems will help you become alert to subtle changes that may point to serious problems. Catching medical problems early offers the best chance of successfully treating them, and keeping your cat happy and healthy.

The Senses

Cats rely on their senses to a much greater degree than do people. They use touch, taste, scent, sight, and hearing to learn about the world around them, and connect with their people. They rely particularly on hearing and sight, and scent and taste to a lesser degree.

Normal aging in the sensory organs affects all cats. In addition, exposure to environmental insults often causes damage to the sensory organs, which means they dim over time. Taste bud numbers decline, and the sense of smell is often the first to show the effects of age, often with loss of appetite. As far as we can tell, though, the cat's enjoyment of the touch sensation—petting, snuggling, and contact with beloved owners—does not change with age. Cats that develop problems regulating body temperature may, in fact, become more likely to want to snuggle in a warm human lap as they get older.

All cats suffer from a certain amount of visual and hearing impairment, says Benjamin Hart, DVM, a veterinary behaviorist at the University of California—Davis. "Certainly that's an impact on behavior." Yet sensory loss usually bothers owners much more than it bothers the pet. Cats are able to compensate for vision or hearing loss to such an extent that we often don't recognize there's any problem until very late in the game.

Aging Eyes

A cat's eyes are designed for a night predator. Vision is arguably the most important feline sense of all. "Visual acuity in the cat is fairly close to that of the human, probably a little less," says Lawrence Myers, DVM, a professor of anatomy at Auburn University. Cats pay exquisite attention to the world around them, and are particularly adept at discerning motion out of the corner of their eyes.

Cats with prominent eyes such as Persians are more prone to damage and chronic inflammation from scratching or bumping their eyes, but this can happen at any age. Cats do not have a particular age-related eye problem, other than nuclear sclerosis, says Harriet Davidson, DVM, an ophthalmologist at Kansas State University. That is a normal change of age that causes the lens in the eye to turn hazy. "It's the reason humans have to get glasses when they turn about forty," says Dr. Davidson. "Your lens is not as flexible, so you can't see up close anymore because it can't accommodate. Elderly animals will have a pupil that looks somewhat bluish or milky in appearance."

Cats can see through the haze and still function well. Nuclear sclerosis is different from cataracts, which ultimately result in complete opacity of the lens and blindness. "Cataracts occur at all ages, but there's more likelihood as an animal ages, just as a person, that cataracts develop," says Dr. Paul A. Gerding, Jr., DVM, chief of the ophthalmology section at the University of Illinois veterinary school.

Glaucoma is another eye problem more typical of older cats. It is extremely painful and, similarly to cataracts, can result in blindness.

Loss of sight doesn't stop her from being a good pet, though. Vision-impaired and blind cats tend to rely more on their other senses, such as hearing, as well as memory of certain landmarks to get around safely. "You can still give them a pretty good quality of life," says Dr. Myers. "Don't go moving the furniture, simple as that."

Aging Ears

The normal feline ear can hear up to three times the range of sounds as those of people. But with age, the delicate structures within the ear begin to lose sensitivity to vibrations. This decline can be accelerated by damage from very loud noises. Chronic ear infections or parasite infestations, such as ear mites, may also damage the cat's hearing.

Age-related hearing loss, termed presbycusis, shows up in any animal if it lives long enough, says George Strain, DVM, a professor of neuroscience at Louisiana State University. "There's a certain loss of nerve cells with time in the body," he says. Hearing loss can't be reliably predicted, but once it starts, it continues to get worse with time.

Cats can't tell us they're hard of hearing. "They compensate by paying more attention to their other senses," says Dr. Strain. "They may become more visually attentive, pay attention to vibration cues, air currents, and things like that." Many times owners don't recognize the cat has lost hearing because it happens so gradually, until suddenly they notice the cat startles when touched or stops running to greet the doorbell.

Aging Taste

Changes in flavor perception are thought to reflect those experienced by aging humans, says Nancy E. Rawson, Ph.D., of the Monel Chemical Senses Center, a nonprofit research institute in Philadelphia dedicated to research in the fields of taste, smell, chemical irritation, and nutrition. "But as a carnivore, the feline's senses of taste and smell are quite distinct from those of the human, and responses to age-associated changes may differ," says Dr. Rawson.

Cats aren't able to detect carbohydrate sweeteners, but can taste and seem to prefer meaty flavors described by people as "sweet." Detection of meaty, salty, and sour flavors doesn't seem to be affected by age. Bitter tastes are more sensitive to aging changes.

Chemical irritations and "mouth feel" influence how well the cat likes or dislikes a flavor. These can be influenced by changes in saliva content, for example, caused by dehydration that commonly develops in aged cats. Disease or medication can reduce or increase the sensitivity of the mouth and tongue, and alterations in taste (and smell) can remain even after the disease is cured and the medicine is stopped. Dental disease creates a hypersensitive mouth, interferes with chewing ability, and produces unpleasant tastes and odors that prompt the cat to refuse certain foods.

Warming foods increases the volatility of tastes and scents to make them more intense and appealing to the aging cat's palate. Antioxidants hold promise for prevention of age-related scent and taste loss, says Dr. Rawson.

Aging Nose

Scent is very important for cats, but few studies have documented exactly what happens to their sense of smell as cats age. Cats do lose smelling sense the older they get, but nobody knows the amount due to aging compared to lifetime damage, says Dr. Myers. "We're just starting to get a handle on how much the vomeronasal organ contributes to the total scent picture for dogs and cats," he says. The vomeronasal, or Jacobson's, organ is in the roof of the mouth between the soft palate and nasal passages, and is thought to be important in the detection of pheromones, chemicals primarily involved in prompting sexual behaviors.

Snuffling foreign objects into the nose can cause damage. Upper respiratory infections as well as endocrine diseases such as diabetes and hyperthyroidism also can be damaging. Age-related losses in the sense of smell result from changes in the anatomy—scent cells aren't replaced as often—and at the molecular level when existing nerve cells and "messenger" molecules in the nose become less sensitive. Reduced salivation or altered nasal mucus composition also impact the way odor chemicals are dissolved and detected, says Dr. Rawson.

"We did a study a number of years ago and published it in the annals of the New York Academy of Sciences that dealt with the lack of the sense of smell in the cat, and the influence of food intake," says Dr. Myers. "A complete loss of vomeronasal as well as olfactory nerve caused the cats not to eat at all. It seems as if the sense of smell gives them some sort of cue that it's edible," he says. "A favorite veterinarian trick is get one of the cheapest, nastiest, smelliest red tuna fish for cats when they stop eating. That does seem to work in a fairly substantial number to start them eating again."

Bones and Muscles

By the time a cat becomes a senior citizen, her bones have begun to lose density and become weaker and more brittle. That means senior cats are more prone to fractures from falls or leaps when they hit the ground.

Cats at thirteen to fourteen generally heal more slowly from a fracture, says James L. Cook, DVM, an orthopedic surgeon at the University of Missouri. "That's when we start to see a lot of the manifestations from arthritis with respect to the joints." Slowed healing and bone loss likely are due to the body's slowed capacity to regenerate bone cells. "Orthopedically, cats are real good healers."

The cartilage cushioning the joints wears thinner and becomes more brittle over time, and the ligaments and tendons connecting the joints can stretch, become less flexible, and tear more easily. Because cats weigh much less than most dogs, the forces placed on bones and joints may not cause as much damage over a lifetime of wear, says Dr. Cook. But obesity will increase the risk for arthritis and strains and sprains.

Cats hide symptoms better, and that makes diagnosis more difficult. "Cats are a little more stoic, so the symptoms aren't quite the same as in dogs," says Dr. Bill Fortney. Cats almost never limp or hold up a paw—they just hide under the bed or refuse to move. "They may not groom themselves very well, they may be more irritable," says Dr. Bill Fortney.

Muscles become less able to use nutrition efficiently. Cats tend to slow down as they age, and a reduction in exercise prompts not only a gradual atrophy and loss of muscle mass but also contributes to bone loss. Older cats that have less stamina and loss of muscle tone may not be able to "make it" to the litter box in time. "Muscle mass is an extremely important metabolic reservoir," says Dan Carey, DVM, a veterinarian with the Iams Company. The body uses muscle as an energy source during illness. Human studies show that ill people with reduced muscle mass don't survive as well as those with a healthy muscle mass, says Dr. Carey.

Digestion

The digestive system includes the mouth, teeth, stomach, intestines, pancreas, and liver. It processes nutrition and eliminates waste. One of the greatest digestion-related problems of aging cats is obesity, or "overnutrition." Older cats don't exercise as much, and their metabolism slows down, so they gain more weight.

Geriatric animals have a decreased thirst response, according to Alice Wolf, DVM, a professor of small-animal medicine and surgery at Texas A&M. That means they are more likely to become dehydrated when ill, or even during routine boarding or hospitalization. The taste sensation is also reduced, which can lead to anorexia—refusal to eat.

Probably the most common intestinal concern for aging cats is hair balls. Hair swallowed during self-grooming is normally passed out of the body with the feces. But because older cats may have more difficulty with motility—movement of waste through the bowels—hair balls can complicate the problem and cause chronic vomiting or constipation.

Aging Teeth

Cats are prone to plaque and tartar formation on their teeth, just like people. They don't indulge in recreational chewing the way dogs do, but may still suffer from broken teeth, especially when the diseased tooth is weakened by resorptive lesions, a type of feline cavity. Tartar and plaque buildup over time causes periodontal disease that can ultimately result in loss of teeth and also impact the health of the rest of the body.

"Having periodontal disease is analogous to having an open wound," says Bill Gengler, DVM, a veterinary dentist at the University of Wisconsin. Oftentimes the gum tissue is no longer attached to the tooth, and the root and bone are exposed. "When that happens, those clusters of bacteria travel through the bloodstream, and are filtered out at capillary beds. This process is called bacterial showering," says Dr. Gengler. The bacteria are predominantly filtered out in the liver and the kidneys, and can damage these organs. It can also lead to heart disease because of the bacteria-laden blood passing over the valves of the heart.

Aging Stomach and Intestines

"The gastrointestinal tract in cats is relatively well protected from the ravages of time," says Dr. Colin Burrows, an internist and professor of medicine at the University of Florida. "In older cats, just as in older people, the ability to digest diminishes somewhat, but it's not frightfully significant." Smaller but more frequent meals often help the cat's body absorb more nutrition.

"The only disease of note in the [older] cat that does not occur in the dog is idiopathic megacolon. This is the constipated kitty," says Dr. Burrows. Megacolon is different from routine constipation, though, and develops as a result of motility problems. The intestines lose their ability to move waste out of the body.

Also, the bacterial population in the cat's intestinal tract changes as she ages, says Dr. Carey. "This isn't as dramatic as in dogs, but in aging cats it does shift toward the undesirable bacteria. In large part they are diarrhea-type organisms that can invade the lining of the intestine."

Chronic constipation or diarrhea are not specifically "old cat" conditions. Obesity, lack of exercise, and hair balls can contribute to constipation. The most common cause of colitis (inflammation of the colon) is stress, which can lead to bacterial overgrowth within the colon. Cats are creatures of habit, and any change in their routine—adding a new pet, or working longer hours, for example—may cause stress-related disorders. Cats may also develop ulcers as a result of kidney disease.

To compensate for changes in digestion, therapeutic diets may help. "Fat restriction may be beneficial because fat absorption and digestion depends on enzymes that are found in the very tip of the villi that line the intestine, and this is the area that's damaged first," says Dr. Dottie LaFlamme, a veterinary researcher with Nestlé Purina PetCare Company. "When you have damage to the intestine, fat malabsorption can occur, and that can lead to worsening of problems."

Aging Pancreas and Liver

The pancreas, located near the liver, produces enzymes vital to digestion, and the production of both gastric and pancreatic secretions decreases as the cat ages. Similarly, the enzymes produced by the liver for metabolizing nutrients and detoxifying the body decline with age.

Inflammation of the pancreas, called pancreatitis, is a recently recognized disease of older cats, although the cause usually is unknown. Stricken cats often develop a triaditis, says Cynthia R. Leveille-Webster, DVM, an internist at Tufts University. That's an inflammation in the pancreas, intestines, and liver all at the same time.

Overweight cats are especially prone to a dangerous condition called hepatic lipidosis, or fatty liver disease, in which fat is moved into the liver and interferes with its normal function. There are several other kinds of liver disease, but the symptoms are all pretty vague and quite similar. "Owners are not going to know that their animal has liver disease most of the time," says Dr. Webster. "And the doctor won't know until after a lot of tests."

The liver will continue to function well, even when not at 100 percent capacity. When a cat needs medication, however, there may be trouble. "You need to be a little more cautious about medications with older animals," says Dr. Webster. "Old pets are often on multiple medications, and drug interactions can affect how they are handled by the liver." For instance, certain drugs can inhibit the normal production of liver enzymes. Therefore, if the liver is functioning at 70 percent and doing well, but a drug reduces that to 35 percent, the body may suffer the consequences. Reduced efficiency compromises the old liver's ability to metabolize medications properly, among other things.

Endocrine System—Hormones

The endocrine system consists of a huge network of glands and organs that produce hormones. The system includes the pituitary, thyroid, parathyroid, pancreas, adrenals, ovaries, and testes.

Hormones are a kind of "messenger" molecule secreted by endocrine glands that are carried by the bloodstream to various distant body sites, with instructions to alter that target tissue's function—speed up or slow down digestion, for instance. They are made either of protein or a type of specialized fatty substance called a steroid, and regulate body functions and coordinate interactions between the different body systems. An excess or deficient amount of a given hormone can cause disease.

Older cats slow down in part because their metabolic rate goes down, says Dr. LaFlamme. Hormone imbalances become more common as the cat ages because of normal wear and tear on the organs, and also because age-related diseases like cancer often target the endocrine system. The most common old-cat endocrine disorders are hyperthyroidism and diabetes mellitus, discussed in Part 2 under their alphabetic listings.

Heart and Lungs

The cardiovascular system carries oxygen and nutrients throughout the body, and removes carbon dioxide and waste materials. The system includes the heart, blood, and lymphatic system.

Old cats most often develop a heart disease called cardiomyopathy, which affects the muscle of the organ. It becomes harder for the heart to work efficiently. Heart failure results when the damaged muscle is no longer able to move blood throughout the body properly. Thromboembolic disease can be a consequence, when blood clots form in the hind legs and cause rear-end weakness, paralysis, and pain due to lack of oxygen.

The respiratory system is composed of the nose, larynx, trachea, bronchial passages, and lungs. This delivery system supplies the body with oxygen, and removes carbon dioxide.

The airways are exposed to damage caused by inhaled allergens, foreign bodies, viruses, bacteria, and fungus, and may result in a wide range of problems. Senior cats are much more prone to upper respiratory infections that can affect the lungs and/or nasal passages. For example, an accumulation of fluid within the chest wall, called pleural effusion, surrounds the lungs and heart, and interferes with their ability to expand. Pleural effusion is most commonly a result of heart failure. Pulmonary edema, fluid within the lung itself, may develop as a result of cardiomyopathy, pneumonia, or cancer.

Immunity

The immune system is composed of the spleen, thymus, bone marrow, and lymphatic system (including lymph nodes), plus specialized cells and chemicals. They collectively work to protect the body against foreign invaders such as bacteria and viruses. For instance, the bone marrow makes the various immune system cells, while the spleen both filters and stores blood and immune cells. How well the immune system works to large degree is dictated by genetics, but also influenced throughout life by nutrition, stress, and exposure to pathogens.

"The immune system changes by seven years in all cats," says Dr. Carey. The thymus gland helps new immune cells mature, but cell replication slows down with age, and the thymus regresses as the cat matures. The immune system also produces chemicals such as interferon and interleukins, which help control the immune system's response. As cats age, the immune function declines. Because of lowered immune protection, geriatric cats

are more susceptible to diseases. They get sick quicker, and have more difficulty recovering.

Cats may be affected by viral infections that suppress the immune system, such as feline leukemia virus and feline immunodeficiency virus. Allergy is also considered an immune disorder in which the system overreacts
to a "harmless" organism or substance, such as pollen or dust.

Golden Moments: Tweety's Drive to Survive

Tweety was one of a litter of seven kittens. Barb Crandall of Eagle River,
Alaska, and her husband had always wanted a Persian. "She was the most
playful one, ducking and hiding, and looked like a little bunny rabbit," says the
elementary school teacher. "She's gold and silver, very pretty, with the flat
Persian face—looks like she's been hit by a Mack truck." She was named
Tweety (the family's male Persian is named Tasmanian Devil or "Taz") because
Barb is a fan of Looney Tunes.

Tweety has always been a very loving cat, but very mysterious. "She likes
to cuddle. She'll let us turn her upside down to pet her tummy," says Barb,
"then puts her paw on your arm to say, That's enough. And at night she loves
to curl up with us, and she'll sleep between my husband, Tom, and myself."

Until two years ago Tweety had been a very healthy, happy cat. Then she
developed what they thought was an allergic reaction—to what, they didn't
know. "She broke out around the nose and chin area with black, crusty-type
material," says Barb. The veterinarian treated her with a cortisone injection,
the rash healed, and Tweety was fine for six months.

"All of a sudden, she broke out again," says Barb. The skin surrounding
her mouth, nose, and chin developed black crusts, and her ears completely
crusted over with scabs. "It was a real mess."

They went back to Dr. Jeff Johnson, a veterinarian practicing at Four Paws
Animal Hospital in Eagle River. He prescribed anti-inflammatory medications
and Clavamox, an antibiotic to fight infection. Despite all efforts to diagnose
the problem over the next six months, it remained a mystery. Keeping Tweety
comfortable began to be more difficult.

About this time, Barb invited her good friend Lynn Alfino to move in while
Lynn developed her writing career. Lynn arrived shortly before Christmas
1999, and because she worked at home, she spent a great deal of time with
Tweety and Taz. "When I arrived I found a really sick kitty," says Lynn.

"We changed her to a prescription food," says Barb, "and that didn't

Two years ago, Tweety developed a mysterious skin condition. *(Photo Credit: Lynn Alfino)*

work. We changed the litter; that didn't work." Skin biopsies didn't show anything, either. "We racked our brains trying to figure out what had changed in her environment," she says. "We finally did the allergy testing, a blood test, and that didn't show any huge spike—only somewhat allergic to milk and rice."

Lynn and Barb scoured all the labels on the cats' wet and dry food. "The stuff that came back on the allergy panel was not even in the food," says Lynn. The list of acceptable foods the veterinarian provided showed that the food Tweety was already eating was just fine.

Over the next year, treatments to manage Tweety's sore skin became less and less effective, until "normal" times between episodes were almost nonexistent—the shots Dr. Johnson gave her lasted two or three days at most. "She would break out in what I call barnacles," says Lynn. "They looked like raised black peppercorns. Barb and Tom brought her in to the vet almost every week at this point."

Because Tweety and Taz were introduced to each other at twelve weeks of age, they'd been together for most of their lives. "He was fairly sensitive to what's going on with her," says Barb. They'd never cuddled together, but Taz stayed in the general area to watch over Tweety as though he wanted to protect her.

"She got so bad in April she was hiding under the bed and wouldn't come out. She'd dropped two pounds to about seven pounds," says Barb. The family agreed that Tweety was miserable.

"She was an emaciated little bald cat with black stuff all over her," says Lynn. "She had lost all her facial hair; her ears were so crusted and tender you couldn't blow on them from six feet away or it would hurt." Tweety wasn't moving, had no interest in people at all. Lynn says, "It was almost as if the look in her eye was, I'm dying . . . kill me now."

At that Saturday appointment Dr. Johnson told them he'd tried everything and had nothing else to·offer. "We think there's some form of an autoimmune scenario with Tweety," he said, and such conditions often are nearly impossible to resolve. "We've talked to a few specialists and done the recommended protocol, but Tweety has just been a challenge."

After returning home to discuss the situation with their children, Barb and Tom made the hard decision to end Tweety's suffering. "Everybody had seen it coming," says Lynn. "It was living with death."

The next day—Sunday—Tom, Barb, and Lynn drove to Home Depot to buy a pickax. "We're on a mountain, and the backyard here is rock with permafrost underneath," says Lynn. "Tom was going to have to dig a grave for Tweety."

On Monday, Barb and Lynn were both upset as they tried to come to terms with taking Tweety back to the veterinarian to be euthanized. "We're both wailing and bawling, when little Tweety came out from the closet where she had been hiding," says Lynn. It was the first time they'd seen her even try to walk in days. The two women looked at each other, and Barb said, "Maybe today's not the day."

Over the next two or three days, Tweety stopped hiding, started eating, and even jumped on top of the billiard table. "I'd never seen her have any burst of activity before," says Lynn. "She was on the bookshelf reading *Moby Dick*—I think she liked the fish!" They continued to hold on to hope, day by day—and then week by week. "I've never met anything that's been so sick with such a drive to survive," says Lynn. "I think the turning point was when she saw the pickax, and thought, Uh-oh!"

They finally figured out that Vetalog injections gave her the most relief. The injection keeps Tweety comfortable for about two weeks, and sometimes three. "It's almost night and day," says Barb. Within twenty-four to forty-eight hours of the injection most of the crusty debris sloughs off and the cat is fine for a while.

She can relapse literally overnight. "You go to bed and wake up the next morning and there's Tweety with peppercorns," says Lynn. But Tweety willingly hops in the kennel, and hunkers down inside for the trip to the vet. "I know that she knows what's coming," says Barb, "but she also knows within the day she's feeling a whole lot better. That doesn't mean she doesn't hiss at the doctor."

After she receives the shots, life goes on for Tweety. She regained the two pounds she lost, her fur has grown back in, and she looks almost chubby. "My son calls her the Poppin' Fresh Dough Cat," says Barb.

With dedicated treatment from her veterinarian and family, Tweety's skin healed and her fur grew back. *(Photo Credit: Lynn Alfino)*

"Barb's a wonderful owner, really cares for the kitty," says Dr. Johnson, "and Lynn's done a lot, too, watching Tweety in the day. Very astute owners help us as veterinarians," he says. "We'll do what we can medically. Quality of life dictates where we go sometimes. Finally this kitty is doing her end of the bargain and the medication is helping."

To this day nobody has figured out why seven-year-old Tweety suffers from the skin eruptions. "But you don't put a child down when they're sick; you treat them," says Barb. "A lot of people aren't in the financial position to do it. I am, thank goodness." She says Tweety just implored her to care for her. "I'll do whatever it takes until Tweety tells me that she's ready, that she's had enough."

Nerves

The brain, spinal cord, and a network of nerve fibers generate and transmit electrochemical signals that connect with every inch of the body.

This regulates and coordinates body systems, and also gives our cats their personality, awareness, emotional life, and intelligence.

A central nervous system change common to older cats is impaired thermoregulation, says Dr. Wolf. Cats are less able to regulate their body temperature, and may be more heat or cold seeking, depending on the temperature around them. For that reason, body temperature must be closely monitored, especially during and after any anesthesia is given.

Age-related degeneration or injury of the brain, spinal damage, and chemical disruptions at the cellular level all have a role in nervous system disorders. Liver failure, for example, may secondarily cause bizarre behavior as a result of chemical imbalances affecting the brain. Feline ischemic encephalopathy and stroke also cause disruption of the blood supply to the brain.

In addition, cats also suffer from spinal injuries that leave them with rear-end paralysis. Embolic myelopathy, a type of paralysis of the rear legs, is caused by side effects of blood clots resulting from cardiomyopathy. It may be permanent, but in some cases is cured with treatment. Uncontrolled diabetes may also affect the nerves and cause mobility problems, which may or may not be reversible.

COMFORT ZONE

- Running water often appeals to cats and prompts them to drink more, which keeps them better hydrated. Drinkwell Pet Fountain (http://www.vetventures.com) has a six-cup capacity and provides continuous running water for the cat. It costs about $50.
- Cats rarely lose the function of their rear limbs. Yet those that do may benefit from a feline "wheelchair" such as those provided by K-9 Carts. The cat's rear legs are supported by a frame over the top of a pair of wheels, while his front legs allow him to move about and tow the cart behind. Product information is available at www.k9carts.com.

Aging Mind

Some felines remain sharp and connected to the world around them throughout their geriatric years. Others aren't as fortunate. "Some of the changes are due to the fact that the animal has an aging brain," says Nicholas Dodman, BVMS, a professor of behavioral pharmacology at Tufts University. "As our pets get older, their thought processes slow down. In humans you talk about senior moments, and I think all our older pets have their senior moments." As cats get older, the blood flow to the brain is reduced, causing a loss of neurons that the body is unable to replace.

While body and health changes often impact the cat's behavior—she hisses and claws when startled because she's deaf, or she urinates outside the litter box due to diabetes—the changes of an aging brain affect both behavior and personality. A Jekyll-and-Hyde transformation can drastically impact the loving bond an owner shares with a pet. Behaviorists believe many age-related behavior problems, such as howling incessantly or getting "lost" in the house, can be ascribed to these brain changes. This condition is called feline cognitive dysfunction, and is characterized by anxiety, personality changes, and problems such as hit-or-miss litter box behavior. It is thought that the cats return to a kitten mind-set, to the time before they learned these lessons. Cats older than thirteen seem more commonly affected, but there's no way to predict how your cat will fare.

Reproduction

"To our knowledge, older queens do not undergo menopause in the same way or with the same physical symptoms that human females have," says Dr. Little. "As they age, their ovaries and hormonal function may not be as good as when they were younger, so we do see a decrease in fertility in queens over about age seven. But they can cycle until the day they die of old age if they are not spayed."

Serious reproductive diseases may develop in cats that have not been spayed, particularly if they are not regularly bred. Intact female cats older than six are highly prone to metritis (inflammation of the lining of the uterus) and pyometra—a life-threatening infection of the uterus. Kidney failure may be triggered by pyometra, because of the body's immune response created to fight the infection. Breast cancer is also a risk in aging unaltered females. Male cats rarely suffer from age-related reproductive disorders.

Skin and Hair

The cat's skin and fur do more than look good. The hair provides a protective barrier that regulates temperature, prevents dehydration, and is the major sensory organ of the body. It also offers a shield from extremes of weather, and from viruses, bacteria, and other disease-causing pathogens. The cat's skin and hair are also an accurate barometer of her health—what she feels on the inside is reflected on the outside.

Normal skin changes occur with age due to a lifetime of exposure and changes in the cat's metabolism. Skin becomes thinner and less flexible, the hair coat becomes duller and drier due to less oil production, and hairs, especially the muzzle and ear rims, often turn gray as the cat ages. The most common skin problem is called miliary dermatitis, a tiny, scabby, bumpy rash, but this is a symptom of a wide range of problems such as allergies and ringworm. It can develop in cats of any age. Ringworm is the most common fungal infection of cats and often affects aging cats more readily because of their less competent immune system.

A number of skin and hair coat disorders arise as a result of other age-related disorders. Diabetes mellitus may prompt hair thinning or loss. Old cats unable to properly groom themselves often develop painful matted fur. Also, any lump or bump on the skin of an older cat is a risk for cancer.

NURSE ALERT!

A new monitoring system to check for blood in the cat's urine is available from Purina Veterinary Diagnostics. Hemalert is dispensed from veterinarians, and comes in packets. The granules are mixed in existing cat box filler, and will change color in reaction to blood in the urine.

Urinary System

Body wastes are filtered from the blood and removed by the kidneys. The bladder collects and stores this liquid waste until it's released from the body through the urethra as urine. Kidneys, the ureters, bladder, and urethra make up the urinary system. Kidneys not only manage waste, they also produce a specialized hormone called erythropoietin, which prompts the production of red blood cells and also helps regulate blood pressure.

As the cat's kidneys age, the tissue deteriorates, the organs slowly shrink, and they gradually lose their ability to function efficiently. "The number one cause of death in older cats is chronic renal [kidney] failure," says Dr. Johnny D. Hoskins, an internist and a specialist in small-animal pediatrics and geriatrics.

Other disorders of the urinary system include urinary tract infections, and urinary stones that affect the bladder, the kidneys, or both. The bladder becomes less elastic and may not empty totally each time the cat urinates. In time, this may lead to increased susceptibility to infections and large bladder or kidney stones in cats.

Urinary tract inflammation and crystals or stones may affect cats of any age, though. Commonly referred to as lower urinary tract disorders (LUTD), the formation of crystals and/or mucoid plugs can cause pain, distress, and sometimes life-threatening blockages. Cats suffering from cystitis (inflammation of the bladder) may have blood present in the urine as well. But older cats develop a more dangerous type of stone.

"The type of stones that tend to form changes from being predominantly struvite in the younger cat to being predominantly calcium oxalate in the older cat," says Dr. LaFlamme. Struvite crystals mixed with mucus typically plug the urethra on their way out of the body during urination. Struvite can be dissolved and prevented by feeding the cat a diet that acidifies the urine. Calcium oxalate–composition stones more typically block the ureters—the conduits leading from the kidneys to the bladder—and require surgery to remove, says Dr. Larry Cowgill, DVM, an internist at the University of California—Davis.

Aging cats almost never develop urinary incontinence, a relatively common physical problem of aging female dogs. Litter box "misses" are more often linked to cognitive dysfunction, where the cat "forgets" how to find the bathroom, says Dr. Little.

FEEDING FOR HEALTH

A percentage of cats are prone to developing urinary crystals or stones. Therapeutic diets are designed to prevent or sometimes dissolve existing crystals. Dietary treatment choices are based on identifying the kind of crystal, and generally are available only through veterinarians. Some commercial products that may be helpful include:

- Eukanuba Veterinary Diets, Nutritional Urinary Formula, Low pH/S/Feline
- Eukanuba Veterinary Diets, Nutritional Urinary Formula, Moderate pH/O/Feline
- Hill's Prescription Diet Feline c/d-s (struvite)
- Hill's Prescription Diet Feline c/d-oxl (oxalate)
- Hill's Prescription Diet Feline s/d (LUTD)
- IVD Select Care Feline Mature Formula
- IVD Select Care Feline Control Formula
- IVD Select Care Feline Hifactor Formula
- IVD Select Care Feline Weight Formula
- Purina Veterinary Diet, UR Urinary Formula
- Waltham Feline Lower Urinary Tract Support Diet

In sum, each system of the body provides support for the whole. A misstep by one can prompt interconnected problems all across the body. Whether sudden or slow and insidious, the various changes in the different body systems collectively contribute to how your cat ages.

That also means that treating one age-related problem can influence the entire body to get better. You can often slow down the entire aging process simply by paying attention and addressing problems promptly as they occur. Aging is inevitable, but you can help your cat do so with grace.

CHAPTER 3

L.O.V.E. for Health

Older cats that become ill typically try to hide how they feel. They also tend to become more seriously ill more quickly, and take longer to recover. "The earlier we see these animals, the more we can do something for them," says Sheila McCullough, DVM. It is vital to pay attention to your cat as she ages, to catch problems before they turn serious.

A good way to keep in mind the special needs of your aging cat is simply to use the acronym L.O.V.E. That stands for Listen with Your Heart; Observe for Changes; Visit the Veterinarian; and Enrich the Environment.

LISTEN WITH YOUR HEART

Never discount that odd "feeling" that something's different, not right. Listen with your heart and your cat will shout louder than words how she feels. That's when you make the extra visit to the veterinarian and explain your concerns. "It's more of an intuitive thing," says Susan G. Wynn, DVM, a holistic veterinarian in private practice in Atlanta. Because of the close relationship you share, you have an advantage when it comes to "knowing" when something's wrong.

A change in behavior is the number one way your cat tells you she's feeling bad from either a physical problem or an emotional upset. Changes in behavior may be sudden and obvious, or may develop slowly and subtly over time.

Think of these changes as a feline cry for help. You need to have a good grasp of what's normal for your cat in order to be able to recognize this shift in the status quo. That includes regularly observing your cat for changes.

Regular veterinary visits are a must. Any time you have an intuitive feeling or a more concrete observation that something's not quite right, validate your concerns with a veterinary visit.

Finally, the environment your cat lives in impacts everything about her. When she begins to age, you have to make appropriate enrichments to her nutrition, exercise, grooming needs, and home life. Don't forget to enrich her mind as well as her body. Follow the L.O.V.E. plan to keep her healthy and happy throughout her golden years.

OBSERVE FOR CHANGES: HOME HEALTH ALERTS

Healthy aging cats see the veterinarian only a couple of times a year. You live with her every day, and you know your cat best. In almost all cases, you will be the first to notice when something is wrong.

Close proximity to your pet allows you to immediately notice any changes that can point to a potential health problem. The major disadvantage to this closeness is that you may overlook subtle changes, or those that have a gradual onset. Veterinarians call sudden problems "acute," and those are the easiest for owners to spot. But conditions that develop slowly over a long period of time, called chronic problems, are more insidious. Changes of a chronic nature creep up on you, day by day, in such small increments that you aren't likely to notice anything's wrong. By the time a problem becomes obvious, the disease may have been simmering for months or even years, and the damage may be permanent.

"The classic emergency I see is the twelve-year-old cat that is feeling badly, and deteriorated over the last twenty-four to forty-eight hours," says Steven L. Marks, BVSc. "The assumption is that the pet has become sick in the last two days, when, in fact, chronic renal failure has been going on for months and maybe years. Now the body can't compensate anymore and the pet's suddenly sick and it's an emergency."

One of the best ways to stay on top of things is to create a log of your cat's normal behaviors. A home health report card provides you with baseline measures against which to compare even the subtle changes in your cat's health. For example, monitor how much your cat weighs. "Even a small amount of weight loss, an ounce or two, will really catch my attention in an elderly cat," says Dr. Susan Little. Should your cat at some point in the future be diagnosed with a particular condition, a home health report card also can help you measure how well the treatment works. That in turn helps the veterinarian make informed decisions if adjustments to the therapy are needed.

Once you have your list, and a benchmark description of "normal," review the home health report card on a monthly basis to check for any changes. If your cat has been diagnosed with a disease for which she's receiving treatment, a weekly or even daily check to monitor changes may be better.

NORMAL VITAL SIGNS

Know what the benchmark readings are for your cat so that you are alerted to a change that might point to a health problem.

- Temperature: This ranges between 99.5 degrees to 101.5 degrees.
- Hydration: Use the scruff test. Loose skin on the neck should immediately spring back when grasped and released, and a delay indicates dehydration.
- Blood Circulation/Pressure: Capillary refill time of 1 to 2 seconds is normal. Firmly press the flat of a finger against the cat's gum, then release, and time how long it takes the pink color to return to the whitened finger-shaped mark. A delay indicates dehydration, low blood pressure, or even shock.
- Heart Rate: 120 to 140 beats per minute.
- Respiration: 16 to 40 breaths per minute.

Behavior Cues

Generate a list of as many of your cat's normal behaviors as possible. The categories will vary somewhat from cat to cat. Be as specific as possible. Examples of categories follow, but don't limit yourself to my suggestions. If your cat gets in the sink every day, for example, or enjoys chasing the dog, include that as a category and describe her routine. Any changes to routine might indicate a health concern that needs attention. For instance, if she used to wake you every single day at five and then suddenly lets you oversleep, perhaps her joints hurt too much from arthritis to jump onto the bed.

- **Favorite Activity:** Describe how she plays. For example, if she loves a fishing-pole toy, does she fetch? Make mad, leaping catches? Play keep-away? Bring you the toy to incite a game? How often does she ask to play? How long does the game typically last? How does she move—at a run or a walk? Does she pounce and leap to the top of chair backs, or climb slowly? Activity monitoring can alert you to painful arthritic changes.

- **Vocabulary:** All cats learn certain words. What are your cat's favorites (*food, play, mousie . . .*) and how does she react when hearing them? A change in reaction to favorite words may indicate hearing loss or cognitive dysfunction.

- **Vocalizations:** Describe what circumstances prompt meows or other vocalizations. Perhaps she goes nuts when the doorbell rings, the can opener whirs, or a neighbor cat visits. How long do vocalizations last? What do they sound like? Are they howls, hisses, yowls, growls? Cognitive/memory changes, hearing loss, and dimming eyesight can change how the cat vocalizes.

- **Interactions/Personality:** How does she get along with the other pets in the household? Describe her relationship to each one. Detail her typical reaction to strangers—ankle-rubbing frenzy or hiding and hisses? Personality changes may indicate sensory loss. If she's deaf or blind, she'll startle more easily and react accordingly. She may also become short-tempered from chronic pain.

- **Sleep Cycles:** When does she sleep, and for how long? Does she have a favorite spot? The sofa, her pillow, windowsill, your bed? What's her temperature preference—cool tiles beside the bathtub or puddle of sunshine? Painful joints may prevent her reaching favorite resting spots on the bed, and prompt her to seek out sunny spots, and sleep for longer periods. Metabolic changes can influence temperature perception and sleep rates. Cognitive dysfunction often reverses sleep cycles, so she's awake at night and sleeps during the day.

- **Habits/Routines:** What is her day like? Does she wake up at noon each day ready to play? Meet you at the front door after work? Beg for a nightly twenty-minute feather-chase game? Is she queen of the cat tribe who keeps others in their place? Loss of hearing or eyesight, painful joints, brain changes, and organ dysfunction may all impact routines.

Body Warnings

Generate a list of your cat's normal body functions. Be as specific as possible. Examples of categories follow, but don't limit yourself to my suggestions. "I'd rather see a case that doesn't need to be seen as an emergency than not see one that needed to be," says Dr. Marks.

- **Appetite:** Does she have a favorite food? Is she finicky or a glutton? How much does she eat (measure the amount), and at what time of the day? Missing one meal usually won't hurt her, but an aging cat shouldn't go longer than twenty-four hours without eating. A change in appetite points to a variety of problems, from metabolic changes to chronic pain or organ dysfunction.
- **Weight Loss/Gain:** How much does she weigh? Is she normal, under-, or overweight? Fluctuations in weight can be a sign of pain, diabetes mellitus, hyperthyroidism, problems of the liver, kidneys, or heart, or dental disease.
- **Water Intake:** How often does the water bowl empty? Measure how much water goes in the bowl, and the amount left at the end of the day to see how much on average she drinks in a day. Increased thirst is a classic sign of diabetes and kidney failure as well as other organ problems.
- **Urination:** What color is the urine? Count the number of times she urinates in a day. How often does she have "accidents"? Lighter than normal could mean her kidneys aren't concentrating efficiently, while darker than normal may indicate dehydration. Blood in the urine can indicate an infection, inflammation, or cancer. "Sticky" urine could be due to diabetes, and greenish urine may point to liver problems. Increased urination often results from increased water intake, and may also prompt more litter box lapses. Inability to properly "pose" may be due to joint pain, and prompt the cat to delay bathroom breaks.
- **Defecation:** What is the color/consistency of the feces? Count how many bowel movements she produces each day. Does she ever have "accidents"? Changes in the frequency of elimination and/or consistency of the stool point to digestive problems or constipation. It may also indicate memory loss—she can't remember where the litter box is—or problems with mobility—it hurts to move/pose so she delays elimination.
- **Skin, Fur, and Claws:** What color is her skin? Is it free of dandruff, sores, and lumps or bumps? Is the fur full, thick, and lustrous? Does she continue to keep herself neat, clean, and well-groomed? Grooming is a barometer of feline health, and cats often stop grooming

when they feel bad. Mats, dingy fur, or debris anywhere on the coat are sure signs she's ill. Metabolic changes often are reflected in the appearance of the skin, claws, and hair coat. Any lump or bump in an old cat is highly suspect for cancer.

- **Eyes:** Are her eyes clear, with no discharge or watering? Squinting or pawing at watery eyes indicates pain, and changes in the appearance of the eye may point to eye diseases such as cataracts, high blood pressure, or glaucoma.
- **Ears:** Do her ears smell fresh? Are they clean? Does she scratch them or shake her head? Stinky, dirty, or itchy ears point to an infection.
- **Nose:** What color is the nose leather? Is it moist and smooth, or dry and chapped? Is there any discharge? Nasal discharge can be a sign of whole-body infection. Changes to the nose leather, as in the skin, can indicate metabolic changes or even nasal dermoid cancer.
- **Respiration:** Is her breathing regular and easy, or does she gasp and strain to get air? Does she have bad breath? Panting or gasping is a danger sign in cats, and points to heart or lung disease. Bad breath may indicate periodontal disease, diabetes, or kidney disease.
- **Gait/Movement:** Does she arise easily from sitting or lying down? Does she refuse to move, or hold up or favor a leg? Is she reluctant to climb? Does she avoid stairs, jump onto or off favorite furniture, or seem fearful of the dark? Does she have trouble navigating unknown territory? Gait or activity changes are strong indications of painful arthritis. They may also indicate vision loss.

Golden Moments: Zoobie's New Life

When a black cat was left at Independent Cat Society, a no-kill shelter in Westville, Indiana, best estimates placed him at two years of age, and he was semiferal when he arrived. That made him difficult to adopt, but he had a home for life at the shelter, says Linda Moore, a volunteer foster mom for the shelter. "They only euthanize when it's in the animal's best interest," she says.

Nine years later, in August, he began having problems with circling behavior. When veterinary treatment for a possible ear infection hadn't resolved the problem by October, the cat was referred to Purdue University. "They couldn't find anything either," says Linda. When it got worse the next spring, he went back to Purdue for a more in-depth screening. "A CT scan found a brain tumor. It was a quarter the size of his brain," says Linda. Unfortunately, Purdue wasn't able to offer treatment.

"The shelter contacted a couple other vet schools, and Dr. Klopp got back in touch with them," says Linda. Lisa Klopp, DVM, is an assistant professor of neurology and neurosurgery at the University of Illinois. "She thought she could do something for him."

That's when Linda first heard about the cat. The shelter wanted him to go into a foster home until treatment could be scheduled, to avoid any possible exposure to illnesses he might pick up there. "I'd given them my name the previous fall to foster older cats, but I'd not heard from them until Sandy Robelia called me," says Linda. The situation seemed oddly coincidental, too, because Linda had only recently lost one of her own cats—solid black, named Natasha—to a brain tumor.

Linda had misgivings about taking the sick cat at first. "I asked Sandy, How can I take this guy and say I'll foster temporarily and then put him back in the shelter? There is no way I can do that! But likewise, I also knew I couldn't afford the bill."

The kitty came to live with her on Easter Sunday. He had several small seizures that week but they were quite different from what she'd experienced with Natasha. "She'd have a grand mal seizure, then pretty much recover from it. He just looked like he was stretching. Then he'd lose control of his bladder, and really couldn't move for a couple days, so I'd have to hand-feed him."

Once Dr. Klopp reviewed the records from Purdue, she wanted to see the cat right away. "She felt he was in imminent danger of hemorrhaging," says Linda. "The tumor had grown down near the brain stem, and she didn't know if she could get it all, or if it would be malignant."

Although the doctor was booked for the next three weeks, she moved him ahead of everybody else, and performed surgery the day after he was admitted. "We got the call and Dr. Klopp was absolutely ecstatic," says Linda. The tumor came out—all of it—in two pieces. Tests showed it was benign.

Dr. Klopp became very attached to him while he was at the university hospital, and once he left ICU, he'd often be found sitting in her lap. "When we went down to pick him up she looked like she was ready to cry," says Linda. "She was calling him Zoobie and he seemed to respond to that, so Zoobie is his name now."

The shelter footed the bill. "They sent out a special appeals letter after the surgery. It all happened so quickly they really didn't have the time before," says Linda. "Within a month they had more than enough to cover Zoobie's bill."

Linda took him back down for his six-week checkup. He was fine. But she

Zoobie has used up several of his nine lives but now is fully recovered from brain surgery and enjoying good health in his new home. (*Photo Credit: Woof Studios* [Jeff Christie])

had fallen in love with the cat, and couldn't bring herself to take Zoobie back to the shelter. "I went ahead and adopted him."

Zoobie is by all estimates around ten or eleven years old, but Linda says since his brain surgery, he acts like a three-year-old. "He goes rollicking around the house with my younger cats and everything amazes him. He loves playing with the cat-dancer toy," she says. "He just about goes berserk for that."

She was a bit concerned about him fitting in with the other animals. "He has no problem with the dog, or with the other cats; he's just incredible," she says. After ten years of shelter life, the black cat is starting his next decade with a permanent home, a new name, and a family that loves him. Zoobie is making the most of it.

VISIT THE VETERINARIAN: WELL-PET EXAMS

No matter what her age is, your cat needs a veterinary exam at least once a year. Vaccinations used to be given automatically each year, and the cat received a checkup at that time. More recently, many veterinarians believe annual vaccines aren't necessary, but since cats age so much more quickly than people do, an annual "well-pet exam" is essential to ensure she maintains good health. The veterinarian listens to the cat's heart and lungs, checks her eyes, ears, and teeth, examines her for parasites, and makes a note of any behavior changes you might have noticed that potentially indicate a problem.

Because senior cats have fewer reserves and can become ill so quickly, the well-pet exam is even more important for them. Once they reach adulthood, each cat year equals about seven human years. Waiting twelve months between checkups leaves them at risk for major health changes. A twice-yearly visit for cats over the age of eight makes more sense. That's the equivalent to a middle-aged person getting a physical about every three years, says Dr. Tranquilli. "It makes all the sense in the world to get more aggressive with checkups, and have the veterinarian ask appropriate questions with regard to overall behavior changes."

Dr. Gengler says you should include a dental check. "You may not be able to do an in-depth exam until the animal's asleep. But at least you can advise the owner that yes, there's halitosis; yes, there's gingivitis; and there's calculus on the teeth so we need to get it off."

It's always best to catch problems early and treat them right away to head off more serious problems. But your veterinarian has a hard time noticing subtle problems if she sees your cat only during a crisis. "The annual health check for older pets is imperative. It's imperative that I put my hands on them, and feel them, listen to them. I talk to Mrs. Jones and say, How are we doing?" says Dr. Marks. "I want to see the pet every year so I've seen him when he's healthy. If something changes, I want to pick it up early."

The top health issues in aging cats include cancer, kidney problems, diabetes, and hyperthyroidism. "As these animals get older, one starts looking at their liver, their intestinal tract, their kidneys, at their heart, and various body systems, looking for those organs that could be failing," says Dr.

Johnny D. Hoskins. Geriatric screening tests help veterinarians go beyond the hands-on exam and examine the cat from the inside out.

Monitoring Tests

Evaluating the blood may uncover abnormalities that otherwise would not be found until it is too late for treatment to help. "I recommend routine blood work be done, and X rays or ultrasounds of the chest and abdomen to make sure nothing's going on that's abnormal," says Rhonda L. Schulman, DVM. A simple test such as a urinalysis, which examines the content and volume of the urine, can alert the veterinarian to kidney disease, liver disease, hyperthyroidism, diabetes mellitus, and other health problems.

"We especially encourage people with cats over ten to see the vet twice a year," says Dr. Little. "It's a change from what we called fire-engine medicine, a reactive response to putting out the fire," she says. "Being proactive requires a good working relationship with a veterinarian who is interested in senior care."

Ideally, your cat should have a first screening test when she's seven to ten years of age and in good health. "By the time they're in double digits, it's time to do some geriatric screening, especially for chronic kidney disease," says Dr. Webster. What constitutes normal varies slightly between cats, and about 5 percent will be outside what is considered a normal range, says Dr. Marks. Having a baseline test is particularly helpful to determine your cat's normal range.

The health of a variety of organs can be determined by looking at specific factors in the blood. A complete blood count (CBC) measures the components that make up the blood. For instance, the hematocrit (HCT), or packed cell volume, is the ratio of red cells to total blood volume. A lower-than-normal HCT indicates anemia, while an elevated HCT is an indication of dehydration, lung disease, or cardiomyopathy. The CBC also typically measures the percentages of the various white blood cells. High or low numbers can indicate anything from infections or tissue damage to cancer or autoimmune disorders.

A biochemical profile measures the various chemicals, vitamins, minerals, enzymes, and other compounds in the bloodstream. Blood urea nitrogen (BUN) is the by-product of protein metabolism, and the BUN level is a good measure of kidney health.

The liver does so many things that many diseases affect it. Therefore, the liver is a solid health barometer for the rest of the body. For instance, bile acids produced in the liver act to absorb fat, so abnormal blood levels of bile acids indicate liver problems. Enzymes produced by the liver are very sensitive, and the levels in the bloodstream will go up if the liver is damaged, says Dr. Webster, but this can also indicate other diseases. "Probably 80 percent of the time you'll find another disease causing that enzyme to go up."

Tests screen only for the *possibility* of a problem, says Dr. Marks. If a liver enzyme is elevated, more specific diagnostic evaluations, such as abdominal X rays and ultrasounds, are required to figure out the exact cause.

Yet checking biochemical abnormalities alone ignores the total animal. When your cat feels great, but has an abnormal lab value on the blood work, Dr. Marks says you have a choice. You can aggressively pursue the cause with further diagnostics, or you can wait a month to repeat the test and, if the result is still elevated, then go further. "I'm not really a fan of saying we have to do *all* these tests on *all* pets over eight years old," he says, but admits that's the easiest way to catch those pets you worry about. It depends on the owner, the comfort level of the veterinarian, and especially on the health of the individual cat.

BLOOD VALUES

Blood Count	Normal Range
Red Blood Cell Count (RBC)	5 to 10 million/microliter
Hemoglobin (Hgb)	8 to 15 grams/deciliter
Hematocrit (HCT)	35 to 45 percent
Mean Corpuscular Volume (MCV)	39 to 55 femtoliters
Mean Corpuscular Hemoglobin (MCH)	13 to 17 picograms
Mean Corpuscular Hemoglobin Concentration (MCHC)	30 to 36 grams/deciliter
White Blood Cell Count (WBC)	5.5 to 19.5 thousand/microliter
Neutrophils	35 to 75 percent
Lymphocytes	20 to 55 percent
Monocytes	1 to 4 percent
Eosinophils	2 to 12 percent
Platelets	3 to 7 (× 10/microliter)

ENRICH THE ENVIRONMENT

When your cat celebrates her seventh birthday, she hasn't any idea, nor does she care, that she's now a "senior" feline. Cats older than seven often have the constitution and attitude of much younger animals. There's no reason she shouldn't enjoy a rewarding and vital life well into her teens. The key is to expect the best of her, and give her the best support possible. That includes good nutrition, exercise, grooming, home-life accommodations, and mental stimulation.

Nutrition

"There isn't any one best food," says Dr. Abood. A number of therapeutic diets address specific diseases, such as kidney failure, once the cat is diagnosed. Dr. Abood says that therapeutic diets are manufactured to have specific nutrient modifications, and that the diets for a given condition are pretty similar no matter who makes them. "When animals do better on one over the other, that's an individual animal variation; that's not a diet difference," she says.

Cats are notorious for hating change, and getting your feline to accept a new diet may take some time. It doesn't matter how great the food is if she refuses to eat it. "If they don't recognize it as food, it's not going to do the job you want it to do."

When the older cat is in good condition, and has a high level of activity, why should you switch to a "senior" diet? Dr. Carey says a food change helps support the cat's physical needs, which usually change before obvious signs of aging appear. The newest senior-label diets are designed to support the cat during these normal but invisible changes of age so she maintains that kittenish behavior, rather than waiting until late in the game when obvious external signs develop. "There's certainly been a proliferation of senior-cat diets on the market," says Dr. Little. "I think they can be beneficial."

Your choices are do-it-yourself diets or commercial products, says Gary Landsberg, DVM, a behaviorist at Doncaster Animal Clinic in Thornhill, Ontario. Many pet owners want to feed natural or even raw-food diets. "Getting ingredients that act as natural antioxidants is a good idea," he says. Commercial pet food manufacturers also recognize the benefits of these ingredients, and employ veterinary nutrition scientists to design diets suited to cat needs. "They are the ones who are doing the research to enhance their food and make it better," he says. "Cats are so prone to thyroid disease, kidney disease, and diabetes, I think feeding the right amount of the premium food is going to make it easier on their organs in the long run. I don't think there's any evidence that raw meats are any better than cooked meats."

Homemade diets fall in the "therapeutic diet" category. If you plan to feed them, they should be designed by a veterinary nutritionist to ensure they're right for your individual animal, says Dr. Wynn.

Because the older pet's metabolism changes so that she typically burns less energy, lower calories are at the heart of most senior diets, says Dr. LaFlamme. "A lot of them also have added antioxidants, or added protein, or added this or that," she says. "But the real key is that diets are formulated to be balanced based on the energy content of the diet and the expected energy intake of the animal. So it's really important that the diet match the individual pet." There's no reason to offer your lap-sitting feline the equivalent of rocket fuel, but if she still swings from the drapes, she'll need the extra calories to keep her healthy. "By the time cats reach fifteen to sixteen years of age, about 30 percent are actually underweight," says Dr. Davenport.

Here's another example. Most regular adult maintenance diets promote an acidic urine to prevent struvite crystals. Yet this is not necessarily the best choice for an older cat, says Dr. LaFlamme, because an acidic urine promotes the formation of calcium oxalate stones—the type more prevalent in geriatric felines. "That may be one reason that cat owners with an older cat might want to switch over to a senior cat food."

Senior diets typically contain highly digestible ingredients to help cats whose digestive system may not be as efficient as when younger, says Dr. Hawley. "By manipulating the nutrients we have the ability to allow them to better absorb things." Other considerations may be added fiber to keep bowels healthy, or softer textures for cats suffering from dental disease. Your veterinarian can recommend a good senior cat product. Make sure the label says the food is "complete and balanced" in accordance with guidelines established by AAFCO (Association of Animal Feed Control Officials).

FEEDING FOR HEALTH

It is impossible to list all of the various cat foods available for mature cats, but you can start with the following list to see if one or more fits your cat's needs:

- Eukanuba Mature Care Formula
- IVD Select Care Mature Formula
- Max Cat Senior
- Nutro Complete Care Senior
- Precise Feline Senior Formula
- Purina Senior Cat Chow
- Science Diet Feline Senior
- Wysong Geriatrix

Exercise

Twenty minutes of aerobic exercise twice a day helps keep cats of all ages physically fit, mentally alert—and out of trouble. A tired cat is a well-behaved cat! But most old felines tend to slow down and may have stiff or painful joints that make them reluctant to move their furry tails. It takes more effort to get her moving at all, let alone to generate the same activity level as when she was a youngster.

Simple movement gives her a much-needed healthy edge, though. Muscles that aren't used atrophy. Muscle mass is the buffer a cat needs to maintain health and recover from injury or disease, and so muscle loss can have risky consequences.

As for the joints, they help feed themselves by spreading nutrients with the pumping action of their movement. A reduction in movement allows the joints to get rusty, become less efficient, and can speed the progression of arthritis. Painful arthritis, in turn, makes the cat reluctant to move—and reduced exercise can lead to gaining weight. In a vicious cycle, obesity puts more strain on the already painful joints, and also predisposes her to diabetes mellitus.

As she ages, your cat may not be physically capable of maintaining the same level of exercise she enjoyed as a youthful athlete. Painful joints aren't helped by the concussive action of leaps and jumps after flying feather toys, so you may need to carefully control her exercise. Rather than a race across the linoleum, entice her to follow you around the house or up and down stairs by dragging a feather lure. Cats are masters of the stretch and bend, and naturally practice feline yoga. Try hiding toys or treats in places she'll have to expend energy to reach—on the top of a step stool, for example, or behind a sofa cushion. If she's trained to walk on a halter and leash, tempt her with a garden stroll to hunt for crickets or butterflies. Find games your cat already enjoys, such as chasing the sheets as you make the bed, and make them part of a daily aerobic workout. The best idea is to maintain a level of aerobic exercise your cat enjoys, so you don't have to fight her every step of the way.

Establish a daily routine for your cat—ten to twenty minutes every morning and evening is a good target, and is much better than one long marathon session on weekends. Don't wait for her to ask you. At the scheduled time, take the leash to her, wake her from a nap if necessary, and get her up and moving. Cats are champion sleepers and won't need an excuse to steal an extra forty winks. With regular exercise, your aging cat will feel better, act younger, and remain healthier for much longer. When you can do it together, it also enhances the bond you share.

Physical Therapy

"Physical therapy especially for geriatrics is absolutely essential," says Dr. Beebe. This includes a wide range of remedies. Cold packs decrease pain and swelling. Heat therapy decreases pain, increases circulation and healing, relaxes skeletal muscles, reduces muscle spasms, and decreases joint stiffness. Exercise helps improve balance, coordination, endurance, and flexibility. Massage increases blood flow and removes lymphatic drainage from injured tissues. Supportive devices range from braces that help protect a nerve-damaged leg to wheeled carts that cradle the rear end of a paralyzed cat and allow her to still get around.

Overweight felines, those suffering from arthritis, or recovering from surgery also benefit from rehabilitation or physical therapy. Your veterinarian may suggest a program to help slim your cat so she regains mobility. Weight loss will also reduce strain on painful joints. In addition, physical therapy can provide mental stimulation that improves her quality of life. Muscle that's lost through disuse will never be regained, so don't delay getting your cat back on her feet, and back into life.

Start slow and gradually build up the duration of exercise. Try setting the food bowl thirty inches away so she must move to eat. At first, reward her just for trying. If she stops and refuses to go on—listen to her. Give her a break, let her rest, and then urge her on.

Enticing blind cats to exercise is particularly challenging. "Sometimes we'll do passive range of motion," says Dr. Cook. That at least keeps the muscles and joints flexible. For instance, the cat recovering from a stroke may have very weak rear quarters, and the simple support of the owner slipping a towel underneath her belly provides enough balance to get her moving. "You can kind of wheelbarrow them, or do dancing with them, so you work the front legs and then the hind legs," he suggests, but be very careful not to overdo. Some blind cats will follow their noses for a smelly treat, says Dr. Cook. Get creative in tempting her to move.

"I think massage is so critical. They really feel better when you work them," says Dr. Wynn. Massage can be an acquired taste, though, and it will likely take repeated sessions before your cat accepts massage at your hands.

Many large veterinary practices now have a massage therapist or physical therapy specialist to work with clients and their animals. Massage targets the muscles and tendons. Injury to these tissues causes a release of chemicals that prompt inflammation, pain, spasms, abnormal contractions, and tightness of the muscles and tendons. That makes it even more painful to move. Massage applies varying pressure to these areas to increase blood circulation. "Basically you're looking for sore spots, and you work at the level of pressure that the animal can tolerate, so you don't cause pain," says Dr. Wynn. That helps nourish the tissue, relieve pain, and promote healing. It is particularly helpful for animals recovering from illness, injury, or surgery.

Different techniques work best for different purposes, and some require special training so you don't accidentally injure your cat. Keep massage treatments to ten- or fifteen-minute sessions. Once a day is plenty, says Dr. Wynn. Listen to your cat and she'll tell you when she's had enough.

Here are a few techniques. Firm, even-pressured palm strokes are called *effleurage.* This technique helps the cat relax when you stroke slowly from the head to the tail, and down the legs to the feet. Use effleurage to begin and progress to *fingertip massage.* Use the flat of your extended fingers held close together, and rub in a circular pattern with enough pressure to move muscle beneath the skin.

Petrissage uses a deeper technique that kneads the muscle to relax the tissue, promote blood flow, and stimulate the lymph system and a release of tox-

A demonstration of effleurage. Stroke your cat all over with the flat of your palm to help relax him. *(Photo Credit: "Cat Massage" by Rogers Staehlin)*

Once he's relaxed from the stroking, progress to fingertip massage. Avoid pressing directly on top of bones—that hurts! Massage *on each side* of the backbone, for instance. *(Photo Credit: "Cat Massage" by Maryjean Ballner)*

ins. Cats must be fully relaxed for this massage technique to be beneficial. Fingers grasp and gently squeeze, roll, and compress the muscle beside the bone, in a bread-kneading motion. Finish each session with the effleurage technique—a head-to-tail petting session that leaves her purring for more.

COMFORT ZONE

Cats may be more willing to try to move around if they aren't frustrated by inaccessibility. Provide ramps or steps so they don't have to make giant leaps that achy joints can't manage.

- C & D Pet Products (888-554-7387) provides carpeted Pet Steps: Single Step is 8½" tall, for $34; Double Step is 13½" tall for $60; and Quadruple Step is 26" tall, for $150
- Pet Classics (www.petclassics.com) offers ramps, feeders, and steps designed for elderly or disabled cats

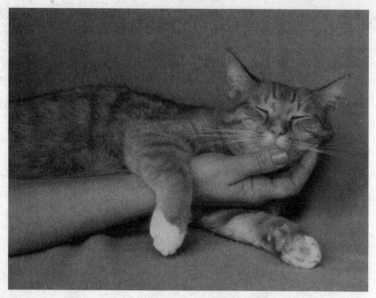

Finish each massage session with a full-body petting, while paying particular attention to all the cat's "sweet spots" he particularly enjoys, such as the cheeks.   *(Photo Credit: "Cat Massage" by Rogers Staehlin)*

Grooming

Fur care is important to your aging cat's emotional health, and also benefits her physical well-being. Cats spend up to 50 percent of their time awake engaged in some grooming activity. Aged cats that become physically unable to stretch and twist due to arthritis or obesity may be unable to reach all the important places. You will need to help her stay clean.

The skin is the outer reflection of inner health. Keeping the fur clean, combed, and tangle-free prevents fleas, ticks, and fungus infections such as ringworm. Feces or urine trapped in the fur is a breeding ground for bacteria and can cause painful inflammation when not removed.

A grooming session also doubles as a home health check for any stray lumps, bumps, or sores that hide beneath the fur coat. Early detection offers the best chance for diagnosing and treating tumors, for example. Besides that, all-over petting can be a feel-good massage or petting session that reminds your cat how wonderful you are.

Good grooming also includes checking the eyes, ears, and teeth. Cats with flat faces and large eyes, such as Persians, are more prone to eye problems. "They are more prone to exposure keratitis," says Dr. Davidson. "That means their eyes stick out so far, and their eyelids don't blink across their eye appropriately, so their cornea dries out." If the cornea dries out, it's more prone to developing ulcers. "It's helpful to use artificial tears in these kitties to keep the eyes more moist. They can be the same type as purchased in human pharmacies."

Persians and Himalayans in particular get a condition called corneal sequestrum. "That's a black plaque that develops on the cornea that has to be treated either medically or surgically," says Dr. Davidson.

Keep hair trimmed away or combed away. Excessive tearing needs evaluation by the veterinarian. "Tears are salty and they will cause irritation on the skin," she says. For eyes that tear more readily, use a clean cloth and warm water on the skin and eyewash inside the eye.

Don't forget to peek inside your cat's ears at least once a week. Cats don't tend to have nearly as many ear problems as drop-eared dogs because the air is able to circulate and keep the ears dry. Cats with very furry ears and folded-eared Scottish Fold cats are more prone to infections because bacteria likes moist, warm places to grow. Keep the fur trimmed around the ears.

Oral disease is a common problem in aging cats, says Dr. Gengler. "It's as important to teach that young animal about dental care at home as it is to teach them about a litter box," says Dr. Gengler. Brush her teeth every day or as often as you can, or provide products such as dental diets or chlorhexidine rinses to help control periodontal disease. "There are a number of different products that are available. You can make amazing strides toward health and a long, quality life span by brushing their teeth."

Accommodations

You need to take into account the special needs your cat may face during her golden years. Adjustments to her environment may be necessary to protect her from injury, or help maintain the status quo and keep her emotionally healthy. Accommodations vary from pet to pet. Think of what's most important to your cat, and make changes that help her continue to enjoy life in as normal a fashion as possible.

If she loses her sight, any change to the surroundings could throw her off balance—literally. Cats mentally map the house and navigate by memory, and rearranging the furniture leaves her without a compass. "Make the house safer for the cat," says Melisa Bain, DVM, a lecturer at University of California—Davis. "If the cat's blind, block off the stairs." Blindness may put her at risk for missing a leap from chair to table, becoming trapped in out-of-the-way rooms, burning in the fireplace, or drowning in the hot tub.

People are often distressed at their pet's loss of hearing or sight, says Dr. Strain, but that doesn't mean the pet suffers. "You just have to protect them from dangers they no longer detect," he says.

Cats with creaky joints or weakened muscles need help to continue their normal routine, because they aren't as flexible or able to manage leaps. "Add extra litter boxes so the cat doesn't have to walk too far," says Dr. Bain. "My cat wants to jump up on the sink, so I put the toilet seat down so she can reach."

Getting on and off favorite perches and resting places is a major issue. Cats used to sleeping on your bed become disconsolate when they are no longer able to manage the leap. "Some people have the cat food bowl up on the washer or dryer, especially to keep it away from the dog. So you may need to sequester that on a lower level," says Dr. Cook.

A wide range of products can make pets more comfortable and maintain their quality of life. For example, you can buy ramps and stairs for easy sofa access; elevated feeding stations so a stiff neck has less distance to bend down; even kitty beds with warming elements to keep old bones and stiff joints limber. "Certainly the temperature can be important with pain associated with arthritis if they're in the garage or outside," says Dr. Cook. "Give them a blanket or move them to a more heated area."

Positive changes in the environment that help your aging cat don't have to cost much. Move the footstool closer to the sofa so she has an extra step to get up and down. "One's only limited by your own ideas," says Dr. Hoskins.

COMFORT ZONE

Try a game of chase-the-bubble to entice your aging cat to get off her tail. Worldwise's Crazy Catnip Bubbles offer a nontoxic, biodegradable bubble solution infused with a special blend of catnip. An 8-ounce bottle costs about $3.50, and is available at www.worldwise.com.

Exercising the Mind

Probably the most important quality-of-life issue is helping your cat to keep her mind active. The old saying, *"Use it or lose it!"* applies for both physical and mental activity. Feline minds become just as creaky with disuse as arthritic joints, so keep the brain and body limber. Engage your cat's interest in the world around her and, of course, in you!

A number of feline brain-teasing toys have been developed that keep the mind active and also encourage physical activity. Try puzzle toys that dispense food as the cat manipulates them. Cats love games of chase and capture, and you can use a fishing-pole-style toy to entice her to "hunt."

Stimulating your cat's mind helps delay the aging process of the brain. Keeping her mind healthy keeps you connected, and strengthens the bond you already share.

Keeping your cat healthy and happy requires addressing *all* aspects of your cat's life. "It's called a holistic modality because you're looking at the physical, mental, and emotional aspects of the animal," says Dr. Beebe. Let L.O.V.E. be the answer.

Golden Moments: Putting L.O.V.E. to Work

Yasmine Galenorn, an author living near Seattle, currently shares her life with four senior citizen cats. Luna and Meercleer are both eight years old; Tara is "probably" ten to eleven; and the queen cat, Pakhit ("Keeter") is eleven. Each cat, though, has aged at a different rate. Although all share the same environment, level of health care, and owner attention, some cats show their age more than others.

For instance, you'd never know that the eight-year-old black-panther look-alike, Meercleer, is a senior. But at the same age, Luna the calico is obviously slowing down. Yasmine says Luna wants to be queen cat, and she thinks the added stress of wrangling over being boss has made her age more quickly.

Luna also has physical problems with a knee injury, and as a consequence has some joint pain that likely will develop into arthritis as time goes on. Yasmine noticed her limping and holding up the leg, and a vet check confirmed that Luna had torn the cruciate ligament, a very common problem in dogs, but rare in cats. Yasmine had to choose between expensive surgery to repair the injury, or forced rest to see if the knee would heal on its own. Confining Luna was a nightmare, says Yasmine. "Every time she cried in the room, I'd feel so guilty I had to go sit with her. She wouldn't sleep unless someone was with her." A follow-up X ray in a month will tell if rest did the trick, or surgery is required. "I'll probably have to do ramps before long for Luna, because she has problems jumping sometimes," says Yasmine.

When Tara joined the family, her teeth were already so bad that even with regular dental care, they continued to decay. "We had to have them all taken

Luna's injured knee makes it harder for her to climb and jump. The eight-year-old will soon be given a boost up with kitty ramps so she can reach her favorite places. *(Photo Credit: Yasmine Galenorn)*

out, so Tara can't eat hard food." Tara now drools all the time, probably due to all her missing teeth. "She'll get drool all over my keyboard, and she'll shake her head and it'll go all over the monitor." Dealing with four cats, it was easiest to offer all of them the same food rather than argue about who got what. "When Tara got soft food, everybody wanted soft food," says Yasmine. "There was going to be a riot if that didn't happen."

Living with four aging cats is all about making compromises, says Yasmine. It's also about staying alert to changes. "I thought that Tara had developed a tumor. I felt this lump on her side, and thought, Oh, my God she's going to die on me!" After checking with the vet, the lump turned out to be Tara's normal kidney. "I never felt so stupid," says Yasmine—but she was even more relieved and grateful. A false alarm is much preferred to the alternative.

Eleven-year-old Pakhit, a longhaired brown classic tabby, still rules the house with an iron paw. Age has just made her personality even more distinctive. "She's very overbearing, and getting grumpier. She's just easier to aggravate and irritate," says Yasmine. "She's more impatient the older she gets, in terms of 'I want it now,' or 'Move over, I want my food now; I want to sit on you,' " she says.

Despite her maturity, Pakhit also sometimes forgets she's not a kitten anymore. "She'll run laps, then try to jump and can't quite hold with her claws, and she'll slide down the wall," says Yasmine. Part of that has to do with her weight. "She's a butterball. With her long hair she looks like this big tribble on legs," says Yasmine. She predicts that ramps and booster stairs—and maybe a diet—are in Pakhit's future.

Today, all four of Yasmine's cats are in relatively good health, and she does her best to keep them happy and healthy by observing for changes, getting prompt vet care, and providing environmental accommodations when necessary. "It helps to listen to your cats," she says. "My cats are my kids." That makes listening with your heart only natural. "If you are tuned in to your pets, you can tell what they need."

CHAPTER 4

Nursing Care

The most important part of your cat's world is you, and as long as you remain a constant in his life, he can live with illness and infirmity and still be happy. Cats aren't concerned about having all their diseased teeth removed or losing their sight to glaucoma—they're just glad the pain went away.

Old cats don't have much time to waste feeling bad—every day, every minute, counts when your feline friend is sixteen. "You hate for them to spend the time they have left in the hospital," says Nicole Ehrhart, VMD, a cancer specialist and surgeon at the University of Illinois. "Pets wake up every day and say, 'This is how I feel today.' If we're making their treatment worse than their disease, even for long-term gain, the pet doesn't understand that."

Based on these considerations, owners can choose (1) curative intent therapy—in which you attack the problem with treatment as hard as humanly possible; (2) palliative care; or (3) hospice. For instance, curative intent therapy would include a kidney transplant that replaces the failing organ; radioactive iodine treatment for hyperthyroid disease, which selectively destroys the abnormal tissue causing the problem; and therapies designed to remove, destroy, and stop tumor growth and cure the cancer.

"With the palliative realm you accept that [the condition] will progress, that quality of life is now reasonable, and so we'll prevent symptoms as long as we possibly can," says Dr. Ehrhart. That might be the best possible choice for an aged feline at high risk for a radical surgery, for example, or for an animal whose cancer is too advanced for other options. It might also be an economical or ethical choice for owners who aren't interested in aggressive treatment and just want the cat to feel good during the time he has left. "Palliative options are minimal hospitalization, and minimal cost in many cases, with nursing care at home," says Dr. Ehrhart.

Hospice is essentially end-of-life care, when medical treatment will no longer help, and the veterinarian explains the end of the cat's life is near. In these instances the owner—or sometimes veterinary staff—provides nursing support at home, keeping him comfortable in a place he knows and loves and with beloved people nearby.

ANGEL'S GATE

In most cases, hospice for pets means the cat is made comfortable in the owner's home. Owners unable to care for their animals' end-of-life needs have few other options, but the hospice movement for pets is slowly gaining recognition. In early 2002, the American Veterinary Medical Association approved guidelines for animal hospice care, and today there are a handful of model pet hospices set up similarly to their human counterparts. Angel's Gate, founded nearly a decade ago by registered nurse Susan Marino and partner Victor LaBruna, was one of the first and is still the largest of its kind.

Angel's Gate (www.angelsgate.org) is a nonprofit animal-care facility where animals who are terminally ill, elderly, or physically challenged come to live out their days in peace, dignity, and love. Marino cares for cats, dogs, rabbits, horses, and critters of all kinds in her Long Island sanctuary. "Our focus is on wellness and quality of life," says Marino. "We provide for the physical, emotional, and spiritual needs of each animal with a holistic approach to caring."

Marino hopes that Angel's Gate will become a model for animal hospices all over the country. Currently she charges no fee for hospice care and relies on private donations to fund the cost of pet food, veterinary visits, acupuncture, massage, swim therapy, and other care options offered to maintain quality of life.

PAIN MANAGEMENT

Everybody has experienced pain at some point in their life, and pet lovers strongly empathize with their cats and do not want them to suffer. But it's very difficult to objectively evaluate pain in animals—they can't tell us, "That hurts" the way people do, says Dr. Marks.

Instead, cats hide their pain and discomfort. This evolutionary trait is designed to protect them from predators that would take advantage of an infirmity. Rather than hold up an injured leg, or whine and cry, cats more likely will hide under the bed. Consequently, owners and veterinarians have to become pain detectives to figure out if the cat is uncomfortable, and to what degree.

Historically, veterinarians have been taught only about disease and how to cure it. "We have never really trained veterinarians to think about pain associated with disease," says Dr. Tranquilli. "We need to incorporate these principles and get the culture changed so new veterinarians learn more about pain and the role it plays in disease processes."

Depending on the type of pain and length of treatment, different medications are available for cats, says Dr. Little. To control postoperative pain for elective procedures such as spays, neuters, or dentistry, drugs like oxymorphone and butorphanol work well. Ketoprofen, an anti-inflammatory drug helpful for arthritis relief, is used often in combination with other pain relievers. More severe pain is assuaged by fentanyl (Duragesic) that's administered in a pain patch, and Dr. Little says the smallest size, used for human babies, can be used for all but the smallest cats. The fentanyl patch often is prescribed for use at home because once applied to the shaved skin, it dispenses pain relief through the skin for three to five days.

Not all pain is severe or sudden. Chronic pain is more typical in older cats, and may be alleviated with something as simple as a heat lamp or warming pad the cat can sleep on. Arthritis is the most common chronic pain syndrome in aging cats.

Postoperative pain may be more severe and require medical intervention. "The majority of the patients I work with are elderly dogs and cats," says Dr. Ehrhart. "Many of them go through what we would consider very radical surgery, and come out with good quality of existence. We're able to manage discomfort very effectively."

She says owners are often surprised at how quickly cats bounce back. Pets typically walk out of the hospital the day after surgery, feeling good, when a similar procedure would put a person out of commission for six weeks. "The degree to which we experience pain has a lot to do with fear," she says. "They don't worry about how long it's going to last, or how much worse it might get. They don't wake up and say, 'Oh, no, I have cancer'— they just say, 'Hey, this is how I feel,'" she says. "We can make them feel decent every day, and they're happy."

OWNER ATTENTION

Illness, whether it involves hospitalization or home care, causes anxiety and stress. "If nobody visited you in the hospital for two weeks, you'd be depressed," says Sheila McCullough, DVM, and so is your cat. Stress makes the immune system less efficient, and depression can cause loss of appetite and refusal to eat or move around. "I strongly believe that owners need to participate in the care of a sick pet."

You should talk to other cat owners, says Dr. Garret. Owners often feel isolated and don't always have the support or understanding of friends or family members. Talking with people who have had similar experiences validates your feelings. "They understand, because they've been through it too," says Dr. Garret. Other cat lovers may offer advice and support for dealing with the situation.

Your veterinarian may dispense medication for you to administer to your cat at home. During your lifetime together, you've probably had experience already giving a pill now and then, or putting drops in his eyes. Care for chronic problems, though, may demand more from you.

Cats recuperating from surgery with mobility problems may need your help being kept clean or getting in and out of the litter box. Diseases such as diabetes or kidney failure may require insulin injections or subcutaneous (SubQ) fluid therapy, which can be administered much more economically at home, and with less stress to the cat.

Restraint

Cats that feel bad may become short-tempered even with a beloved owner. It's impossible to explain that you're giving him pills for his own good. Struggling to get necessary medicine down the cat's throat increases his stress level and may make him even more ill. Safely restraining the cat prevents either one of you from being accidentally hurt, and can make medicating him less traumatic.

Your veterinarian can demonstrate using an effective restraint for your particular cat. Usually, an extra pair of hands makes medicating go much more smoothly. One of you restrains while the other medicates.

The restraint technique you choose depends on which part of the body requires attention. For instance, a muzzle wouldn't be appropriate if you needed to treat a wound inside the mouth.

Here are some of the most common types of restraints.

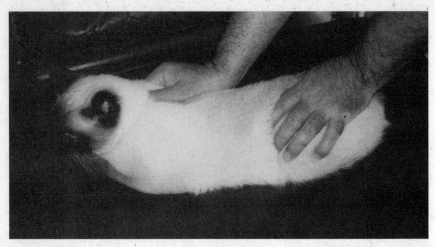

To "scruff" the cat, grasp the loose skin over the neck and shoulders and gently hold her in place against the table surface. That may be all the restraint needed for a second pair of hands to apply the necessary medication. *(Photo Credit: Amy D. Shojai)*

- **Muzzle:** Yes, there are muzzles designed for cats. The commercial muzzles typically cover the entire face and are fixed behind the ears, and prevent your cat from biting out of fear or discomfort during treatment. When you don't have a commercial cat muzzle handy, a pillowcase works nearly as well and also contains the claws. Place your cat inside the pillowcase with the body part that needs treatment exposed through the opening. Oftentimes, simply being inside the bag helps calm the cat.
- **Stretch restraint:** Restrain the cat by gently pressing him against the tabletop or floor as you grasp the loose skin at the back of the neck—scruff—with one hand. Capture both hind feet with the other hand. Then gently stretch him out flat against the table surface.
- **Kneeling restraint:** This is one of the best techniques for medicating cats, especially when you are by yourself. Place the cat on the floor between your knees, facing outward. Then put one hand on top of the head, and the other beneath his jaw to hold him still.
- **Collar restraint:** Commercial cone-shaped collars that surround the pet's neck like the elaborate ruff of an Elizabethan noble are called Elizabethan collars or E-collars. They come in a variety of sizes to fit any pet. However, some cats have trouble eating or navigating with them on. A newer alternative, called a Bite-Not Collar, is

For cats that object to being medicated, the "stretch restraint" works well to contain any struggles. Scruff the cat with one hand, capture both rear paws with the other, and gently stretch the cat out flat against the table surface. That keeps both the teeth and front claws from doing any damage. *(Photo Credit: Amy D. Shojai)*

more similar to the stiff cervical collars designed for people to wear after neck injuries. These collars are used to prevent cats from pawing head wounds or from chewing body injuries. They are available at most pet supply stores or from your veterinarian.

- **Body restraints:** A baby's T-shirt provides the cat with freedom to move while keeping him from bothering healing wounds, stitches, stomach tubes, or catheters. His front legs go through the armholes, his head through the neck, and the loose end is safety-pinned behind his rear legs beneath the tail.

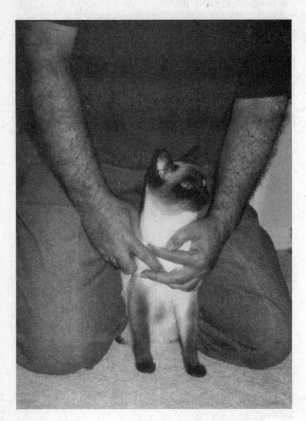

When you must medicate the cat without help, place the cat between your knees as you kneel. That helps confine his movements. *(Photo Credit: Amy D. Shojai)*

Medication

Giving cats pills is notoriously difficult, but often you can request another form of medicine and make treatment easier on you both. A pill may be turned into a liquid, or compounded into a flavored treat. Some medicines can even be turned into a transdermal preparation that is smeared on the skin and absorbed.

Medicating your cat often becomes a quality-of-life issue for cats, and may negatively impact the bond you share. If your cat hides from you out of fear of being pilled, don't be shy with your veterinarian about asking for alternatives. After all, not only the cat's comfort but also his life may be at stake.

- **Topical treatment:** Topical application—that is, on-the-skin treatment—usually comes as an ointment, salve, or spray and is the easiest to administer. Pain medicine may come in the form of a patch

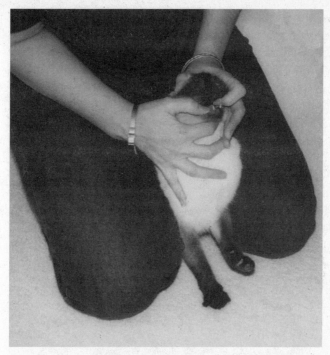

Once the cat is confined in the kneeling restraint, you can
more easily pill him by placing one hand over the top of his
head, and the other beneath his chin. Slip one finger into the
side of his mouth to prompt the cat to open wide. *(Photo
Credit: Amy D. Shojai)*

that's stuck onto a shaved area of the cat's body. Tapazol, a drug used
to treat hyperthyroid cats, can be compounded into an ointment
that's smeared on the inside of the cat's ear and absorbed into the
system that way. Take care the cat doesn't groom away topical medicine before it has a chance to do the job.

- **Liquid medicine:** Applicators similar to eyedroppers or needleless
  syringes often come with liquids, and tend to be easier to give than
  pills. Draw up the prescribed amount and then tip your cat's head up
  toward the ceiling. Insert the tip of the applicator into the corner of
  his mouth, and squirt the medicine into his cheek, keeping his
  mouth closed. You may need to stroke his throat a bit and keep his
  head tilted up until you see him swallow. Cats usually lick their noses
  after they've swallowed, so watch for that cue.

- **Pills:** Cats hate pills. Although dogs readily take pills hidden in a hunk of cheese, cats usually see through the ruse. Or they may take the treat, but you'll find the pill later in your shoe. When pills are needed, circle the top of your cat's muzzle with one hand, pressing his lips gently against his teeth just behind the large, pointed canine teeth. That prompts him to open wide, and when he does, push the pill over the hill of his tongue with your other hand. Aim for the V at the center of the tongue. If you fear for your fingers, use a pill syringe (pill gun or pill dispenser), a hollow plastic tube that places the pill at the back of his throat. Then close his mouth, and gently hold it closed while stroking his throat or gently blowing on his nose to induce him to swallow. It helps to put butter or margarine on the pill to help grease its trip down his throat. Watch for the nose-licking cue that tells you he's swallowed. Sometimes it works best to offer a favorite treat, such as a bit of tuna, immediately after the pill, so the cat swallows the treat, pill and all.

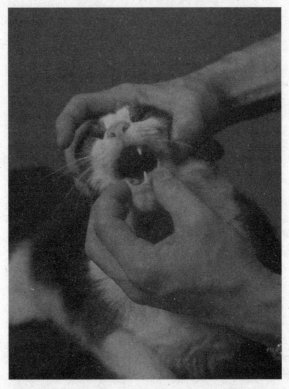

Press the cat's lips gently against his teeth to prompt him to open wide. *(Photo Credit: Amy D. Shojai)*

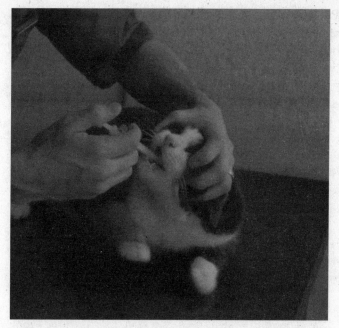

A pill syringe works well to administer medicine to a reluctant cat. The same technique applies when using a liquid medicine given with a needleless syringe. *(Photo Credit: Amy D. Shojai)*

- **Eye medicine:** Eye medicine usually comes as a liquid or ointment. Tip his head toward the ceiling, gently pull down the lower eyelid, and drip or squirt the recommended amount of medicine into the cupped tissue. Then release the eyelid and allow your cat to blink. That spreads the medicine evenly over the surface of the eye.
- **Ear medicine:** The feline ear canal is shaped like an L with the eardrum right at the foot of the L. Keep the cat's head tipped with the affected ear aimed at the ceiling so that gravity will help get the medicine where it needs to go. Liquid and ointment medicine is dripped into the canal. Be sure to gently grasp the cat's ear flap to prevent him from shaking the medicine out. Use your free hand to massage the base of the ear. That spreads the medicine deeper into the canal. Cats with itchy ears tend to enjoy this, and may lean into the massage. Painful ears, though, may require a few treatments at the veterinarian's to get him to the point of allowing you to medicate him at home.
- **Injections:** Medicine administered by injection can provide quicker relief, and for certain conditions such as diabetes, injection

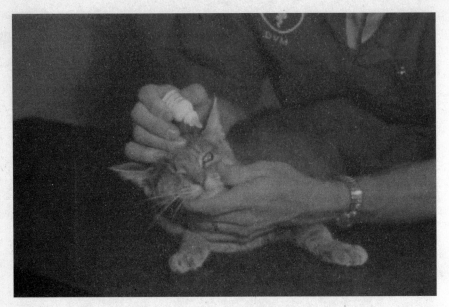

Gently pull down the cat's lower eyelid, and then drip in the liquid medicine. It may take two pairs of hands to treat the cat's eyes safely. *(Photo Credit: Amy D. Shojai)*

is the only option. Needles can be scary to pet owners, but cats don't seem to be nearly as concerned. For an injection, draw up the specified amount of medication into the syringe. Point the needle at the ceiling and gently thump the syringe so any air bubbles float to the needle and can be squeezed out with slight pressure on the plunger. Watch for a small drop of fluid to appear out of the needle, which means air is expressed and you're ready to give the injection. Place your cat on a countertop, grasp the loose skin over the shoulders with one hand, and insert the needle horizontally with the other. Depress the plunger to give the shot, withdraw the needle, and briefly rub the spot to help remove any sting and help the medicine to be absorbed.

Fluid Therapy

"We've taught hundreds of people to give fluids at home, from the very young to the elderly, and I've not met anybody who could not learn the technique," says Dr. Little. Fluid therapy is one of the main things you can do to make cats with kidney insufficiency comfortable, give them a continuous quality of life, and stabilize their disease. "It makes a tremendous dif-

The key to medicating feline ears is hanging on to the ear flap (pinna) so that the cat doesn't shake out the liquid before it has a chance to do its job. *(Photo Credit: Amy D. Shojai)*

ference," says Dr. Little. "It empowers people, too. Owners are doing something very powerful."

All the proper supplies are available from your veterinarian—the IV kit with the plastic line and large-gauge needle, and appropriate fluids such as saline for kidney disease, dextrose (sugar) solutions to feed, or a balanced electrolyte solution for other conditions. Injecting fluid into the veins requires special training, but once your veterinarian demonstrates, it's easy to administer subcutaneous—beneath the skin—fluids to your pet at home. When your cat requires fluids regularly, it's not only less expensive to administer them at home; it is much less stressful for your cat.

- Warm the fluids to body temperature by running warm water over the bag. That makes the experience more pleasant for the cat.
- Suspend the bag higher than the cat, so that gravity helps the fluid run into the right place. You can use a coat hanger to make a holder that fits over the top of a door or cabinet.
- Spread a towel or favorite blanket, or set the cat's bed on a tabletop,

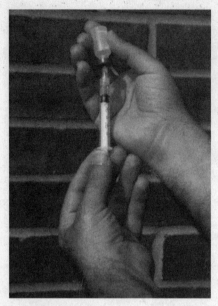
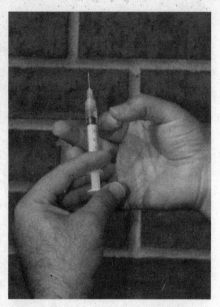

Left: Injectable medications come in a vial. Insert the needle into the vial and pull back on the plunger to fill the syringe to the prescribed level. Your veterinarian will explain exactly how much to give for each dose. *Right*: Once the syringe is filled, withdraw the needle from the vial and point it toward the ceiling. Thump the syringe once or twice to dislodge any air bubbles in the liquid—they'll rise to the end of the needle so you can carefully squeeze them out with the plunger. *(Photo Credit: Amy D. Shojai)*

to pad the surface for your pet to lie down and get comfortable. An ironing board makes a great treatment platform. He'll need to stay still for up to twenty minutes, so make the place as comfortable for you both as possible. A position in front of a window may help distract him. If he's too antsy, have a second person on hand to help manage him, or you can place him in a pillowcase or "cat bag" restraint or wrap him in a towel. Ask the veterinarian if a heating pad underneath a couple of layers of blanket is a good idea.

• Pets that need fluid therapy will have lots of loose skin, and you need to insert the needle so that the fluid drains into the space right under the loose tissue. Anywhere on the body will work, but the best locations to place the needle are right between the shoulder blades or right above the ribs. Grasp the skin with one hand and "tent" it— draw it up off the solid muscle. Then press the sharp end of the needle firmly into the skin, between where your hand holds the flesh

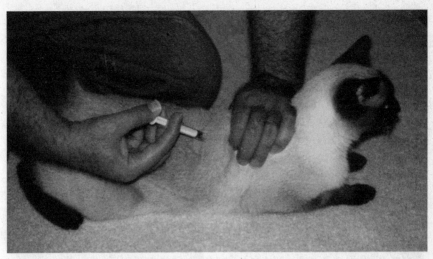

Grasp the loose skin over the cat's neck and shoulders to form a "tent" of the tissue. Insert the needle at the base of the tented skin, horizontal to the cat's body, and then depress the plunger to administer the medication. Remove the needle and gently rub the exit. Grasping the scruff also prompts the cat to be more willing to hold still. *(Photo Credit: Amy D. Shojai)*

and the solid muscle of the pet's body. You'll need to push pretty hard, because the needle has to be pretty large to feed enough fluid in, and cat skin can be tough. Push it at a horizontal angle level with the body until you no longer see any of the needle, but only the plastic head that houses the plastic IV line. Don't be surprised if the pet flinches a bit—but once the needle is in place, he should settle down and won't be much bothered by the therapy. Hint: alternate needle sites to prevent scar tissue from forming that may make subsequent treatments more difficult.

- Once the needle is in place, let go of the tented skin and let it fall back into place. Open up the release valve on the plastic line, so that the fluid begins to drain down and into the needle. Some cats object if the liquid flows too fast, so adjust the speed to accommodate the comfort of your pet. Watch the container of fluid until the amount your veterinarian recommends has been given. A severely dehydrated pet may need 30 milliliters per pound, while for other conditions, 10 milliliters per pound once a day may be enough.

- As fluid runs into the skin, you'll soon see the skin start to balloon with liquid. This does not hurt the pet, although it may feel a bit cool, and will tend to settle and spread out under the skin. The fluid will be gradually absorbed into the body and the balloon will deflate.

- Shut off the valve on the IV line to stop the fluid, and then gently remove the needle from your pet. It's normal for a small amount of fluid to leak back out of the injection site—especially when given over the shoulders. Giving fluid over the ribs with the needle inserted downward will reduce this loss. You can also help the injection site hole to close by rubbing and massaging the place. Offer your cat a scrumptious treat afterward to help associate the treatment with good things.

COMFORT ZONE

Ask your veterinarian about the new "indwelling catheters" designed for subcutaneous (beneath the skin) administration of fluid. Dr. Martin G. St. Germain of Practivet (www.practivet.com) developed the unit, called the Greta Implantable Fluid Tube (GIF-Tube). The nine-inch silicon tube is surgically implanted just beneath the cat's skin, and a small skirt of material is sutured in place to hold the tube steady. An injection port is attached to the outside portion of the tube. The veterinarian will change the port each month, but the tube itself can remain in place for up to a year. A needleless injector connects to administer fluids through the port. That allows you to give fluids to your cat without poking him with a needle.

Golden Moments: Caring for Kricket

Karen and Len Holden of Cedar Hill, Texas, currently share their lives with three senior citizen cats. Tiffany (aka "Tiff the Terror") is the baby at eight. "She is our perpetual kitten. It's like having a two-year-old loose in your house twenty-four/seven," says Karen. Pumpkin, an orange gentle-giant of a cat, is twelve. "He is the most laid-back guy you will ever come across." The two cats are great pals, and usually leave the oldest cat alone.

Eighteen-year-old Kricket is a Persian/Manx and the matriarch of the cat clan. She still rules the roost. "She can be very grumpy with the other furkids," says Karen, "but with Len and me she is very loving." Kricket has overcome many challenges in her long life. The black-and-gray tabby survived the bite of a water moccasin snake, being hit by a car, and even was lost for six weeks before returning home. "We should have named her 'Timex' because she takes a lickin' and keeps on tickin'," says Karen.

The cat has led a more protected indoor-only life since moving in with the

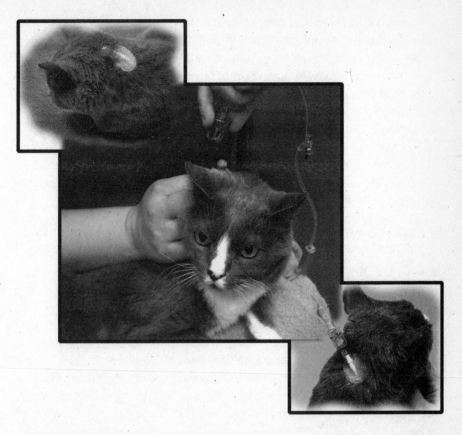

Cats suffering from kidney failure greatly benefit from fluid therapy that replenishes the water their body is losing. In the past, owners gave the cat fluids by inserting a needle beneath the skin, but many people are reluctant to deal with needles. An innovative system designed by a veterinarian eliminates the needle. Instead, the GIF-Tube catheter is surgically implanted beneath the skin so owners just hook up the fluid line to a needleless port.   *(Photo Credit: PractiVet Inc.)*

Holdens. When their granddaughter Danielle was born, Kricket became the baby's protector. "She'd hiss at anybody who came close!" says Karen.

Today the elderly cat is still determined to get her way. "In bed at night, she will paw at my shoulder until I turn over and face her. She'll rear up like a horse and come down on the tap light, and turn it on and off, until I give up and get out of bed." The pair is so close that Karen immediately knew Kricket needed prompt medical help when she became sick last November. Her personality changed, she began drinking and urinating too much, refused to eat, and acted very depressed.

Since it was after the regular clinic's hours and Kricket couldn't be seen until morning, Karen called another facility. "The Desoto Animal Hospital said to bring her in immediately," says Karen. Dr. Erin F. Barcevac examined Kricket and diagnosed her in the early stages of kidney failure.

A therapeutic diet was prescribed to help take the strain off the cat's kidneys. "The vet says the main thing is to keep her eating," says Karen. Foods for Tiff and Pumpkin are also available, and Kricket alternates and grazes from three brands on the "kitty snack bar."

At first, fluid therapy (a sterile saline solution) was administered twice a week at the hospital. The treatment helped Kricket maintain a good attitude. "She was still quite alert, active, extremely affectionate, and had the appetite of a bear coming out of hibernation," says Karen.

But the veterinary visits—Kricket screamed and complained throughout the fluid therapy—were stressful for all concerned, and the cat's kidney values continued to go up. "The fact we couldn't get her stabilized was discouraging," says Karen. Kricket had started out weighing ten pounds, and despite a good appetite, she'd dropped down to seven-and-a-half pounds in a very short time.

Dr. Barcevac explained that more frequent fluid treatments would be even more helpful. Cat owners often learn to administer subcutaneous fluids at home, which is usually less stressful for the cat. However, it does require using a needle, which didn't appeal to Karen. She learned that a new alternative to "needling" the cat was available. Dr. Barcevac suggested implanting a subcutaneous catheter so that Karen and Len could give Kricket fluids at home.

The couple debated long and hard about the catheter implant. They were apprehensive at the thought of anesthesia because of Kricket's advanced age. "I think Len could do it with the needle, but the catheter would make it much easier on Kricket," says Karen. "Dr. Barcevac showed us the catheter. It looked like a little soaker hose." The doctor promised to make Kricket a little stretchy T-shirt to wear over the catheter to help protect it from cat claws until Kricket grew accustomed to it. Karen and Len decided to go ahead with the procedure.

The catheter was put in place in mid January, and Kricket came home that same day. She was to be given a liquid antibiotic (Clavamox) as a precaution against infection, and to receive fluids twice a week. "She came through everything, but was tremendously stressed," says Karen. Before they left the clinic, the veterinarian demonstrated how to administer the fluids, though Kricket was not at all a cooperative patient.

Once home, the cat—now wearing a bright red kitty T-shirt to protect the catheter—settled down into her familiar bed. That evening, giving the Clavamox was a piece of cake, and Kricket made a couple of trips to nibble food during the night. Karen was greatly encouraged.

The next morning, Kricket again took her Clavamox without a fight—as if she knew it was making her better. "Usually medicating Kricket requires an army," says Karen. The spark wasn't yet back in her eyes, but the cat did bat a toy, and gave head butts and love nips to Karen. Surprisingly, Kricket resisted any idea of having the T-shirt removed. "She let me know that just because a girl is under the weather doesn't make her less fashion conscious!"

Two days later, the first fluid session at home did not go well. Dr. Barcevac had suggested giving Kricket some Benadryl to slightly sedate her prior to the session, but the stress of being pilled made things even worse. "She screamed as if it was painful, tried to bite, scratch, and escape," says Karen. The experience made the Holdens dread future sessions—especially since the vet had recommended increasing therapy from twice to three times weekly.

In the meantime, Pumpkin began to play nursemaid to Kricket, keeping her company and refusing to leave her side. "It was as if he became her guardian," says Karen. Always before he'd either ignored her, or seemed bent on aggravating her. Kricket usually put him in his place. "She is a growly, snarly, hissy, grumpy little old lady cat who swats any cat who gets within reach. Pumpkin has always given her a wide berth," says Karen. She was amazed to see how solicitous Pumpkin became, and even more surprised Kricket accepted his watchful presence.

Meanwhile, Karen wasn't at all happy about the innovative treatment. "I was really regretting having the catheter implanted, and wondered why we'd put her through this." Karen says the vet must have sensed her feelings, and told her she would not remove the catheter before a two-week trial was done.

Before the next fluid session, Karen sought suggestions from other cat owners with fluid-administration experience. "The fluids went so much better!" says Karen. Following advice, they warmed the fluids, slowed the rate of administration, and played a tape of the Dallas Symphony Orchestra. "Kricket was in her bed with Len massaging the back of her little neck and me massaging the bridge of her nose and speaking softly to her—she took it like a champ. She actually enjoyed it, and she knows she feels better immediately afterwards. It's working—slowing the drip made a huge difference," says Karen. The following week, they increased the treatment to three times a week.

The increased fluids almost immediately improved Kricket's demeanor. She started to come looking for breakfast instead of waiting to be served. She reestablished her position as queen cat by pestering Tiff the Terror,

When Kricket developed kidney disease, her family overcame their anxieties and learned to give her fluid therapy. *(Photo Credit: Karen Holden)*

smacking the white cat's gray ears each time she came within reach. And afterward, she slept like a log (snores and all), awoke, and demanded more comb time with lots of head butts.

Even more telling, Kricket started purring like a freight train throughout the fluid treatment. Karen and Len knew they were out of the woods when Pumpkin left Kricket's side and returned to his position in the bay window to watch the birds.

Ten days after the catheter had been implanted, a checkup showed that Kricket's kidney values had gone down significantly, and she'd gained another half pound to reach eight-and-a-half pounds. Len and Karen were thrilled at the news.

"I would recommend the catheter implant to anybody," says Karen. "But I would warn them to be prepared for some bumpy roads."

The subcutaneous catheter implants are still quite new, and as with any innovative therapy, unforeseen problems could potentially develop—and hopefully will be corrected should that happen. Some cats have developed infections from the implant, for example, which means special care must be taken to prevent this.

"I'm not saying all our problems are past. I am sure we will face more as time goes by, but for now, things are good for Kricket—and for us," says Karen. She says Dr. Barcevac and everyone at Desoto Animal Hospital, from the front desk all the way to the back, has been compassionate and supportive. "I just wish every animal had access to such loving care."

Nutritional Support

Nothing is more important to your aging cat than good nutrition. Old cats have fewer reserves, and going twenty-four hours without food can tip the balance of health into decline. Good nutrition is vital not only to maintain the older cat's health, but also to support him during illness and help him recover.

Reduced sense of smell due to age, or a stopped-up nose, can make a particular taste seem more intense, says Nancy E. Rawson, Ph.D., (of the Monel Chemical Senses Center, a nonprofit research institute in Philadelphia dedicated to research in the fields of taste, smell, chemical irritation, and nutrition.) "The frequent complaint of elderly patients that the food 'tastes too salty' or 'doesn't taste right' is linked to this altered perception," she says, and aging cats likely experience similar changes in the way foods taste. In elderly humans, odors of a given concentration are perceived as half as intense as they are to younger people, so boosting the smell and flavors of foods are helpful for elderly cats.

Feeling bad for any reason often prompts cats to stop eating. Even healthy cats dislike change. When your cat needs a new diet, perhaps to address a heart condition, kidney problems, or just to change over to a senior formula, it can be tricky to cajole the cat to eat. Cats, especially those that are overweight, tend to develop devastating liver problems as a result of fasting, so it's vital that your aging cat continue to eat. Use one or more of these techniques to keep your cat well fed.

- **Switch foods slowly:** Nothing upsets the aging cat's feelings (or tummy) more quickly, or prompts him to snub the bowl with more determination, than an abrupt diet change. If a switch is in order—whether to a quality "senior" product or a therapeutic diet for a health condition—do so gradually. Offer a 50/50 mixture of the new diet with the old food for the first week. Then give him a third of the old mixed with two-thirds of new food for another several days, and finally feed the new food exclusively.

- **Offer alternatives:** The new diet may be state-of-the-art, but it's worthless if the cat won't eat it. If he still refuses after the gradual switch, ask your veterinarian about comparable alternatives. Several pet food companies offer lines of therapeutic foods, and your cat may prefer one brand to another. Some cats want variety, so offering two flavors allows them to choose.

- **Soften the food:** This is particularly helpful for cats with painful or missing teeth. Dry diets can be difficult for senior cats to manage. Change to a canned or soft-moist formula, or soften the dry diet by adding a cup of water for every cup of dry food. Avoid milk; that gives some cats diarrhea and gas.

- **Increase the smell:** Scent stimulates the feline appetite. Palatability of the food is dictated not only by taste and mouth feel, but also by smell. You may be able to spark his appetite by making the food more pungent. Try adding warm water or an unsalted chicken broth in a drizzle over the food, and heating in the microwave for a few seconds. The warmth unlocks the aroma and the temperature may also help tempt the appetite.

- **Offer intermittently:** Older cats may not be able to eat too much at a time. Also, the "appetite centers" in the brain will shut down if the cat is offered food for too long. Many times, cats are more willing to eat two or three bites at a time if you then take away the food for an hour or so before offering more.

- **Give some contact:** Cats are more likely to eat for an owner than they are in the hospital surrounded by strange people, sights, and smells. Perhaps it's the loving bond they share that prompts cats to eat better when stroked on the head and neck by the owner, or hand-fed the meal one fingerful at a time. When your cat refuses food, a bit of one-on-one attention may be the answer.

- **Tube feeding:** Chronic-care and critical-care patients that refuse to eat for two or three days are candidates for tube feeding. It's nearly impossible to force-feed a cat, even when he's weak from illness. The most effective way to get nutrition into these cats is to place a tube into the stomach, through which a soft diet can be fed. This requires anesthesia. One end of the large-bore flexible gastrotomy tube opens into the cat's stomach, while the other exits through the abdominal wall in his side. The tube makes it possible to feed for weeks or months at a time—often necessary with chronic liver problems. Usually, a high-calorie soft diet is fed one syringeful at a time, and can be managed by the owner at home.

FEEDING FOR HEALTH

Getting concentrated and highly palatable nutrition quickly into the sick cat makes a big difference in how quickly he recovers. Most "recovery"-type foods are available only through veterinarians. Examples include:

- Eukanuba Veterinary Diets, Nutritional Stress/Weight Gain Formula, Maximum-Calorie/Feline
- Hill's Prescription Diet Feline a/d
- IVD Select Care Development Formula
- Waltham Feline Convalescence Support Diets
- Waltham Feline/Canine Rehydration Support (a glucose-electrolyte drink to help counter mild to moderate dehydration)

Wound and Bandage Maintenance

Any wound from an injury or surgery is subject to infection from the contamination of bacteria. Foreign material that infects wounds or bandages thrives in moist, warm environments. Therefore, the best defense against complications is keeping wounds and bandages clean and dry.

- **Clean the area:** Most times the injured area is shaved and cleaned by the veterinarian. You just need to monitor the site for discharge, heat, or swelling—any of which may point to infection. The best way to clean a wound with the least amount of discomfort is using cool water to flush out debris. That way your hands never have to touch the place, which can be very tender. However, cats are notorious for their distaste of getting wet. Your veterinarian may provide you with a cleansing solution, such as the non-stinging antiseptic Betadine Solution. Dilute this 50/50 with distilled water to the color of weak tea. Put the diluted Betadine Solution in a plant sprayer, and use to spray the wound site to disinfect. Pat dry with gauze pads or a clean, lint-free cloth.
- **Protect the bandage:** There are a variety of bandages designed for different injuries, and your veterinarian will show you how to change

them, if necessary. Primarily, your job is to keep the bandage clean
and dry. It's best to keep cats with bandages confined indoors to
avoid contaminating the bandage.

- **Prevent licking and chewing:** Cats dislike anything "stuck" to
  their fur or body, and most will try to remove a bandage. A collar restraint prevents the wrong kind of attention. You can often stop licking of suture sites or bandages by applying strong-smelling Vicks
  VapoRub. The menthol tends to be off-putting. A cat that ignores his
  bandage and then suddenly decides it must come off may have an infection brewing under the cover, or the bandage may be too tight.
  Ask your veterinarian to check the situation.

COMFORT ZONE

Cats recovering from illness or injury may not be able to reach the litter box
in time, or may have trouble getting in and out. Bathroom accidents are not
only frustrating for owners, but they can impact the cat's health as well.

- Save yourself frustration and aggravation by confining the cat to an
  easy-to-clean area, such as a cat carrier, or a small room with
  linoleum.
- Provide a temporary litter box with lower, more accessible sides.
  Disposable foil cookie sheets from the grocery work well.
- Protect carpet and furniture by putting down sheets of plastic and
  spreading disposable diapers or products like Depend undergarments
  to catch the urine.
- Bath Wipes are alcohol-free premoistened wipes with skin condi-
  tioners. They are soothing to inflamed skin, and come in resealable
  packages, available at www.eightinonepet.com.
- 3M Cavilon No Sting Barrier Film is a liquid barrier that dries quickly
  to form a breathable, transparent coating to the skin. This human
  product is designed to protect intact or damaged skin from urine,
  feces, other body fluids, tape trauma, and friction—and it is also
  ideal for pets with incontinence problems. Ask your veterinarian to
  order this spray product for you, or contact www.3M.com, and
  search for "health products + incontinence".
- Products such as Dri-Dek elevate the pet from the floor to keep her
  away from "accidents." The waffle-shaped material comes in sheets
  that can be fitted to your size needs. Contact www.dri-dek.com.

The definition of a "good" quality of life varies between individual owners and cats. How well or poorly a cat functions during illness or convalescence is influenced by veterinary support and your own care for him.

Cats consider their humans to be surrogate moms. "When they see their owner, they know that protection is coming, that security is coming, that 'My owner/companion is here.' That makes a big difference for them," says Dr. McCullough. Caring for these aging and sometimes ill pets by nursing them at home can be a loving and meaningful experience for you both.

CHAPTER 5

Advanced Care Options

Because so many of us consider cats to be part of the family, we want to prolong that relationship for as long as possible. To do that, more and more owners seek a very high level of care, thereby spurring veterinary medicine to ever greater heights to answer the demand.

The local veterinarian has all the necessary training and skills to care for your aging cat throughout a healthy old age. Specific health problems of geriatric cats, though, often benefit from the expertise of a veterinary specialist.

VETERINARY SPECIALISTS

After eight to ten years of study to attain their DVM or VMD (general practitioner's degree), veterinarians can continue with three to seven or more years of further study to qualify as a "board-certified specialist" in a particular health discipline. There are more than twenty specialty boards, referred to as "colleges," which provide certification. A veterinary specialist is said to be a "diplomate" of a particular college specialty. The designation for a cat specialist, for instance, would be Dr. Stephanie Lord, DVM, DABVP (feline), which stands for diplomate of the American Board of Veterinary Practitioners, with a feline specialty. Feline specialists have a particular expertise in cat care.

In general, veterinary specialists have a wider range of equipment, such as ultrasound and MRI (magnetic resonance imaging) for diagnosing and managing health problems. Specialized equipment and treatment techniques are often too expensive for a local veterinary office to afford. Therefore, most advanced treatments are available only at veterinary teaching schools—there are twenty-seven in the United States—or at multiple specialty practices usually located in larger cities. Often, mobile practices bring specialists and their advanced technology, such as cardiac Doppler ultrasound and orthopedic surgery, to the general practitioner's office.

The specialists' training provides them with the skills necessary to perform advanced surgical techniques and treatments, from radioactive iodine therapy (for hyperthyroidism) and kidney dialysis to chemotherapy and cataract surgery. You will find the same kinds of specialists in veterinary medicine as practice in human specialty medicine.

There are currently only three certifications available in complementary alternative veterinary medicine: acupuncture, chiropractic, and homeopathy. "A new certification program in physical therapy was just started at the University of Tennessee," says Dr. Beebe. The American Holistic Veterinary Medical Association provides a list of qualified complementary alternative practitioners on their website at www.ahvma.org/.

People now recognize that veterinarians are physicians practicing in a medical field, and understand why a general practitioner would want to refer them to a veterinary specialist. Dr. Marks says it's quite common for people to tell him, "I wish my grandmother had gotten the care that you're providing for my cat." There are a few differences, though, that you might not expect. "People have no problem calling me at three o'clock in the morning, which they would never do with their physician, even for their child!" says Dr. Marks.

The strong correlation between human and veterinary medicine also has some negative effects when a human family member's medical experience has been less than pleasant. "When I say *chemotherapy* they say, 'Oh, no!' " says Dr. Kitchell. Pets treated with chemotherapy rarely have the side effects we've come to expect with the human treatments. They don't lose their fur, for example.

Specialty care tends to be more costly, just as it is in human medicine. Surgery or radiation therapy can be expensive, while herbal medications and diet changes might be comparatively less. Never hesitate to ask your veterinarian about options. Universities may be seeking candidates to participate in reduced-cost experimental trials, or they may offer delayed payment plans. Dr. Kitchell says some drugs are no longer under patent, which makes them not only affordable alternatives but also offer very similar results to the patented drug. Any therapy you choose must be right for you and your cat, including the state of your pocketbook.

SPECIALISTS FOR AGING CATS

- Behaviorists (American College of Veterinary Behaviorists, or ACVB)
- Dentists (American Veterinary Dental College, or AVDC)
- Diagnostic imaging specialists, including cancer radiologists (American College of Veterinary Radiology, or ACVR)
- Eye specialists (American College of Veterinary Ophthalmologists, or ACVO)
- Feline specialists (American Board of Veterinary Practice—Feline, or ABVB [feline])
- Internists, including cardiologists, neurologists, and cancer specialists (American College of Veterinary Internal Medicine, or ACVIM)
- Nutritionists (American College of Veterinary Nutrition, or ACVN)
- Skin specialists (American College of Veterinary Dermatology, or ACVD)
- Surgeons (American College of Veterinary Surgeons, or ACVS)

GERIATRIC RESEARCH

Veterinary science is constantly changing. Medicine evolves as past breakthroughs become old news and fresh information is discovered. Sometimes doctors find that information they've relied on for years is incorrect. Other times new research builds on the past to give a more complete understanding of medical issues.

Today, we know more about caring for senior cats than ever before. Much of that has to do with our new perception of pets. According to surveys, more than 84 percent of pet owners consider their cats their children. This unique relationship means cat lovers take better care of their cats than in the past. Today, owners want a comparable level of veterinary care for their pets to that which is available for their human family members.

While younger felines more typically develop acute (sudden) diseases and conditions, such as a broken leg or cat bite abscess, older ones more typically suffer from chronic, long-term health concerns. Acute problems are often best addressed by surgery or other "allopathic" treatments, but chronic disease doesn't always respond as well to these traditional Western medical therapies. Some "old-fashioned" methods, such as herbal treatments, acupuncture, and nutritional supplements, offer great potential for maintaining quality of life. "Acupuncture and herbs, the two mainstays of Traditional Chinese Medicine (TCM), work together to achieve healing in the elderly cat by improving the homeostasis of the body, rebalancing it, and helping to stabilize and slow down the degeneration of body systems," says Dr. Beebe.

"Western medicine is very powerful and effective for certain things. If you're bleeding to death, you can't give herbs and acupuncture. You need Western medicine for that," says Dr. Beebe. Yet when surgery and state-of-the-art diagnostic tools are combined with alternative methods, that offers the best of all worlds. Alternative approaches are often ideal for keeping the old cat feeling well during chronic problems like cancer or arthritis. "Most of these holistic systems have been around for several thousand years. Western medicine has been around for a hundred and fifty," says Dr. Beebe. "There doesn't have to be a choice between them."

A 1999 survey by the American Animal Hospital Association indicated that about 30 percent of respondents used some form of complementary and alternative veterinary medicine (CAVM). At that time, seven of the twenty-seven veterinary schools had some educational program in CAVM; 87 percent of respondents believed that acupuncture, nutraceuticals, nutritional supplements, and physical therapy should be included in the curriculum; and 61 percent thought herbal medicine should be included. Owners and veterinarians agree that CAVM has a place in the care of our pets.

NUTRITION RESEARCH

Research is an ongoing process that is never complete. Feline geriatric research is particularly daunting because it requires large numbers of cats to study over a great many years. This is not only very expensive, but finding large populations of old research animals is nearly impossible. Instead, researchers often contact veterinarians and ask for volunteers from among their senior cat clients. Because there are fewer studies conducted, research that is available has a much greater impact on the health of aging felines.

The major commercial pet food companies maintain their own colonies of animals specifically for answering questions about feline health. A number of changes are now being made to "senior" cat foods to address the needs of aging felines.

When senior cat foods were first developed, the focus was on reduced calories, based on the premise that older pets don't require as much energy.

The most important nutrient of all is water. Cats tend to drink much less water than they need for health, and many of them are drawn to running water. Rather than leaving the faucet running, a commercial "water fountain" often stimulates the aging cat to drink the necessary amount.   *(Photo Credit: ©Veterinary Ventures)*

They aren't as active; many have been spayed or neutered, which may slightly decrease their metabolism; and often they're overweight. "We can replace those fat calories with some fiber and slap a label on it, and you've got a whole new realm," says Sarah K. Abood, DVM. Consequently, the label "senior" has been regarded as more of a marketing ploy than being particularly helpful to older cats.

One of the biggest changes in the past few years in understanding senior needs is new thinking on protein requirements. "Dietary protein has absolutely no role in causing kidney disease, so there's no benefit to reducing protein," says Dr. Carey. "It wasn't as big an issue in cats, because you can't reduce protein in cats very much because of their high requirements." Studies by many nutrition scientists indicate older animals are at risk for developing other problems if they don't eat enough protein.

"Cats tend to break down protein at a steady rate whether you feed it to them or not," says Grace Long, DVM, a veterinarian at Nestlé Purina Pet Care Company. If they don't get enough protein, they burn their own muscles for fuel. For this reason, DM Diabetes Management Feline Formula, introduced in July 2000, combines very high protein with low carbohydrate content to allow some diabetic cats to live normal lives without insulin injections.

Dental health also benefits from nutritional research, says Bill Gengler, DVM. Plaque is a scummy material that collects on teeth and eventually crystallizes into calculus or tartar. Once calculus mineralizes, it cannot be brushed away—it must be scaled away with dental instruments by the veterinarian. "If we can prevent or at least delay this biofilm from crystallizing, we have more opportunity for it to be brushed away or worn away by chewing," says Dr. Gengler.

Sodium hexametaphosphate (sodium HMP) helps fight crystal formation and is now added to some cat foods and treats. Another dental innovation in food incorporates a woven edible fiber that makes up the kibble. "It doesn't break apart as quickly so the tooth goes in and out of it several times. That has a mechanical abrading or scrubbing activity," says Dr. Gengler.

Food Restriction

No long-term feline longevity studies have been conducted, but research from the dog side has implications for cats. A canine longevity study, conducted by Nestlé Purina PetCare Company, began fourteen years ago with six-week-old Labrador retriever puppies. Basically, the research looked at the effect food restriction has on dogs over their natural lifetime. "Food restriction is the only nutritional manipulation that is known to extend life," says Dr. LaFlamme. The study involved two groups of twenty-four puppies each, fed identical diets. One group was fed 25 percent less of the food for their entire life, says Dr. LaFlamme. This resulted in a significant reduction in orthopedic problems in the group fed less food, and these dogs also lived longer.

The dog results appear to parallel the results of an earlier study in rodents, and researchers believe that staying thin throughout life also would improve longevity in cats. "One would expect that, because obesity is linked to a large number of problems," says Dr. LaFlamme.

Antioxidants—Vitamin Age Protection

In the past few years, antioxidants have been found to offer great benefits. Influencing the immune system using diet is a new frontier. "As cats age, the immune function declines," says Dr. Carey. "However, if you use the correct blend of antioxidants, you can actually reverse some of that."

Antioxidants are vitamins that protect the body against oxidation. "Oxidation is the metabolic version of rust," he says. "For example, sun exposure is the result of ultraviolet radiation causing oxidation and damage."

Our bodies use oxygen to help release energy. By breathing, we constantly bathe all of our tissues in oxygen. Yet oxidation by-products are responsible for damage to the tissues. The youthful body is able to keep oxidation and its by-products in proper balance. "With age, the ability to manage those oxidative processes decreases," says Dr. Carey. This balance tends to tip toward increased oxidation, which further speeds tissue damage, hinders the immune system function, and increases the effects of aging.

When the cat is given the right balance of vitamins, the oxidation process is put back in balance and aging is slowed. "Vitamin E is one of the antioxidants that do this. In cats it works quite nicely," says Dr. Carey. Research that measures the immune response on the cells themselves has shown that 250 milligrams per kilogram of vitamin E in the food can give the cat the immune competence of a much younger cat. "But if you go too high, you lose the effect," he says.

In experimental studies, antioxidants lessened the severity of age-related hearing loss in rats. William W. Ruehl, VMD, Ph.D. says antioxidants may also prove useful for senile cataract treatment or prevention. Dr. Ruehl is director of clinical pathology for Antech Diagnostics, a veterinary laboratory in northern California. "We're going to see research just explode with regard to the antioxidants and cytokines and interleukins and these immune stimulators," says Dr. Abood. She predicts that pet food companies will apply all of this research even beyond "senior cat" diets. In other words, if it's good for old cats, why not feed it to younger cats so they also get the benefits?

Since certain cancers show oxidation damage to DNA, theoretically, antioxidants should also help protect against cancer. Early studies seem to indicate that antioxidants reduce DNA damage, but it's still too early to say for sure.

BRAIN RESEARCH

Wouldn't the proper nutritional antioxidant mix also protect the brain, and keep cats "thinking" young? Yes, says Debbie Davenport, DVM. In fact, a diet for dogs developed by Hill's does just that. It contains a mix of antioxidants, along with other nutrients such as folic acid and L-carnitine. Studies at University of New Mexico, the University of Toronto, and in-home tests with dog owners have shown that Prescription Diet Canine b/d improves learning ability and alertness in older dogs, significantly reduces house-soiling accidents and disorientation, and improves sleep patterns and interaction with owners. Researchers found that cognitive ability in these old dogs also improved when their brains were "challenged" with new things to learn.

It is believed that aged cats with similar cognitive dysfunction may also benefit from antioxidant-enriched foods and keeping their minds agile.

"We're not nearly as far along with the feline product as we are with the canine product," says Dr. Davenport.

The difficulty is twofold: first, it is hard to find a large enough number of cats of the appropriate age to participate in feeding trials, she says. Second, researchers historically have used dogs, and aren't sure how to devise appropriate cognitive tests for felines and train the cats to perform them.

There simply haven't been as many studies of cognitive disorder in cats as in dogs, says Kelly Moffat, DVM, a veterinarian at Mesa Veterinary Hospital in Mesa, Arizona. "They've looked at brain changes, and they've found that some cats seem to have the beta amyloid deposition that is similar to the dogs or people that are showing [Alzheimer's-like] behavioral signs."

Two years ago, Dr. Moffat began collecting data from cats over the age of eleven to track age-related cognitive changes, and so far, has gathered information from over 150 cats, including some as old as twenty-one. There is a similar study being conducted by Melissa Bain, DVM, at the University of California—Davis. Preliminary results support many veterinarians' opinion that aged cats do, indeed, suffer from similar senility problems as aged dogs.

The onset appears to happen later (since most cats are longer-lived than dogs), and also may develop less frequently. But that may be a perception difference on the part of owners, says Dr. Moffat. "Dogs know a lot more commands, and I don't think we hold cats to that." Dog owners may therefore notice the dog "forgetting" a command more readily than cat owners noticing a more subtle behavior change.

Along with a better understanding of feline senility problems is the availability of new treatments that may reverse some of the symptoms. Drugs such as Anipryl have been used successfully in both dogs and cats with the problem.

DRUG RESEARCH

New drugs become available all of the time, and those designed for treating old-pet health concerns are at the forefront of veterinary research. However, testing and approval of new medicines take a long time and great expense, and some never reach veterinary approval. Medications that might also be used for humans receive the most research funding. Therefore, veterinary medicine commonly "borrows" from the human pharmacy to offer a wider range of treatment options to aging cats. When a drug has not been officially approved for use in pets, it is referred to as "off-label" or "extra-label" use.

A drug does not necessarily need to be officially approved for veterinary use. For example, the drug deprenyl, also known as selegiline (brand name Anipryl), is approved for dogs suffering from cognitive disorders to help reverse the signs of canine senility. Although not approved for feline use, the drug has been used safely off-label and helped a percentage of cats with similar symptoms. Another example is heart medications used to treat common aging-heart conditions. ACE-inhibitors (angiotension-converting enzyme), such as Atenolol, block nerve receptors on the heart and blood vessels to correct the irregular heartbeat caused by disease. Cancer drugs for cats are almost always the same ones used in human chemotherapy treatments, as are most intravenous fluids, antibiotics, and many of the pain medications.

"In the veterinary market we can prescribe anything we want to," says Dr. Myers. "Off-label use is very important for veterinarians. We have to be sensible about it," he says. "It's not something you should abuse, but we can prescribe all sorts of things that physicians cannot." The FDA allows veterinarians to prescribe medication in circumstances where it's needed, as long as they explain to the owner that the drug is being used off-label, what the side effects may be, and how it will help.

CLOMIPRAMINE

Separation anxiety has long been recognized in dogs, and the drug clomipramine (Clomicalm) has been FDA approved to treat this problem. It's currently also used in humans to treat panic and anxiety disorders. It works by inhibiting the reuptake of serotonin, one of the neurotransmitters in the brain associated with good moods. Separation anxiety has only recently been recognized in cats, and older pets tend to more often suffer from this condition. Clomicalm is already being used off-label in cats for feline anxiety disorders and aggression with some success. Now Tracy Kroll, a veterinary resident and researcher at Cornell University College of Veterinary Medicine, has begun a Novartis Animal Health trial in March 2002 to pave the way for possible future FDA approval of the drug for feline use.

Herbal Options

Herbs have been used for centuries as medicines in both human and animal health. "Herbs are very good at helping to stabilize failing systems," says Dr. Beebe. "Chinese herbal medicine is really good for geriatric animals because it has minimal side effects." Old cats that already suffer from cancer or failing kidneys, for example, have greater difficulty handling the more powerful Western drugs because they must be processed through the kidneys and liver.

Herbs not only treat the problem, but also have the ability to tonify (strengthen) ailing systems. Very few herbs have been through safety or efficacy tests, though, and only a handful have any sort of FDA endorsement at all. In effect, one could say that *all* herbs are used off-label, and the best ones for feline health care have been proved by the test of time.

The majority of herbs have a large margin of safety, but they are not benign. "If they were, they wouldn't be causing an effect, and what good would they be?" says Dr. Beebe. Keep in mind, too, that just because an herb is "natural" does not necessarily mean it is safe. For example, pennyroyal has often been touted as a topical flea repellent but it can also cause spontaneous abortions in cats. While Saint-John's-wort is used as a natural sedative, it also can cause photosensitization and make the cat more susceptible to sunburn. Some herbs may cause dangerous drug interactions when used with other medicines. For instance, *Ephedra sinica* used as a decongestant can be very dangerous for pets (or people!) with heart conditions.

Herbs are not regulated in the same way as commercial drugs. Different manufacturers may offer the same herb products, but one is several times stronger than the other. Some consumer investigations into "natural" products indicate that without regulation, it's difficult to be assured the labeled ingredients are really in the bottle. Therefore, you must enlist the aid of a veterinarian knowledgeable in their use, of their interactions with other drugs, of the reputation of various manufacturers, and of the individual animal's problem to choose the correct herbal treatment.

Pain Management

Cats do not react to pain in the same way that people do. Typically, cats simply hide and stop moving when in pain, and become very good at hiding any discomfort. For this reason, until relatively recently cats weren't thought to experience pain to the same degree as humans. Yet managing pain effectively is at the heart of maintaining a good quality of life for aging cats.

Part of the problem is that cats do not metabolize common pain medicines such as NSAIDs (nonsteroidal anti-inflammatory drugs) in the same way as people and dogs. These can be toxic to cats. So even when a veterinarian knew a cat was suffering discomfort, she didn't always have good options to help relieve the pain. For instance, Rimadyl is one of the newest drugs approved specifically to address arthritis pain in dogs. "A lot of the nonsteroidal anti-inflammatory drugs are tricky in cats," says Susan Little, DVM. "I don't use Rimadyl in cats; some people do. But you're always running the risk of adverse reactions."

The Companion Animal Pain Management Consortium, launched in early 2001, was established to study and better understand the mechanisms and treatment of pain. Pfizer Animal Health supported the development of regional "pain centers," created at each of the veterinary schools at University of Tennessee, University of Illinois, and Colorado State University. Veterinarians in a variety of disciplines—oncology, orthopedics, anesthesiology, ophthalmology and others—seek to help pain in various ways. At Illinois, anesthesiologist William Tranquilli, DVM, says each group has been asked to identify their three most prevalent pain issues, and share their expertise. He hopes that this will help them learn better ways to alleviate pain.

Owners must be involved in the process as well. "We suggest that practitioners give owners a chart for them to track how the animal is behaving before and after medication to determine what changes they see," he says. For instance, maybe your cat asks to play with a fishing-pole toy more often, or once again runs to dinner when kibble hits the bowl. "It gives a tool to the owner that encourages them to actually pay attention to what's going on, on a daily basis, and see if things are getting better with medication."

Eventually, the consortium hopes to gather the information into a formal pain-management program that can be shared with other universities, large referral practices, and at veterinary conferences. It is hoped that pain management might someday become a new veterinary specialty. "Just like we now have pain physicians, we may have veterinarians specializing in pain management in the future," says Dr. Tranquilli.

COMFORT ZONE

Harp music has been used in human medicine, particularly in hospice situations, to alleviate pain and distress. Susan Raimond, an author, music therapist, and concert violinist and harpist, lectures with the International Harp Therapy Faculty in Richmond, Virginia. She has been a pioneer in harp therapy for animals.

Music, especially from the harp, lowers heart rate and blood pressure, slows respiration, increases endorphin levels (natural pain control factors produced in the brain), and possibly increases longevity. Add harp music to your pet's environment as a stress reliever and pain modulator, or simply to improve his quality of life. It will help you feel better, too!

Acupuncture

Acupuncture is now an integral part of veterinary medicine, endorsed by the American Veterinary Medical Association, says Dr. Beebe. Veterinarians can be certified by IVAS, the International Veterinary Acupuncture Society, or by the American Academy of Veterinary Acupuncture (AAVA) to ensure they have the proper training for animals.

Acupuncture employs an ancient method for relieving pain without the side effects of drugs. Typically, long, thin needles are inserted into the body to stimulate certain points that affect various systems of the body. Acupuncture was developed in ancient China and has been used for several thousand years to successfully treat a wide range of health problems in both people and animals.

"All the mechanisms of acupuncture are not understood," says Dr. Beebe. Traditional Chinese Medicine holds that all living things contain an energy flow called *qi* (pronounced "chee") that moves along specified pathways (meridians) throughout the body. The meridians connect to all the organs, skin, muscles, and nerves, and illness is described as an interruption or imbalance of this natural flow. Acupuncture corrects the imbalance and returns the cat (or person) to health by stimulating specific points found throughout the body along the meridians. Each point is associated with a particular body system.

Magic? Not at all, although it does sound odd when we're more accustomed to giving drugs to fix a problem. MRI (magnetic resonance imaging) tests have shown that a needle inserted in one part of the body somehow does have an effect on other areas. Certain parts of the brain light up during acupuncture, when measured using an MRI. For example, needling the outside of the foot (the part associated with the eyes) causes the same reaction in the brain as if the eyes saw a flash of light.

"Stimulating specific points on the body can cause the release of certain chemical factors in the blood," says Dr. Beebe. Studies have shown that acupuncture stimulates the release of natural painkillers called endorphins, can reduce nausea, and even can affect heart rate and blood pressure.

Holistic veterinarians believe acupuncture helps the body heal itself by stimulating circulation, relieving pain, and improving organ function, especially the failing organs of older animals. Many times a cat benefits most from using the best applications from each world. "If you have a system of medicine that does not cause harm, that is relatively free of side effects, and could potentially save a life, you don't have to believe in it or understand all of it," says Dr. Beebe. "A good doctor always offers all the options."

SURGERY

Kidney disease and chronic renal failure is one of the top causes of death in old cats. When they are healthy otherwise, cats with kidney failure benefit from an organ transplant. Kidney transplantation is available at University of California—Davis, University of Pennsylvania, University of Wisconsin, and a few other veterinary specialty centers.

Hemodialysis is also extremely beneficial and becoming more available, says Larry Cowgill, DVM. Acutely damaged kidneys may have the ability to regain function, if given enough time to heal, and dialysis gives them that time. Dialysis temporarily takes the place of the kidneys and cleanses the blood of toxins. Dr. Cowgill began the pet dialysis program at Cal-Davis in the early 1990s, and today they are able to treat any pet bigger than two kilograms. "The program has grown and grown," he says. "We now have a second unit opening in San Diego at the University of California veterinary medical center." Other programs are available across the country, including one at the Animal Medical Center in New York and Tufts University in Massachusetts.

Other senior cat care advances include surgeries to treat chronic constipation problems (megacolon), cancer surgeries that remove brain tumors, orthopedic procedures that restore function to arthritic joints, and cataract surgery that can restore vision. Cutting-edge heart treatments such as open-heart surgery are available in only a handful of veterinary teaching institutions, such as Colorado State and University of Pennsylvania.

Experimental and cutting-edge treatments can be hard to find and are often expensive. If your veterinarian doesn't offer alternatives, it's up to you to ask. "We should not be afraid to offer the best care," says Jeff Johnson, DVM, a general practitioner with Four Paws Animal Hospital in Eagle River, Alaska. "It depends on what the client wants to do." The owner should understand the pros and cons, and what home care may be required, before making these care decisions.

Research into feline longevity and health care is still very new. Studies of age-related disorders in other animals, including humans, stand to benefit our cats as well. In the best of all outcomes, both humans and their special cats will enjoy longer, healthier lives—together.

Golden Moments: Zepp's Last Chance

Five years ago, attorney Marc M. Gorelnik, from El Cerrito, California, decided he wanted to adopt a cat. While visiting the San Francisco SPCA, he fell in love with a twelve-year-old longhaired feline. "He weighed about eighteen pounds, and had very light fur with darker on top—a cameo color," says Marc. "He was really sweet, crawled up in my lap and purred and purred. He was very mellow and affectionate."

The cat's original name—Peach Pie—didn't seem to fit, so Marc settled on Zeppelin, or Zepp for short, because of the cat's size. Zepp's heart was as big as his furry outside, and he constantly wanted to be held and petted. "He'd follow you from room to room, wanted to be in your lap, and was all over you when you were on the phone," says Marc. "He was almost a nuisance at times, he was so affectionate."

The first four years together, Zepp had no health problems. "He was a very low-maintenance cat," says Marc. When the cat's weight crept up to twenty pounds, it was easily managed with a reduced-calorie food until he slimmed down to a svelte sixteen to seventeen pounds.

When he was sixteen, though, Marc saw a change. "He'd always had a great appetite. I noticed he wasn't finishing his food, was lying around and keeping his distance. He just didn't seem to feel comfortable." The veterinarian ran blood tests on Zepp, but they were from the low- to high-normal ranges, nothing that convinced the doctor that treatment was necessary. She suspected he might be hyperthyroid, and recommended periodic rechecks to monitor the situation.

Meanwhile, Marc decided to get Zepp a pal—a Maine Coon kitten. He contacted various breeders in January, interviewed and decided on one, and made arrangements to choose a kitten.

Zepp continued to have good days and bad days, and Marc grew more and more concerned. "He'd never had any health issues at all, and he very obviously was not feeling well." After further tests in March, the veterinarian was persuaded Zepp was hyperthyroid, and Marc was referred to a local practice to receive what is known as an I-131 radioactive iodine procedure.

"It took a long time to get an appointment, so we put him on Tapazole," says Marc. Tapazole is an oral medication to counter the effects of the hyperactive thyroid gland. "The doctor said there might also be a kidney issue, but we'll deal with it after taking care of his thyroid."

When specialists reviewed Zepp's symptoms and tests prior to his I-131 treatment, they told Marc the cat was in advanced chronic renal failure. "Then

Zepp essentially crashed. I knew immediately this poor cat was dying," says Marc.

Zepp was hospitalized and given fluid therapy. Marc was dispensed a couple different kidney diets, and instructed how to give subcutaneous fluids at home. "But he didn't improve at all. He wasn't eating; his weight was dropping like a stone, down to about thirteen pounds," says Marc. "My family urged me to get a second opinion, so I made an appointment at University of California—Davis."

Zepp weighed only twelve pounds by the time he was seen at Davis, and had suffered a lot of muscle wasting. Marc brought copies of the previous lab work, and they ran additional tests as well. All his kidney values had climbed. To counter his weight loss, they placed an esophagostomy tube to get some food inside the cat.

Dr. Ellen Macdonald, a resident and internist at the teaching hospital, told Marc there wasn't much they could do. They'd try to stabilize Zepp and perhaps improve his quality of life for the time he had left. "I was beside myself, and in tears through most of this," says Marc. "They said short of transplant there's really nothing that can be done."

Marc was given instructions how to feed Zepp a slurry of food through the tube. "It was real easy to medicate him, but he needed to be fed three times a day." He found a local vet tech willing to come during the day, and Marc handled the morning and evening food and medication.

Despite intensive care, Zepp continued to decline, to the point he was unable to get out of the litter box once he climbed inside. He was rushed back to the Davis hospital on a Friday. "I thought it was his last trip. I was trying to be realistic about it," says Marc. "He had lost quality of life. This was no way for him to live."

At the hospital, Dr. Macdonald asked if a transplant was a consideration. They could run the tests to see if Zepp passed the criteria. Marc asked surgical resident Dr. Ian Holsworth to look at Zepp and his tests. Only a couple minor tests were lacking to qualify him for the procedure. "And they had a slot open," says Marc, still very emotional remembering the events. If the last tests were okay, Zepp had a chance to get a new kidney. Marc knew it was the one, final chance to save Zepp's life.

He took the sick cat home to wait for the phone call that would mean life or death—and Zepp got his miracle. Three donor cats were good matches. Zepp was admitted on Saturday morning, and surgery was performed by Dr. Holsworth and Dr. Clare Gregory the following Wednesday. "They called to tell me everything was fine, and the donor cat was also doing fine," says Marc.

Part of the arrangement of the transplant procedure is that the owner of the recipient cat also adopts the donor cat. Newton, a seventeen-month-old gray tabby, was Zepp's savior. "Newton is a fabulous cat," agrees Marc. "He is aggressively affectionate, and loves to be rubbed on the belly, but he is brutally strong. My brother says Newton is hard like a tabletop with fur. He's been neutered but still has the tomcat physique."

Newton is the best thing that's ever happened to Roger, the brown mackerel tabby Maine Coon kitten that arrived. They are constant play buddies, chasing each other and wrestling.

It took about a month for Zepp's new kidney to become fully functional. He came home with the feeding tube still in place. "He was not good when he came home," says Marc, but once the feeding tube was removed he became a different cat altogether.

Today, his kidney is fine. His extravagant displays of affection have not returned, and he's still relatively quiet compared to before his illness. "But his quality of life is back," says Marc.

Since the transplant Zepp has faced other challenges. Most transplant cats get both prednisolone and cyclosporine daily for the rest of their lives to prevent organ rejection. But he developed diabetes, and it is a balancing act to regulate him because the antirejection drugs also affected insulin/glucose levels. "I don't mind giving him insulin shots. It's easier than dealing with giving him a pill," says Marc.

His experience has taught him that veterinarians are very busy, and unable to offer the detailed attention an owner could give your pet. "Trust your instincts," he says, and educate yourself to what's involved in the health needs of your cat. "If you have an older cat these things are going to happen," he says. "Try to know your limits and try to know your cat's limits in terms of what they can take."

He would do everything again in a heartbeat. "Fortunately, I can afford it, so I did it. And I'm glad," he says. "Zepp has brought me such joy. Looking at Zepp right now, lying on the couch a couple of feet from me, grooming himself—it's worth it when you see that. When you see him doing normal cat things and enjoying it, it's worth it."

CHAPTER 6

Making Choices

Today we are privileged to enjoy sharing the company of our cats for longer than ever before. Of course, even two decades of time together isn't enough. Most cats will not outlive their owners, however. That is a sad fact we must accept when we welcome a pet into our heart.

As they age, we know our cats *may* develop a health problem or disability. We understand that someday we *will* lose them to death. If anything, that makes the short time we share with them even more precious. But as our strong connection with special cats grows stronger year after year, making choices about her life and death becomes ever more difficult. Is it selfish to want to prolong her life? When is the right time to say good-bye? Cost of care, concerns over her comfort, and guilt about making these choices can make your last weeks or months together even more difficult.

There is no wrong answer. Take a moment to look at your cat, stroke her soft fur, and smile through any sadness because you know she trusts you to make these decisions for her. She's not worried. She won't "blame" you, no matter what choice you make on her behalf. And what's more, it doesn't matter what other folks think, or what they'd do—every situation is different, and what applies to others may have no bearing on your situation. Give yourself permission to say, Yes, this is hard. It hurts. In a strange way, it's supposed to be hard. It wouldn't be so difficult if you didn't care so much.

A hard decision is often the right decision when it comes out of love for your cat. Take comfort because the best any of us can hope to do is to make informed choices with the best information available at that time. *Any* choice you make that's based on love and concern for her welfare *cannot be wrong.*

THE FINAL GIFT

Cats are born, live for a time, and then they die. Accidents may tear them away from us while they're young. Some drift off in the gentle sleep of old age and never awake. Others linger in pain, begging for relief with silent eyes. These last need our help, a gift that comes with equal measures of love and pain—that is, giving them a calm, dignified, and gentle death through euthanasia.

When do you know the time has come? When you begin asking yourself that question, it's time to consider the possibility that the end is drawing near.

Does she still like her life? Does she enjoy being with you? How many more days will she have that are as good as or better than today? "I think that's one of the most meaningful measures," says Susan G. Wynn, DVM. "If today is really bad, and almost every day following this is going to be as bad, it helps for you to make that call."

When pain or illness consumes her with little hope of recovery; when your cat knows her fight is done; when prolonging her life offers no hope for enjoying that life; these are determinations only you, as your cat's best friend, can make. People who are closely bonded to their special cats just *know* when the time is right. Listen to your heart, and your cat will tell you when she's ready to say good-bye.

Preparing for the End

Veterinary oncologists routinely deal with owners struggling with life-and-death decisions and ultimately grief. "For me, grief counseling is part of the therapeutic process," says Dr. Kitchell. "We know what the outcome is going to be. It's just a question of how long it takes to get there."

"The best situations are when a client is emotionally and mentally prepared, and they've had time to think about their options," says Dr. Garret. "If you see it coming, you can plan things." For the most part, geriatric cats with chronic diseases such as cancer or kidney failure will not overcome their illness. Treatment actually gives back time the cat wouldn't otherwise enjoy. Treatment offers the owner time to come to grips with the reality of eventual loss. "Prolongation of life isn't really my primary goal," says Dr. Marks, "but if that quality of life leads to quantity of life, then that's tremendous."

Dr. Garret says the best time to talk about pet loss is before you lose your cat. "The diagnosis of a terminal disease is often the time that the grieving process starts," says Dr. Garret. An important part of the veterinarian's job is to talk to clients about their thoughts and feelings, and help them through the process to make the right choices for themselves and their animals.

It's common for owners at some point during a chronic treatment to ask about what to expect as the end draws near. That's beneficial because it helps eliminate surprises, and helps you prepare. Typically, veterinarians will explain treatments and the average prognosis at the time of your cat's diagnosis. There's no way to predict survival with any accuracy, but the doctor can offer an average life expectancy based on the condition and the chosen treatment. "If it's a cancer, I'll explain that we can prolong the life very comfortably but not cure them, and in the end, you will lose her to this disease," says Dr. Garret.

In some instances owners prefer to euthanize the cat while she's still feeling good. For example, a brain tumor could prompt a seizure or hemorrhage that causes a traumatic, scary, or painful death that they don't want to risk their children witnessing. "That's a horrible memory, with no beauty to it at all. They'd rather talk it over with the family, and plan a euthanasia, have the family there, have her favorite toys there," says Dr. Garret. "When she's fighting a terminal illness, any time is the right time to decide to put her to sleep."

But remember, this is your choice to make, and many people can't make this decision as long as the cat looks and feels good. "I respect that, too," says Dr. Garret.

Talking to Children

Being present for the euthanasia can be a gift to both the adults and children in the cat's life when the passage into death is painless, calm, and loving. The loss of a beloved cat typically is the first experience children have with death and losing someone they love. Dr. Kitchell believes it's very important that children are involved and a part of the process. "It hurts to see this," she says, "but it would hurt anyway to lose somebody if you love them." The bond is often deeply shared by children in the cat's family as well as adults, and this needs to be recognized.

Children learn valuable lessons from the death of a pet. Parents shouldn't fear including them, says Dr. Kitchell. "This is not just about the biology. The relationship has to be honored and has to be respected. This is about the spiritual side of that bond between a person and an animal."

Your children are most affected by the way parents, as role models, react. "When they see the parent afraid of death, they're going to be frightened, too," says Wallace Sife, PhD. Instead he advises parents to explain that all things must die, that even though cats live shorter lives, we become better people because of the wonderful love that we've shared. The younger your child is, the easier it will be for him to accept that death is a normal process, and that your cat will go to kitty heaven.

Dr. Sife warns that trying to help cushion the pain with euphemisms may backfire and terrify the child. "Parents will say, 'God wanted him so much that he had to take him.' And the child then wonders, What about me? Doesn't God love me?" He cautions that using terms like *put to sleep* could have serious ramifications, as when that child needs to be put to sleep for a tonsillectomy. "I have counseled terrified children because of this," he says. Older children take less at face value. It's much better and more truthful to place a special pet in a whole new category, where her memory lives on in our hearts to make us better people.

When children are old enough to truly understand, bring them into the decision-making process of euthanization. "The parent is going to decide," he says, "but let the child feel they're a part of it." This is a decision based on love and connection with the cat that should be made by everyone who loves the cat, rather than the adults announcing what will happen without consulting the children.

It's especially important that teenagers be included. They typically will oppose any decision made by parents, but they need to understand how the process works. If the teenagers strenuously object, put the decision on hold for a day or so for them to become used to the notion. "The feeling of working together, and memorializing the beloved pet, can even help unify families that are having problems," says Dr. Sife. When mutual love drives the decision, there's no conflict.

Right Time, Right Place

You have choices when deciding to end your cat's life. Do you want to be present for the euthanasia? Or do you want to remember her as she was, and not be present for the end? "Having owners there is a culmination of the pet's life," says Dr. Garret. "It's a very peaceful process. They feel like they were with them to the last minute." Veterinarians should respect your wishes, whatever you decide. "It's very important to feel in the end that you had the sort of good-bye that you wanted," says Dr. Garret.

In some practices, veterinarians will euthanize animals at the owner's home. If you feel that would be more comforting for your cat, don't hesitate to ask. In nice weather, it's even possible to have an outdoor euthanasia, says Dr. Garret. Other owners don't want to be reminded each time they walk into the room that Fluffy died there.

Euthanasia at home gives the other pets in the family the opportunity to say good-bye, and to understand what has happened. It sometimes helps them to see the body after she's passed away, so they don't spend days or weeks searching and crying for their lost friend. Grief in pets is technically considered to be an extreme form of separation anxiety.

If you prefer to bring your cat to the clinic for euthanasia and are worried about other pets grieving, ask if you can bring them along, suggests Dr. Garret. She recommends you wait until after euthanasia, though. "The person's whole attention should be spent on their pet that they're saying good-bye to." Another option is to take the body home and allow the other cats and dogs to investigate.

Some surviving cats and dogs howl and cry, while others don't even sniff the body. Be prepared for any reaction, or no reaction at all. After she's gone, the other pets may recognize the body is not the same cat anymore. Truly, the part that made her special has left.

In most cases, euthanasia takes place in the veterinarian's office. It often is a sad day for your veterinarian, too, says Dr. Garret. "You've known her for two years—but you know it's the right thing, that it's time. There are times we cry. You can cry because you feel bad for the owners and you're saying good-bye to the pet yourself," she says. "The time when I can go through euthanasia without feeling any emotion is the time I'll quit. I don't want to get to that point." Euthanasia is a culmination of everyone's relationship together in helping an animal to die comfortably and peacefully, with all the loved ones around her, including the veterinarian.

Golden Moments: Arthur's Broken Heart

Bonnie Cheak, a programmer/analyst in Westminster, Maryland, loves her cats without reservation. She's spent many years caring for cats that have developed everything from diabetes and cancer to liver disease, high blood pressure, and stroke. She knows cats develop affection not only for her, but for their cat friends, and may mourn them as deeply as any human. Arthur is a prime example.

The tiny gray tabby weighs almost seven pounds and has lived with Bonnie since he was eight. "People think he's a Scottish Fold because the previous owners broke the vessels in both his ears," she says. Despite his rocky first home, Arthur is very sweet and affectionate. "He's my baby," says Bonnie. Arthur is over twenty years old.

He's been through a lot in two decades. In 1997, Arthur developed a tumor on his neck, nearly overnight. He was diagnosed with cancer and received chemotherapy through April 1999. The lymphoma immediately went into remission and hasn't returned—and Arthur's whiskers also grew back.

Bonnie says the cancer was nothing compared to Arthur losing his lifelong kitty companion, Deerface, in May of 1999. "He was looking in corners. I'd

Arthur's human—and feline—family helped him get over his broken heart. At age twenty, he's learned to love again.
(Photo Credit: Courtesy of Bonnie Cheak)

open a cupboard and he'd immediately run over to look to see if she was there," says Bonnie. "They just loved each other dearly. He'd scream and cry when he couldn't find her. I really thought it would kill him." Arthur also began showing health problems and was diagnosed with chronic renal failure. Bonnie believes stress over mourning Deerface had a lot to do with it.

Bonnie keeps a sharp eye on Arthur's health, but today he's doing very well. "He still jumps up on the counter—pretty good for an old cat," says Bonnie. Various medications to support his kidneys, fluid therapy at home, and regular blood pressure checks help keep him physically fit.

As far as his emotional health, a new love has healed Arthur's broken heart. "Now he's attached to my little five-year-old, Katie, and he'll actually chase her up the stairs. They clean each other and kiss each other," says Bonnie. She believes cats not only can mourn; they can love again—when given the chance.

UNDERSTANDING EUTHANASIA

Before the time comes, ask your veterinarian to explain the usual procedure so you're prepared. Private rooms are generally provided so that you have time alone with your cat before, during, and after the euthanasia. Usually a catheter is placed in the vein as a first step, to make it easier to administer the euthanasia solution when the time comes. Chronically ill cats may already have an IV catheter in place.

Dr. Garret prefers to place the catheter in the back leg so you can interact with your cat's face throughout the procedure. Sometimes the cat will be sedated first, and that makes her very sleepy. You may prefer to forgo the sedation so that she remains alert up to the end, and you are better able to interact with the friend you know and love during your good-byes.

The veterinarian will return after you've had time to visit. As the drug takes effect, it relaxes the cat and she'll sometimes involuntarily urinate, so if you want to hold her on your lap, cuddle her in a towel. If she's not been sedated before, she may receive that injection now so she's relaxed and has a smoother transition. Then a slow IV injection of the euthanasia solution, an overdose of a barbiturate anesthetic-type drug, is administered. It can be very quick-acting.

Usually the cat will die within only a minute or two, and the veterinarian will listen for a heartbeat to confirm that she's gone. There may be a few involuntary muscle spasms, or last-minute breaths, says Dr. Garret. "But it's not them. They're gone at that point. It's just an automatic response by the body."

Most people wish to spend some time alone with their pet afterward. Don't hesitate to ask for this consideration if it's not offered.

The way the euthanasia is managed will influence the way you feel about the experience in the future. Don't be reluctant to ask questions, or make requests for you or your cat's comfort. "About 60 percent of owners who have their animal put to sleep will change veterinarians," says Dr. Fortney. There are a variety of reasons for this. Perhaps the most telling is that some just don't like going back to the practice where they put Fluffy to sleep.

VALIDATING GRIEF

Elisabeth Kübler-Ross documented the five stages of grief people feel at the loss of a human loved one. You will feel similar emotions after losing a beloved pet. The stages are denial; anger; bargaining—"I'll do X, Y, Z, if only he'll be okay"; depression; and finally acceptance.

Grieving is a normal human process, and major loss of any kind will produce bereavement. But Dr. Sife says that pet bereavement has unique qualities, because we share very different parts of our lives with pets. "We have to understand specifically what the bond was, why it is so valid to grieve this way, and not belittle ourselves or doubt ourselves," says Dr. Sife.

Many cat owners look on their pets as dependent children. Even more, an old cat represents milestones in the owner's life—the cat was a childhood playmate, accompanied you to college, was there for your wedding, or your divorce, and perhaps helped you through the loss of a spouse. Losing her feels like losing a part of yourself.

Pet bereavement may not receive the same level of sympathy and support as from losing a human family member, and that makes the loss even more profound. "Many people resent that we can bereave so deeply for a pet. They will take it personally and get very judgmental or offensive," says Dr. Sife. He says that reaction stems in part from society's negative view of death, which makes it difficult to openly express grief, especially for "only" a pet.

Individuals who have never experienced a close relationship with a pet will have the most difficult time understanding your pain. "There's a dimension of life they can't appreciate," says Dr. Kitchell. When one family member was much closer to the lost cat than others, they may be unable to handle the emotional fallout. "For people who don't have that capacity to understand the bond, it's as if they go through life color-blind."

There is no right way to experience grief. Each person's experience will be different, and the process can be short or long. The stages of grief are not necessarily sequential—you may feel depression, then denial and anger, for example. "You do not have to experience all these stages to successfully grieve," says Dr. Garret. While the cat's death may throw you into deep denial, your husband may simply get angry—or come to terms with her death much more quickly than you can.

Guilt is common. Whatever choices you made, guilt often stalks you afterward. Have faith that you made the best possible decision at that time.

Delayed grief may also knock on your door. In these cases, you feel no emotion at first, and feel odd, empty, or even guilty for lack of distress. Delayed grief may come days, weeks, even months later, when the sight of Fluffy's catnip mouse you find under the bed prompts an emotional meltdown.

All of these aspects of grief are normal.

Close family members and friends who want to help you through your grief may not know how to give support. They'll say, "Don't cry." Or try to diminish the reason for the pain by saying, "It's only a cat." "That, of course, only intensifies the pain," says Dr. Sife, and can permanently damage friendships and relationships. "The important factor here is that someone is hurting. And if we are good humans, whether we agree or disagree with the reasons, we give compassion."

So how do you help someone who is hurting? What is the *right* thing to say to help a friend, comfort a family member, or guide your child through their grief? If you loved the cat, or are a pet owner yourself, you can relate to the pain from firsthand experience and can commiserate. If you're not a pet owner, just ask how you can help. Tell them you know they're experiencing something terrible, and that you don't really understand the depth of the pain. Tell them you care for them. Say you want to be there for them.

A supportive, nonjudgmental presence can be the most important ingredient in the healing process. Listen to cherished stories about the special cat—the way she always nibbled noses or pounced on toes each morning to wake them, how she'd chase the laser light forever, the way she snuggled into their lap and purred.

When you are the person in pain, please know that you are not alone. Every person reading this book loves or has loved a cat, and understands the grief of losing a beloved feline friend. You may feel a buzzing numbness, an aching absence that something priceless is gone from your world. It may catch you by surprise when entering a room—and she's not lounging on the cat tree, or ambushing your ankle to greet you. Her food bowls are still on the kitchen floor, with the last bit of water or kibble she left behind. You put on a shoe—and find the sparkle-ball toy she hid inside, and burst into tears, knowing it's the last time you'll ever play a part in her game. Maybe you "feel" her leap onto the bed at night as you doze off to sleep, or "see" her out of the corner of your eyes. These are all normal experiences, and common to people who have shared a particularly close bond with their pet.

It's normal to feel awful. It hurts like crazy, but you are not going nuts. Aren't other things, such as work or people, supposed to be more important? No. Your cat and your grief for her loss are just as important, only in a different way. She had a unique impact on your life, or you wouldn't miss her the way you do. "It's much better to validate those emotions than to just cover it up," says Dr. Garret. Always remember there is no guilt or shame in being a caring person. Never let anyone make you feel wrong for honoring your pet with tears.

The best help for grief-stricken pet owners is support from people who've experienced loss too. You are not alone. Talk about your feelings. Share stories about her with other pet lovers. Local veterinarians or animal shelters may offer grief support groups that meet in your area. A number of veterinary universities host pet-loss support hot lines. If you are on the Internet, pet sites provide pet-loss support groups where you can share stories, cry a little, receive—and give—support to other pet lovers going through the same emotional journey.

At times the grieving process becomes prolonged, and people need help to get through it. In fact, the loss of a pet may sometimes trigger other very deep-rooted and unresolved problems in the person's life that they may not even recognize, or have repressed, says Dr. Sife. "Then they're overwhelmed with grief, and they can only see it as the loss of the pet, which is intense by itself," he says. "That's where it takes a professional counselor who is professionally trained and capable of identifying and helping the person."

HONORING THE MEMORY

How you commemorate your special cat's death can help you get through the grieving process. You will need to decide what becomes of her body. When your cat was treated by a teaching hospital at a university, you may be asked about allowing an autopsy, especially if it's an un-usual case. This could be considered a legacy that will help the lives of other cats.

Your veterinarian should have suggestions for taking care of her body, and may provide services for clients who do not have the ability or re-sources to make other arrangements. Rural areas with property available may offer the opportunity for a home burial. Be aware that some cities have laws prohibiting burial of pets within residential areas, so check with offi-cials in your area. A home interment allows you to create a memorial grave site in a setting familiar to the missing cat friend—perhaps beneath a fa-vorite tree she loved.

Pet cemeteries provide a "formal" burial arrangement. That may in-clude the plot, casket, a gravestone or marker with inscription, or even a burial service. These cemeteries can be expensive, though. Cremation has become a popular choice, particularly for urban pet owners. It's typically less expensive than a cemetery. The pet's ashes can be kept in a container of your choice in your home, garden, or even scattered in a memorial cere-mony. Ask your vet for a local referral for a pet cemetery or crematorium service.

Funeral ceremonies, memorials such as planting a tree, or making a charitable donation in memory of a beloved pet offer wonderful memorials for the departed cat. Some veterinarians will make a paw impression for you, or you may wish to keep a lock of fur. There are no wrong choices. "Little things like that really help an owner through the grieving process," says Dr. Garret. A formalized type of memorial can be particularly helpful to children. "We have to show children that bereavement is a loving process of remembrance," says Dr. Sife.

After the death of a cat, some people want another cat right away, while others may never be ready for another pet. Each person has a different time frame. But cats seem to have their own time frame, and often our "next" feline love chooses us. It's not uncommon for owners to say that the deceased cat "sent" the new one. If that happens, rejoice and enjoy your new friend, not as a replacement but as a legacy to her memory. After all, other cats need you, and such unselfish love should not be wasted.

Death is a natural process. It will come despite our best efforts to delay the inevitable. But it does not have to be scary, or painful, or bad—dying can, in fact, be a beautiful, loving experience for both you and your cat. "We are the best memorials that we can create for our pets," says Dr. Sife. "If we can make our lives better because of them, that is a wonder-ful tribute."

COMFORT ZONE

Memorializing your cat can be a comfort to you and tribute to her life. Memorials can be expensive purchases, such as a grave marker, or something as simple as creating a scrapbook full of memories. There is no right or wrong way, and creative remembrances that are individual to your cat will mean the most.

- Write a letter or poem to your cat. Tributes can be posted at www.in-memory-of-pets.org/tributes.asp or other sites. She can even be honored in a "virtual" pet cemetery, such as www.rainbowsbridge.com, and www.mycemetery.com.
- Donate money in your pet's honor to a worthy animal organization.
- If your friend is grieving, send a note of sympathy. Hallmark launched its Pet Love Greetings line in 1995 that includes sympathy cards, and other cards are also available. You could purchase a blank card with a cat illustration on the front and send a personal note.
- Commission a portrait from an animal artist.
- Inscribe a headstone, grave marker, or other keepsake with your cat's name. Garden Grace (877-252-1221, www.gardenstones.net) offers pet memorial slate stepping stones, and Reflections in Time (252-514-4494, www.reflectionsintime.net) custom-engraves slate and glassware for pet memorials and wall plaques.
- Make a pawprint impression. World by the Tail (970-223-5753) sells a kit for about $10 with molding clay that's baked in the oven. Pawprints (800-827-6985, www.pearhead.com) also offers a kit.
- Choose an urn or container for cremation remains. Pro Connection (877-4-OUR PET, www.proconxn.com) uses fossil stones with inside storage for the pet's tag, lock of fur, toy, or cremated ashes. GoodWorks (888-586-8400, www.4goodworks.com) custom-designs porcelain urns and decorates them with a photo of your pet. BrandNew Memorial Markers (800-964-8251, www.brandnewpetmarkers.com) are hardwood urns with a custom copper plaque with the pet's personal information.

Golden Moments: Midgie's Legacy

Five-year-old Midgie came to live with Wendy Braun of Albany, New York, ten years ago. The frightened black-and-white cat lost her owner and needed a new home. It took a little over a month to bring the beautiful cat out of her shell, and then Midgie claimed Wendy as her special person.

Midgie's lessons of love will stay with her owner forever. *(Photo Credit: Wendy Braun)*

When chronic medical problems required Wendy to be hospitalized, Midgie refused to move from the door until she returned. Wendy says it made an important difference in her well-being. "I believe Midgie was sent to me," she says, and as each year passed, the bond between the two became stronger.

Then last April, Midgie began wheezing, and the veterinarian diagnosed asthma. "I told myself medication would take care of her. But something told me she didn't have a whole lot longer to live," says Wendy.

Wendy's brother recommended she put the cat to sleep and get a healthy cat that needed a home. "But she was my best friend," says Wendy. The cat had been there for Wendy during her own illnesses, the death of close friends, and an extremely traumatic separation and divorce. Their deep love and special relationship made the thought of losing Midgie even more difficult. "It was the first time in my whole life that I cried," says Wendy. She was determined to support her friend during this time of need.

Midgie fought being medicated, so Wendy devised creative schedules and a treatment box that the cat readily accepted. Wendy also learned to value the affection they shared during crises as much as the love felt during the peaceful times. "That's a hard lesson to learn when you're frightened," says Wendy.

Eventually the cat stopped fighting and relaxed. "It was a whole different love. She literally put herself in my hands," says Wendy, still moved to tears at the memory. Knowing the end was near, Wendy asked her veterinarian what to expect. "I had never seen an animal die, and Midgie didn't need me being hysterical," says Wendy. "She needed to draw on the love that I had for her rather than my fear."

Midgie died at home, in Wendy's arms, and felt her friend's love until the end.

Dealing with the aftermath was difficult because other people didn't understand or support her feelings. Wendy chose to honor the cat's memory, despite what others thought. She took three days off from work, sought out grief counselors, posted to Internet message boards to talk about her loss, and slowly the pain grew less as she began to dwell more on happy memories.

A box with a picture of a tuxedo cat that looks like Midgie holds her ashes, and has a place of honor in Wendy's office. The treatment box has become a planter memorial to the cat, and Wendy is making a scrapbook to hold pictures, a lock of her fur, and special favorite toys, like a feather Midgie loved.

"Cats bond with us at a level that most human beings don't get to." Wendy knows that Midgie will always be a part of her heart. "I miss her quiet, steadfast, peaceful, mature nature. Even though it's sad she's gone, I've learned to enjoy her legacy," says Wendy. Midgie taught Wendy how to grieve, and then heal without giving up on love. "You can love in death as well as life."

PART TWO

A-to-Z Health Concerns

Arthritis

Arthritis is a degenerative disease of the joints. It's caused by inflammation and degradation of the cartilage, resulting in increasing pain that interferes with mobility. Unlike dogs, cats with arthritis often show few if any symptoms until the condition has become severe, says Kathleen Linn, DVM, an orthopedic surgeon at the University of Wisconsin. She attributes that to the cat's lighter weight and athleticism. "Cats are very good at protecting things that hurt. They can have terrible arthritis on X rays and you'd never know."

Because of their habit of hiding infirmities, cats are less likely to be diagnosed with arthritis—but that doesn't mean they aren't suffering, says Dr. Little. You just have to look for the condition. "I see a lot of cats with arthritis," she says. "In the past it was attributed to getting old, when in reality kitty may not want to go down three flights of stairs to get to his litter box because his hips hurt. We have to start realizing there may actually be a medical reason that can be treated, instead of just blaming it on old age."

Specialized tissue called cartilage cushions the ends of the bones that form joints, and allows the bones to move freely against each other. A joint capsule encases the cartilage and contains a fluid-producing membrane that lubricates and maintains cartilage health. The natural motion of the joint pumps this synovial fluid where it's needed.

Injury to the cartilage from trauma, such as broken bones, predisposes the cat to arthritis as he ages. Damage and inflammation develop when the bones fit imperfectly in the joint and erode the cartilage when they rub to-

---

SENIOR SYMPTOMS

Cats rarely vocalize pain. "They're very stoic creatures," says Dr. Linn. "Owners frequently don't think their animals are in pain until they're having a really tough time getting around." Look for:

- Overall reduction in activity, sleeping a lot, and simply not moving at all, especially in the morning. Movement warms up the joints, and mobility often improves later in the day.
- Reluctance to jump up onto or off of the couch, the bed, or the countertop, or use the stairs.
- Failure to groom.
- Limping or holding up a paw or leg.

---

gether. Damaged cartilage releases inflammation-causing enzymes, which interfere with elasticity and the ability of the joint capsule to nourish and repair itself. The resulting pain causes cats to stop moving, and that causes even more damage when loss of motion reduces the distribution of the synovial fluid.

Loose or torn tendons are more common in dogs but can also occur in cats. Tendons and ligaments normally hold the bones in place, and tears cause joint instability that leads to arthritis. For example, a torn anterior cruciate ligament can cause knee instability that eventually results in arthritis.

It's hard to say which cat breeds are more prone to arthritic changes because no specific studies have been done. Greater weight places more stress on the joints, so larger cats such as Maine Coons and those that are overweight tend to have more arthritis. Any cat can develop it, though, and they become more prone the older they get.

The most common area affected is the hip, which may develop as a consequence of dysplasia. This is a developmental disease in which the hip joints do not fit correctly. Lightweight and athletic cats often compensate and may never show problems, but as they age, they're more likely to experience discomfort. Elbows, back, and knees also may develop arthritis. Affected cats typically have trouble keeping themselves well-groomed because it hurts them to stretch and flex to reach everywhere.

Arthritis usually is diagnosed based on symptoms and X rays. Once arthritis is diagnosed, therapy consists of any one or a combination of surgery, physical therapy, medical management (drugs), weight control, and acupuncture.

AGE-DEFYING TIPS

Arthritis almost always develops as a result of joint injury earlier in life, so prompt repair or treatment prevents problems later. Once your old cat has any degree of arthritis, you can slow down the progression and even reverse some of the signs, says Michael G. Conzemius, DVM, a veterinary surgeon at Iowa State University.

- Keep kitty active. Low-impact exercise is ideal to help keep joints from stiffening. Entice him with a treat or ribbon lure to keep him moving.
- Keep cats thin. Added weight puts more stress upon joints. Regular exercise along with a reduced-calorie "senior" diet helps reduce or control weight.

NONSURGICAL TREATMENT

James L. Cook, DVM, recommends a triad approach to the nonsurgical management of arthritis. This includes weight control, exercise, and pain relief such as medication, acupuncture, or other therapies.

The first thing to realize is that a cure is not possible. Arthritis won't get any better once the damage has been done. But the severity of the symptoms can be lessened. "Our goals are to decrease pain, increase function, and increase quality of life and slow down progression," says Dr. Cook.

Owners have to monitor the cat's treatment in order to measure success. Improvements can be subtle, so keep a chart that logs and compares progress of symptoms, says Dr. Cook. That record helps the veterinarian decide if a particular therapy is helpful or not, and adjust the treatment accordingly. Since you live with your cat, and are more closely attuned to his well-being, your input is vital to helping the cat maintain quality of life. "The last thing I want to do is change things that may be working," says Dr. Cook. You can use a form such as the Arthritis Report Card (page 124) to keep track of the cat's status.

Weight Control

"Weight loss for cats is important," says Dr. Linn, and is probably the most critical aspect of the triad approach. "A lot of cats look like basketballs and always have a hard time getting around."

Great care must be taken with reducing diets, though, because a crash

ARTHRITIS REPORT CARD
Patient:
Month:

Week 1

Attitude   Normal   Depressed   Agitated   Comments:

Appetite   Normal   Decreased   Increased   Comments:

Body Condition   1 2 3 4 5 6 7 8 9   Weight (optional):
**Purina Body Condition System™—www.purina.com

Activity   Type   Walking   Running   Playing
                Duration
                Frequency

Pain   At rest   0 1 2 3 4 5 6 7 8 9

                Morning   0 1 2 3 4 5 6 7 8 9

                Walking   0 1 2 3 4 5 6 7 8 9

                Running/Playing   0 1 2 3 4 5 6 7 8 9
**visual analog scale: 0 = no pain to 9 = severe pain

Medications: Type   medicine   dose   given   days missed
                        name   how
                                              often

---

diet in cats can cause life-threatening liver problems called hepatic lipido-sis, or fatty liver disease. If the cat is already at a good weight, he should maintain it, says Dr. Cook. "We give owners the little Purina body condi-tion score, and tell them we want them somewhere around a 4 or 5, which is the leaner ideal on that scale."

Exercise

The second part of the triad is moderate exercise. "It's better for them to get up and move around than to just lie around the house all day," says Dr. Linn. Dogs are easier to exercise, and swimming is considered an ideal

---

FEEDING FOR HEALTH

Reduced-calorie diets are helpful to slim down an overweight cat and help take the strain off arthritic joints. Regular "senior" formulas may do the trick, but in some cases a veterinary-supervised diet is required. Some foods also contain ingredients designed to help ease the discomfort of achy joints. Some options include:

- Eukanuba Adult Weight Control Formula
- Eukanuba Veterinary Diets Nutritional Weight Loss Formulas Restricted-Calorie/Feline
- Hill's Prescription Diet Feline r/d (reduction diet)
- Hill's Prescription Diet Feline w/d (weight diet)
- IVD Select Care Feline Weight Formula
- Nutro Max Weight Control Formula
- Precise Feline Light Formula
- Max Cat Lite
- Purina Veterinary Diets, OM Overweight Management Formula
- Waltham Feline Calorie Control Diet

---

activity for loosening arthritic joints. Cats, though, rarely care for water sports and may also be reluctant to walk on a leash. "Slow walks on a leash are fairly low-impact. It doesn't bang on the joints," says Dr. Linn.

Even old cats can learn new tricks, though. Choose a figure-eight style harness and get the cat used to the idea first simply by petting him with the leash and harness. This helps him associate pleasant things with the equipment and also identifies them with his own comforting scent. Leave the halter and leash out in the room for him to sniff and investigate at his leisure. Try to entice him into a chase game with the end of the leash—if he identifies it with a toy, it won't seem so scary. After a day or two, fit the halter on the cat, leave on for a minute, reward him with a game or treat, and then remove it. Repeat this exercise several times a day over the next few days, gradually increasing the amount of time he wears the halter. Finally, hook on the leash, pick up the end, and follow your cat around the house. Once he's used to this, you can begin to guide him with gentle tug-releases on the leash to keep him moving. A halter and leash allows your cat to be safely walked around the house or even in the backyard, which may inspire him to exercise a bit more to investigate all the new smells and sights.

Teaching a reluctant cat to accept the halter and leash takes quite a bit of patience. A more painless method capitalizes on the cat's own instincts. "About the most useful way to get a cat up and moving is to play," says Dr.

Linn. "Find something she wants that gets her attention as much as possible. You have to find out what motivates the cat." Use a treat, a feather toy, the beam from a flashlight, or some other enticement to lure him into action. Fishing-pole toys work well for many cats. Avoid making him leap for the lure, which can jar the joints. Keep the toy on the ground so that he can stalk and chase and pounce but doesn't overdo.

Ten minutes several times a day is a good start, says Dr. Conzemius. Small amounts daily are much better than marathon sessions once a week. Massage before and after exercise can help keep muscles from tightening, which can make your cat reluctant to get off his furry tail. It also doubles as a nice bonding exercise.

NURSE ALERT!

- A number of arthritis medications are available. Nearly all are in pill form, and will require you to pill your cat one or more times a day.
- Many cats enjoy and benefit from massage, especially from someone they love.
- Following surgery, you may be required to keep incisions or bandages clean, restrict your cat's movement, or encourage him in physical-therapy activities.

Medication

Each arthritis medication has advantages and disadvantages, says Dr. Cook. What works best for your cat may not be helpful for another, but you won't know until you try. Generally he recommends a three-week trial on any medication. The results are monitored, and if it's not working, another drug can be tried.

NSAIDs—nonsteroidal anti-inflammatory drugs—are a class of medication that can really help arthritic dogs and people. Aspirin is the best known of these. The drugs work by affecting the production of certain enzymes that are involved in joint inflammation and pain.

But cats are much more difficult to treat for pain because they lack the enzyme that breaks down many of the most common NSAIDs, says Dr. Linn. "Consequently, cats can be poisoned by a number of analgesics. Tylenol kills cats, and aspirin isn't so hot either."

Aspirin *can* be given to cats but only under a veterinarian's supervision, and care must be taken not to overdose. It's not the best choice for pain relief anyway—Dr. Little says aspirin is effective only in relatively mild cases of arthritis. Carprofen, trade name Rimadyl, is approved for dogs, and with care it can be used off-label in cats. "I don't use Rimadyl in cats, but some people do," she says.

"Metacam (meloxicam), made by Janssen Animal Health, is another one licensed for dogs, but there is a feline dose," says Dr. Little. The manufacturer's feline recommendations call for an initial injection (0.2 mg/kg), followed by a daily oral dose (0.1 mg/kg) for four days. "There is an oral liquid form of Metacam available in Canada," she says. "It is hard to recommend meloxicam for chronic conditions, since cats are very sensitive to the gastric and renal side effects of these nonsteroidal anti-inflammatory drugs."

Dr. Linn says Ketoprofen is probably the most commonly used NSAID in cats. It's also currently used off-label. "It certainly isn't approved for use in cats, but a lot of the folks I know who medicate cats with analgesics have liked it."

Another group of drugs—steroid—can help ease feline arthritis pain. "Cats are very steroid-tolerant as a species," says Dr. Little. "Occasionally I'll use prednisone for advanced high-inflammatory effect, because cats tolerate prednisone on the whole better than most of the NSAIDs, and you have less risk of a problem with prednisone in a cat." The dose varies, but generally the lowest dose possible that keeps them comfortable is given.

Nutraceuticals

Today, a variety of nutritional supplements—nutraceuticals—are used like drugs to treat a wide range of health conditions. Also called "functional foods," these substances maintain or improve health beyond what ordinary nutrients in the food provide. Nutraceuticals include herbs, enzymes, animal extracts (i.e., liver), and other chemical compounds such as vitamins or microbial products including "good" bacteria found in yogurt, for example.

Some of the newest "senior" diets contain nutraceuticals said to benefit joint health. You can also add appropriate supplements to your cat's diet. For example, Dr. Linn says essential fatty acids, specifically the omega-3 fatty acids, can alleviate arthritis pain. "A lot of folks prescribe a combination supplement called DermCaps," she says. Products that contain green-lipped mussels (perna mussel), such as Glyco-Flex, are helpful because they contain glucosaminelike compounds. They also smell fishy, which is very helpful when trying to medicate cats.

A group of compounds are thought to help diseased cartilage work a little better, and may slow or stop the progression of arthritis. "We've actually done some of the research here, and other labs have verified that . . . glucosamines work as an antidegradative," says Dr. Cook. He particularly likes using these products because they have no side effects and can be used alongside other medications.

Dr. Little agrees. "Glucosamine and those related products have been used in cats for a long time." Compounds such as chondroitin and glucosamine also have anti-inflammatory properties, says Dr. Conzemius. "They can reduce swelling, and that can help with the pain." Some products work better than others. "The glucosamine HCL is probably the best," says Dr. Cook, because it's better absorbed into the joint compared to the others.

You can buy glucosamine HCL or other products over the counter, but you should be aware that the nutraceutical industry is not well regulated. The effectiveness and quality of products varies greatly from brand to brand, says Dr. Linn, and not all the label claims on products have been found to be truthful. A glucosamine and chondroitin sulfate combination product, called Cosequin, is one of the few that's actually been tested in scientific trials, and it is most often recommended by veterinarians. It is, however, more expensive than many health-food products.

Dr. Cook suggests looking on the label specifically for 500-milligram dosage of glucosamine HCL. The general dose is about 10 milligrams per pound of body weight, twice a day—so a fifteen-pound cat would get a total of a third of a 500-milligram capsule once each day. "With the glucosamine in cats, you sometimes you have to break up the capsules, or you can get somebody to compound it. I've not seen [over-the-counter products dosed] below 500," says Dr. Cook. "Once we're getting a good effect, then we try and figure out the minimal dose that's effective, and back them off over time."

Acupuncture

Acupuncture is not a drug, but can act like one to relieve the pain of arthritis. It can be used with drugs, or neutraceuticals such as Cosequin. "Acupuncture is a good choice for arthritis in cats," says Dr. Little. The insertion of needles in proscribed locations throughout the body prompts the release of natural painkillers called endorphins. Most cats tolerate these needles quite well.

"Some animals don't tolerate the medication, or the owners don't like medication," says Dr. Fortney. "As long as the diagnosis has been made and there is some science, I've seen some success with acupuncture. It's a matter of combining whatever it takes to improve the quality of life. I think that's very appropriate."

COMFORT ZONE

- Stair steps or stools help arthritic cats reach the bed or cat tree perch when they can no longer make that leap. Commercial ramps are available in different sizes from places such as www. catfurniture.com, but it's simplest and most economical to position a chair, hassock, or cardboard box for access.
- Move food bowls and litter boxes to an accessible location to eliminate the need to jump up or down for dinner. Set the bowl on a shirt box so the cat won't have to bend his sore neck clear to the ground.
- Cut down the high sides of litter boxes, or provide a low-sided pan, so arthritic cats can more easily climb in and out.
- Cats love basking in a puddle of sunlight, and heat helps relieve joint pain and keeps the cat more limber. Heated beds help ease the pain of achy, stiff joints, or you can use a well-shielded (with a blanket) heating pad. Several orthopedic and heated cat pads, beds, and snugglers are available from pet product outlets.
- The Snuggle Safe plate-size pad (available from Drs. Foster & Smith) can be microwaved, then slipped beneath the cat's bed to warm without electricity. Or you can fill a couple of socks with dry uncooked rice and microwave. They'll hold the heat and work great as kitty bed warmers.
- Situate a lighted lamp above the cat's bed to provide an economical and effective heat lamp.
- Fill a box with towels or blankets fresh from the dryer once a day for five minutes to warm up the muscles and relieve stiffness and pain.

Acupuncture is particularly helpful for cats because it has no side effects, says Dr. Linn. "It's very noninvasive; it's safe." Be sure you work with a veterinarian certified in acupuncture to ensure the most benefits to your cat.

SURGICAL TREATMENT

Cats almost always do quite well with the triad strategy, so that should always be tried first, says Dr. Conzemius, but surgery is a viable option when medical management isn't enough. Today, more owners than ever before pursue advanced treatments such as surgery. "There's more surgeons that can do these techniques, so it's more available to people. And owners are becoming better informed about what the disease is and the treatment options."

Femoral Head Ostectomy (FHO)

Cats with severe arthritis in their hips have worn the cartilage right off the bones. "It always looks to me like that highly polished marble in lobbies. You can imagine that hurts," says Dr. Linn. There's no cartilage left to protect with nutraceuticals or anything else.

The state-of-the-art surgery for dogs is a total hip replacement in which the joint is completely replaced with prosthetics. However, "joint replacement in cats would be difficult," says Dr. Conzemius. Prosthetic joints are not made small enough to benefit cats. "There are other surgical options that can be considered," he says, "for example, femoral head and neck excision for the hip [also called femoral head excision arthroplasty]." This eliminates the bone-on-bone rubbing.

The surgeon removes the ball part of the ball-and-socket joint in the hip, and closes the joint capsule over the socket. Cats form a little pad of scar tissue, and the hip joint is then supported entirely by the muscles. "It's a highly successful procedure, very good at getting animals out of pain," says Dr. Linn. The success rate is between 80 and 85 percent. Many veterinarians in general practice are very familiar with FHO, so you don't have to go to a special center for orthopedics.

Cats may be prescribed a narcoticlike drug called butorphanol for postoperative pain relief, says Dr. Linn. "It makes cats smile. Makes them purr, they *love* butorphanol." Another option, fentanyl (Duragesic), is a narcotic that is administered by means of a skin patch. "We don't usually keep an animal on narcotics for arthritic pain long-term. But it can be useful if they've been injured or have had surgery," says Dr. Linn.

BOTTOM LINE

The cost for arthritis treatment varies depending on the specific product, procedure, and part of the country in which you live.

- Cats are much smaller than most dogs, which means medicine dosed by weight often is much more economical for them. Cosequin, for example, would cost approximately $6 a month for a fifteen-pound cat.
- "A femoral neck and head excision (FHO) runs about $1,100 per side at University of Wisconsin," says Dr. Linn. It would likely cost quite a bit less performed in a general practitioner's office.

Golden Moments: Accommodating Punkin

Michelle West of Toronto was breeding and showing Abyssinians when she attended a cat show and saw her first Scottish Fold. "She was the most beautiful cat I'd ever seen," says Michelle. The breed is known for the endearing ears that fold forward toward the face and look like a little cap on the cat's head. "I called the lady who raised her; I just had to have a kitten." When the lovely folded mother cat had a litter in September, Michelle chose a calico

Despite her arthritis, Punkin manages just fine—with a few helpful accommodations from her owner. *(Photo Credit: Michelle West)*

baby when she was four months old, and named her Punkin. "It was love at first sight!" she says, and Michelle has been breeding Scottish Folds ever since.

Punkin celebrated her thirteenth birthday last year. "She is a typical Scottish Fold, very sweet and loving, and a real mushy kind of cat. But she was raised with a group of rowdy Bengals, so she's scared of everything." Bengal cats tend to be rambunctious and outgoing, and they must have taught Punkin early in her life to avoid noisy situations.

Michelle first noticed that Punkin was walking stiffly when she was about five years old. The condition has become progressively worse the older she's grown. "Scottish Folds are prone to having various joint problems," she says. The natural mutation that causes the cartilage in the ears to fold may also predispose the cats to other cartilage or joint problems unless care is taken in the choice of breeding matches.

"When they discovered the first Scottish Fold in 1951, they were breeding folded-eared cats to folded-eared cats," says Michelle. "Their kittens had all kinds of spine problems, stiff joints and stiff tails, short tails and club feet, spina bifida, that kind of thing. They realized very quickly if you breed a fold to a straight-eared cat, you didn't get these problems," she says. Today, ethical breeders avoid these health problems in their cats by breeding folded-eared cats with straight-eared cats. "But there's a lot of folded to folded in every Scottish Fold's background, because they all started with just one cat," says Michelle. "That's probably part of the problem with stiffness that they have."

Many cats get stiff and hunched up when they're older, says Michelle. "We don't know if Scottish Folds have normal arthritis, or if it's something special to folds." Carol W. Johnson, DVM, Ph.D., of Kalamazoo, Michigan, is collecting histories and X rays on affected and asymptomatic cats to help determine how widespread Scottish Fold Osteodystrophy (SFO) is within the breed. All submissions remain confidential. The ultimate hope is to find out whether or not the problem is associated with the fold gene, and/or find families of cats within the breed that do not get SFO so that selective breeding will prevent the problem in future generations.

Punkin's problems first showed up in her stiff back legs, and then she began to hunch over as though her back was painful. "It seemed to come and go," says Michelle. It was especially bad during pregnancy, perhaps because of the extra weight and strain on her joints. "She had a really rough time," says Michelle, and she finally stopped breeding her. More recently, Punkin has developed knobs on the insides of her wrists. "Like small marbles, they're smooth. They're so bad now that even when she's at rest you can see the little knobs sticking out there."

Over the years, Michelle has made adjustments to help keep Punkin comfortable and maintain her quality of life. "I put little boxes everywhere right by the bed so she never has to jump more than six inches. And I put a step stool and table by the window so she could go up steps. That does seem to help."

She also found information and advice on the Scottish Fold E-mail list, in particular about changing Punkin's diet. When a new senior-cat food came out that included glucosamine and chondroitin, Michelle decided to give it a try. "I healed my own arthritis with glucosamine and chondroitin, so I'm a big fan," she says. Michelle offers a mix of different foods to her cats, so for Punkin she added 50 percent of the new food to the cat's previous diet. "I started on her birthday last year, so it's been just about a year, and she's much better. It has really worked for her," says Michelle. Punkin no longer walks all hunched up, she's not as stiff, and she's much livelier and plays more.

Michelle has also noticed that the cat's ability to groom herself has declined, probably because she's not as flexible. "She used to be one of those cats that if you touched her, she'd clean her whole body for twenty minutes," says Michelle. "She's mostly white, and she kept herself sparkling clean and perfectly smooth. Now she's starting to develop little mats around her neck and under her chin—and she's a shorthaired cat. So now I have to brush her for the first time."

Also, Michelle has never had to clip her cat's nails. "I teach them to scratch like maniacs, and it keeps the nails in perfect condition. But because of her arthritis, Punkin can't scratch so much." She's noticed problems with the nails getting too long, especially on the back toes, and curling into the tender flesh of the pad. "It seems to be a slippery slide. Once she gets stiff, she can't clean herself as well, so therefore mats, and she can't scratch and therefore toenail problems," says Michelle.

She knows that Dr. Johnson wants Punkin's body to study when she dies. "I hope she's going to live another ten years," she says, but she's made the necessary arrangements for when the time comes. She hopes learning from Punkin will help advance understanding about SFO and help other cats.

Today, taking care of the beautiful cat and accommodating her senior needs doesn't feel like a hardship to Michelle, or to Punkin. "Her quality of life is just fine," says Michelle. "We're great together. She really loves me and I really love her."

Blindness

Cats can become blind at any time, but it occurs mainly when they are older. Vision loss often is gradual, but may be sudden, complete, or partial. Injury or eye disease such as infections, cataracts, or glaucoma can frequently cause blindness. "The greatest problem we see in aging cats is hypertension secondary to renal [kidney] problems," says Paul A. Gerding, Jr., DVM. Hypertension can also develop as a consequence of heart disease. "It's far more common to see vision loss due to retinal detachment because of hypertension than anything else."

Even if the cat loses vision, the owners typically aren't aware of it—at least not at first. "They can be down to their last bit of vision, and in their own home they compensate very well," says Dr. Gerding. Blind cats remember the layout of the house, and rely on sound and scent landmarks to get around. Vision loss typically causes problems when they're in unfamiliar surroundings. Owners may suddenly realize there's a problem if they rearrange the furniture, for example.

Catching vision loss in the earliest stages offers the best chance of preserving the cat's sight. Specific drug treatments and sometimes surgery are available for glaucoma and cataracts, discussed further in the chapters on those topics. Eye infections and inflammation may also respond to prompt medication.

Similarly, cats suffering from kidney or heart disease often benefit from antihypertensive drugs, says Dr. Gerding. "If you catch it early and treat it medically, you may catch it before the retina completely detaches, or it may reattach so there's still some viable vision afterward."

SENIOR SYMPTOMS

"Usually you'll see vision loss in an unfamiliar environment. They'll have memorized their own home or yard if they've been there the last five to ten years," says Dr. Gerding. Symptoms of vision loss are therefore noticed more in an unfamiliar environment. "Cats tend to become a little more withdrawn if they lose their vision," he says. Look for these signs:

- Hides, and her activity level decreases
- Shows reluctance to navigate stairs or jumps, especially in unfamiliar places
- Becomes clingy
- Bites when touched unexpectedly
- Moves more slowly and cautiously
- Pupil of eye stays dilated

ACCOMMODATION

When blindness due to disease or injury can't be reversed, you need to adjust your cat's environment to help her better cope in a sightless world. Blind pets compensate for the loss by relying more on other senses, and won't be nearly as concerned about the deficit as the owners, says Harriet Davidson, DVM.

Cats prefer the status quo anyway, and this becomes even more important when they can no longer see. Don't rearrange the furniture. Keep things in the same place so the cat can map the house, and doesn't become disoriented. "Keep their food, water bowl, and bed always in the same spot so the animal knows where his things are at all times," says Dr. Davidson. Cats don't tend to run into objects, but they may decide to stop moving altogether in a strange landscape.

"The animal's behavior will change somewhat in that they will sometimes become more dependent on the owner," says Dr. Davidson. "They tend to stand very close and follow you around more." That can be a problem, especially for elderly owners if the cat stays underfoot and causes falls. To counter this tendency, try providing a safe, cat-friendly retreat such as a bed or cat tree in each room.

Cats that have always loved to be the center of attention may become

---

COMFORT ZONE

- Sound is much more important to blind cats. Try attaching a bell to the collar of other pets in the home, so the blind cat can more easily find them. It may also be helpful for you to wear a bell, or speak to announce your presence to avoid startling the cat.
- Offer toys that have a sound, such as balls with bells inside or a noisy paper sack, or scrunch up wads of paper she can hear and "dribble" across the room.

---

reserved once vision is lost, especially when guests visit. That's only natural, says Dr. Davidson. The cat's sense of self-preservation keeps her out of harm's way—under the bed—instead of beneath the feet of guests, where she might be stepped on.

As long as the environment stays the same, blind felines become adept at compensating and may still be able to accurately judge well-known leaps simply by memory. But take care to block off danger zones, such as the basement stairway, to protect your blind cat from an accidental fall. If you must pick up and carry the cat, set her down in a place she recognizes— near her litter box, for example—or she may become disoriented. Setting her on high, unfamiliar surfaces could cause her to fall off because she doesn't know where she is. Also, warn visitors that the cat can't see, and to avoid startling her. Frightened cats often bite out of reflex, and you want to protect friends and family—and your senior kitty. Interestingly, other cats often seem more tolerant of blind cats than they are of others that can see.

A blind cat is still a very happy cat. She can enjoy and remain engaged in life and the world around her. "People are told by a neighbor that when they're blind, you have to put them to sleep," says Dr. Gerding. Nothing is farther from the truth.

Golden Moments: Blind Stubbornness

Rudy is a ten-year-old fawn Abyssinian, but she doesn't act the least bit old. "Abys are kittens forever!" says Linda Weber, a children's book author from Reno, Nevada. Linda shares her home with seven cats, aged two, six, eight, nine, ten, seventeen, and nineteen, but Rudy rules the roost—even though she is mostly blind. "She still runs through the house at ninety miles an hour," says Linda.

Rudy began having problems with her eyes at age four, as a result of an

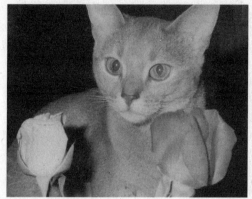

Rudy still acts like the kitten she was (left photo)—even though she now has very little vision left (right photo). *(Photo Credit: Linda Kay Weber)*

earlier upper respiratory infection caused by a common herpes virus. "We had to fight to keep her alive. She didn't seem to have any immunity to herpes," says Linda. The illness started with congested lungs and a stuffy nose, and got progressively worse. "We thought we were going to lose her then, because she couldn't eat or drink."

Rudy managed to fight her way back from this near-death experience. But then the infection got into her eyes. "She was healthy except for her eyes, and these things kept growing and growing through the corneas." In many such cases, owners finally decide to put the cat to sleep. "That wasn't an option with her because she was just fighting too hard to survive," says Linda. "That seems to be a quality in fawn Abyssinians. They seem to be extra stubborn."

The infection caused chronic inflammation of the cornea, which resulted in a corneal sequestrum—a growth of dead tissue on the cornea. This dark plaque interferes with the cat's ability to see, and treatment involves removing the bad spot and patching with tissue. "She ended up having three surgeries on her left eye and two on her right eye to remove them," says Linda.

Each time the surgeon would remove the sequestrum from each cornea, and pull up the inner eyelids and stitch them shut to give the corneas a chance to heal. "Rudy would be completely blind for a week," says Linda. "We'd put her in the funnel collar, and she'd use that as a white cane, stomp around the house and run into furniture with it to figure out where the furniture was. She'd walk along the back of the couch, scraping it against the wall, but I think she was doing that just to annoy us." At the end of the week the stitches were removed, the eyelids opened, and she could see again.

But two years later, after she'd had two surgeries on the left eye and one on the right, Rudy's left eye was so thin that it ruptured. "Fortunately, it coagulated right away and didn't completely drain, but it was scary," says Linda. "We lived in Fresno at the time, and the ophthalmologist was two hours away in Stockton." The surgery to fix the damage left her blind. The left eye had too little remaining cornea, and that eye developed cataracts. "The right eye has a skin patch across the middle of it," says Linda.

The last surgery didn't seem to bother Rudy any more than the previous ones, until the stitches were cut. "She was tense because she knew what was happening," says Linda. But this time when her eyelids opened up, she didn't relax into happiness; she stiffened up again. "You could feel her anger. It radiated out of her in waves," says Linda. "When her vision didn't come back, she got mad that we'd broken the rules. I don't blame her. She showed us that she was pissed, literally, and sprayed the house."

Rudy eventually adapted to the loss, and she is a very happy cat most of the time. She's got just enough sight in that right eye that she can see where she's going, says Linda. "The ophthalmologist compared it to looking through a full Coke bottle with a label in the way—I don't know how she does it."

Rudy still manages to leap to her favorite sleeping perches on top of the furniture. "She fakes depth perception to know how far to leap," says Linda. "She loves to be up high." It takes two eyes to judge depth accurately—the brain processes vision from each individual eye and automatically makes the necessary calculation. To compensate, Rudy gets more than one "reading" with her single, damaged eye by moving her head into different positions. "She'll spend about thirty seconds stretching her neck out, and then pulling it back so that one right eye has moved a distance of about two inches," says Linda. "Somehow in her brain she has used that to fake the depth perception you get of two eyes side by side. Then she'll leap flawlessly and land on top of the eight-foot-tall entertainment center."

Despite being virtually blind, Rudy enjoys life to the fullest and keeps the rest of the Abys in line. So far her innate stubbornness has brought her through multiple challenges. "I expect Rudy to live to be about thirty," says Linda.

Brain Tumors

Although cats of any age can develop them, brain tumors are more commonly considered a disease of older animals. "Typically the cats with brain tumors are anywhere from nine to fourteen years of age," says Lisa Klopp, DVM, a neurologist at University of Illinois. Even when tumors are quite large, cats can appear to be "normal" on a neurological workup. Symptoms of brain tumors are often chalked up as simply behavior changes of old age, when the cat becomes less active, more vocal, hides, or has litter box problems. As with any tumor, prompt treatment offers the best hope of remission and/or recovery.

Pets are more likely to develop certain types of brain tumors. "I think now everybody agrees we see by far more meningiosarcomas, tumors of the covering of the brain. That's true especially in cats," says Dr. Klopp. Meningiomas usually can be removed. The biggest issue for the surgeon is the location and how accessible the spot is. The majority of these tumors in cats develop in locations that you can get to, she says—in the forebrains.

The symptoms depend on the location of the tumor. "By far the most common presenting sign is seizures," says Dr. Klopp. Another sign is when the cat stops jumping up. Of course, this could also be an indication of arthritis. Vascular injury—a stroke—mimics the signs of a brain tumor, but the symptoms of a stroke typically improve over time. Symptoms due to a brain tumor tend to get progressively worse. An inflammatory disease, such

---

SENIOR SYMPTOMS

Symptoms of a brain tumor are vague, and vary according to what part of the brain is affected. Symptoms may grow progressively worse, or very suddenly turn bad. Watch for:

- Seizures, by far the most common symptom, which are typical of the forebrain,
- Any behavior change, often similar to cognitive dysfunction symptoms.
- Head tilt, weakness, circling, or muscle atrophy on one side of the face, typical of tumors of the brain stem.

---

as encephalitis, can also cause these signs, and sometimes a spinal tap or test for antibody levels in the blood (titer) will be checked for specific diseases.

A general neurological workup may include an MRI—magnetic resonance imaging—that shows the veterinarian the inside of the brain to determine if it's structurally abnormal. "It's pretty straightforward now that we have the imaging techniques," says Dr. Klopp.

TREATMENT

Owners of pets diagnosed with brain tumors may opt either for palliative care—keeping the cat comfortable perhaps with antiseizure medication until the end—or treating to get rid of a tumor. Surgery, radiation therapy, and chemotherapy from the cancer arsenal may be helpful, alone or in combination. Surgery is usually the treatment of choice.

"I don't see people who aren't committed," says Dr. Klopp. "They say, 'I just want it out. I want to know it's not growing in my cat's brain.'" The nice thing about cat brain tumors is they can be treated, and after surgery they don't tend to come back. "Frequently they can be considered curable," says Dr. Klopp. "Cats can live for years after having a meningioma." Because most patients are already senior citizens, adding two or more years of quality of life is a significant benefit.

The drawback with surgery is that it can be expensive. "You're talking about a pretty big emotional and financial commitment for the owner," says Dr. Klopp. While radiation or chemotherapy is an option, she says she's not had much luck with chemotherapy for brain tumors in pets. "It's not my first choice," she says, but she will offer it as adjunct therapy or if clients can't afford or don't want surgery. "It depends on the client and patient individually. I'm not going to offer brain surgery to every single case that has a brain tumor. The goal is to give them back a happy quality of life, and if I don't think I can do it safely, I'm not going to offer that."

It can be difficult to avoid damaging normal tissue with radiation therapy. Yet an innovative method is now available at University of Florida's Evelyn F. and William L. McKnight Brain Institute. The system uses a three-dimensional ultrasound guidance system to pinpoint the location of the tumor and target radiation beams precisely, while sparing the surrounding tissue.

With the new technique, pets can be treated in one high-dose treatment, rather than through repeated sessions over a period of weeks. Radiation therapy requires anesthesia to keep the pet in the proper position, so the single treatment session avoids the repeated doses of anesthesia that may be risky in geriatric cats. The procedure costs roughly the same as for traditional veterinary radiation therapy, but a limited number of animals may be eligible for subsidies or free follow-up care and imaging.

"So far we've done a total of twenty-two animals, including both cats and dogs," says Nola Lester, BVMS, a clinical instructor in radiology with the University of Florida College of Veterinary Medicine. "In some cases we've seen fantastic results and the tumor completely disappears. In others, this is not the case."

BOTTOM LINE

"I'm probably pretty cheap," says Dr. Klopp, of University of Illinois. "The majority of the cost is the aftercare."

- Most brain tumor surgeries performed by Dr. Klopp, with follow-up care, run about $2,000.
- Traditional veterinary radiation therapy costs approximately $2,200, though the amount varies in different parts of the country.

Golden Moments: Fixing Phantom's Pain

Phantom, a beautiful blue Persian show cat, had just celebrated his eleventh birthday two years ago when his owner, Judy Miley, noticed a problem. "When I showed him in the American Cat Fanciers Association (ACFA) he was the third best cat in the nation," says Judy. "You get really close to your cat when you travel with him all the time. He's just one of the family."

So when Phantom suffered a seizure, she was concerned. "My vet really didn't know what was causing them, and said, 'Just keep an eye on him.' " Medication was an option if the seizures became frequent, but Phantom had only one more in October—and the five-month interval between the two episodes didn't call for drugs.

"Then he started acting odd," says Judy. "He'd give me very low, deep-in-his-chest meows, telling me, 'Mom, help me,' and he started hanging his head way down low when he walked, as if he had a terrible headache." Yet another set of X rays of Phantom's head still didn't reveal any problems. The veterinarian knew something was wrong but didn't have the proper equipment to find out. Judy, who lives in Lafayette, Indiana, told her vet, "I'll do anything to try and find out what's wrong with him." Because no neurologist was available at the veterinary school at Purdue University, right across the river, Phantom was referred to neurologist Dr. Lisa Klopp at the University of Illinois.

In early November, Judy and her husband, Fred, traveled to the school for Phantom's appointment, and Dr. Klopp gave the cat a full neurological exam. Dr. Klopp still found nothing, but she recognized that Judy and Fred knew Phantom best, and that something was surely wrong. "She offered to do an MRI on him to see what we'd find," says Judy. The test would cost $380.

They left Phantom overnight for the test and drove home. The next day, Dr. Klopp called to say that she had the results, and Judy returned to the clinic, this time with her daughter, Denise, for moral support. "Denise is an RN, and she loves this cat, too. And she knows how I feel about my cats."

The MRI clearly showed that Phantom had a tumor in his brain. "My daughter and I both sat there and cried. It was terrible," says Judy. The tumor was also producing fluid that encompassed three times the space of the tumor itself. "It was pressing his brain outward into his skull," says Judy. Phantom's tumor, shaped like a cone, was located between the two spheres of his brain. The fluid it produced filled the space between and was splitting the two spheres apart.

Certain kinds of brain tumors have a better prognosis than others, but the MRI didn't diagnose what type Phantom had. A biopsy—analysis of tissue from the tumor—would be required, and that would require surgery. At the same time, as much of the tumor as possible would be removed. "Dr. Klopp said the surgery would cost between $2,000 and $3,000."

The proposed expense rocked Judy, but she was more concerned about potential surgical risk to Phantom because of his age. "So we thought hard about it for a short time, but then we said yes. Do what you need to do. See if you can help him and give him a chance."

Phantom stayed overnight, and his surgery was performed the next day. Unfortunately, the tumor was in a position that made it impossible to remove. Only enough was taken for the biopsy, but Dr. Klopp was able to extract all of the fluid and relieve the pressure on the cat's brain. "We had to wait for the biopsy tests to come back," says Judy. It was good news. "It was a meningioma. And it was nonmalignant."

The whole family was relieved at the news. Phantom stayed in the hospital for only three days and was ready to come home. Dr. Klopp explained the further treatment options available to address the tumor. Radiation treatment was suggested as the best option. It would include anesthesia each time to ensure the exact same spot was targeted.

The radiation would run $1,300 to $1,500 on top of the surgery. The estimated final bill, including surgery, radiation, medications, and exams, would be about $5,000. "My husband and I said, 'Absolutely. Go ahead. Let's see if we can stop the growth of that tumor and the production of the fluid.' "

Radiation treatments began right after Thanksgiving. Phantom stayed at the hospital, undergoing sixteen sessions of radiation, one every day of the week—and came home to be with Fred and Judy on weekends.

Phantom's being away from home was rough on everyone. Phantom didn't want to eat when he was at the hospital, and he dropped from ten pounds down to six-and-a-half pounds during the treatment regimen. "Dr. Klopp would bring him turkey and ham, feed him baby food, and try to get him to eat," says Judy.

The final treatment occurred right before Christmas. Before Phantom went home, Dr. Klopp did a second MRI to check the status of his tumor. It was the same size, but the treatment had prevented any return of fluid.

Judy worried that with all of the invasive treatments, the sweet personality she loved about Phantom might somehow change. The biggest problem, though, was the food issue. "Phantom acted like he was absolutely starving, but he forgot what to do and how to take it into his mouth," she says. But once the anesthesia was fully out of his system, he started eating again.

"Now he's back up to almost eleven pounds," says Judy, eight months later. "He doesn't hang his head anymore, and he runs and plays with my other cats. He's like he was before anything ever happened." Phantom's most recent MRI, performed at the end of July 2001, showed the tumor in his brain had shrunk, and only a tiny, insignificant amount of fluid remained.

At the time of the surgery, Dr. Klopp wouldn't guess at Phantom's prognosis. After his surgery and the biopsy, she estimated he'd live at least a year or

Phantom's lovely fur was shaved for his surgery. He's now fully recovered. Once the fur came back, nobody could tell he had ever had brain surgery. *(Photo Credit: Courtesy of Judy Miley)*

more—but there was no way to tell. Now that the radiation treatment has been so successful, "She's not putting any time limit on him at all," says Judy. "We're going to do another MRI in the spring to keep an eye on it."

Other than the tumor in his brain, which no longer causes him any problems whatsoever, Phantom's health is excellent. "They find nothing wrong with him," says Judy. "His treatment was worth every penny. I'd do it again if I had to, if only to take him out of his pain." After all, with Phantom eleven years old and counting, Judy says every single day is a gift.

Cancer

Feline cancers can strike at any age, and the kind that is often associated with feline leukemia virus (FeLV) and feline immunodeficiency virus (FIV) tends to strike young to middle-aged cats. But cancer mostly strikes older cats, and 80 percent of tumors found in cats are malignant. The Veterinary Cancer Society says cancer accounts for nearly half of the deaths in cats over the age of ten. Cats can develop many of the same types of cancers that affect people, but three are most common: lymph gland cancer, skin cancer, and fibrosarcoma.

"Owners of cancer patients are in a state of shock," says Barbara Kitchell, DVM. "It's the C-word, the chemotherapy, the horror, the fright." The good news is that a number of cancers can be easily treated, some can be cured, and in all cases, treatment can help maintain the cat's quality of life.

Nearly 90 percent of lymph gland cancers are caused by FeLV, and affect the lymphatic system and blood cell–forming organs such as bone marrow and spleen. Skin cancer, the second most common type, usually affects the face and head, often due to overexposure to sunlight. Fibrosarcoma is a malignancy of the connective tissue of the body, with a wide range of subtypes—collectively referred to as soft-tissue sarcomas. Vaccine-associated fibrosarcomas are included in this category. Breast cancer is also very common in cats, and Siamese are reported to have twice as much risk as other breeds. Other common old-cat cancers include digestive-tract tumors, oral tumors, and bone cancer.

SENIOR SYMPTOMS

Signs of cancer vary from type to type depending on what part of the body is primarily affected. In general, the Veterinary Cancer Society lists ten common signs of cancer:

- Abnormal swelling that persists or continues to grow
- Sores that do not heal
- Weight loss
- Loss of appetite
- Bleeding or discharge from any body opening
- Offensive odor
- Difficulty eating or swallowing
- Hesitation to exercise or loss of stamina
- Persistent lameness or stiffness
- Difficulty in breathing, urinating, or defecating

The cells of the body die and are replaced all the time in a normal process called mitosis, in which a cell divides into two identical cells. Sometimes the new cells mutate for unknown reasons. Instead of duplicating the parent cell, abnormal, fast-growing cancer cells take the place of healthy ones and interfere with normal body functions. A breakdown in the immune system can allow tumors to grow either in one isolated place (called benign) or proliferate throughout the body (malignant).

Occasionally certain families of cats show a predisposition for cancers, but these show up pretty early in the cat's life. Cancers are more likely to develop as a consequence of a lifetime accumulation of injuries or insults, says Dr. Kitchell. "We're seeing the extremely old geriatrics, like the nineteen-year-old cats that come in with cancer," she says. "We tend to see more carcinomas in the elderly, maybe because carcinomas appear most often in epithelial tissues [such as skin]." Skin, lungs, and bladder tissues are more likely to be affected by contact with the outside world, so damage from the sun over a lifetime ultimately causes old-age cancer.

There's an added concern with geriatric cats. "When you reach that advanced age, you lose a lot of reserve capacity in a variety of your organs, like your liver and kidney function," says Dr. Kitchell. "We have to be so careful with what we try to give to very geriatric patients when we try to treat them."

Encouraging news from researchers at Purdue University suggests that the "oldest-old" among pets, similarly to very old humans, seldom develop lethal cancers. Cats that don't develop cancer until very old probably have a better chance of surviving it because of the same extreme good health that has allowed them to live so long. "Just because they're old doesn't mean they shouldn't be treated," says Susan G. Wynn, DVM. "If you take, for instance, a twelve-year-old cat with lymphoma, we've had lymphoma cats live another four years or longer."

REDUCING RISK

Many feline cancers are associated with feline leukemia virus (FeLV) and feline immunodeficiency virus (FIV). A number of preventive vaccines are available for FeLV, but it has taken many years to develop similar protection against feline AIDS.

Dr. Niels Pederson, DVM, an international authority on these viruses at University of California—Davis, and immunologist Janet Yamamoto, a professor at University of Florida, first identified FIV in 1986. Dr. Yamamoto has since worked with Fort Dodge Animal Health to develop an effective vaccine, resulting in the USDA approving the first FIV vaccine in early 2002. Take these steps to protect cats from FeLV and FIV, and reduce their risk of associated cancers:

- Keep cats indoors to reduce exposure from infected cats.
- Quarantine and test new cats before introducing them to resident cats.
- Consider FeLV- and FIV-preventive vaccinations for high-risk cats— those adopted as strays or from shelters, those living in multicat households, and cats allowed outdoors.

DIAGNOSIS

We often are anxious to get that "thing" removed from our cat as quickly as possible, and the key to successful treatment is early intervention. But removing the tumor before knowing the full diagnosis can be dangerous, cautions Nicole Ehrhart, VMD. "You may disrupt tissue planes that might have been barriers for spread of that tumor," she says. "What could have been a perfectly curable cancer with just surgery alone has been compromised." Without an advanced diagnosis, a hurried surgery could result in spreading the cancer so it's harder to treat, or cannot be treated at all.

She says the best first step in diagnosing lumps is a needle biopsy. Usually no anesthetic is required, and it involves merely inserting a needle and withdrawing a few cells. "They look at them on a slide or send them off to a pathologist," says Dr. Ehrhart. The needle biopsy offers a good indication if caution is needed with further tests—perhaps taking just a tiny piece of the tumor for laboratory analysis. That not only identifies the cancer, but also "stages" the tumor so the doctor knows how advanced it is and can best recommend treatment options. When the cancer is on the inside, an ultrasound, X ray, or other imaging technique may be used to locate the tumor. A newer technique called lymphosyntigraphy injects radioactive tracers into the body. Cancer cells tend to absorb these compounds, which makes them easier to locate.

A detection technique from human medicine, called TRAP (Telomeric Repeat Amplification Protocol), is now available for veterinary use. The test detects telomerase, an enzyme that helps cancer cells re-create themselves indefinitely. Activity of telomerase appears to be a unique feature of noncancerous tumor cells that turn into malignant cancers, says Dr. Kitchell. Since normal cells don't usually produce the enzyme, its presence is an indication of cancer. Dr. Kitchell's study on cats, published in the *American Journal of Veterinary Research*, showed the presence of telomerase activity in twenty-nine of thirty-one malignant tumors, and in only one of twenty-two benign tumors studied over a two-year period. She hopes that an in-house veterinary test kit for early detection of cancer will become available for local practitioners in the near future.

Once cancer has been diagnosed, owners have several decisions to make. Although that can be scary and emotionally draining to you, your cat won't know why you are upset. She feels the same as she did yesterday, and isn't worried about the future. Also, Dr. Ehrhart says that cancer is almost never an emergency, so you should carefully discuss the options with your family and the veterinarian and figure out what you want to do.

Having a good relationship with your cat's doctor is very important, because you can ask questions and feel comfortable taking her advice. Dr. Kitchell says oncologists must be able to temper their clinical knowledge with empathy for the patient. "It takes both to be good at this job," she says. Part of the doctor's role is to help you make the best choice for your cat's individual situation. "What's right for you might not be the right choice for the next person," says Dr. Ehrhart. "We will support whatever decision you make."

Flexibility is built into treatment plans because not all owners have the same goals for their cats. "Some clients want to cure the animal of cancer," says Dr. Kitchell. That allows the doctor to offer very aggressive therapy. "I also have patients who just want him to live until kids come home from college to see him in the summer."

No matter what the goal, though, nobody wants the treatment to make the cat feel bad. "These animals should feel *well* during therapy, they should feel *well* after surgery, they shouldn't feel worse. We have the ability to make them feel good every single day," says Dr. Ehrhart.

TREATMENT

Veterinary oncologists use the same treatments to remove, shrink, or stop the cancer growth as human doctors do. Surgery, radiation, and chemotherapy are employed singly or in combination, with the goal of keeping normal tissue untouched. Several new therapies are also available that may help.

Dr. Kitchell says it's hard to say what's most common or "normal" for cancer therapies because each patient is different. Trial and error is often the name of the game because it's not possible to predict how every cat will react. "If it works for this patient, we keep going. If it makes the animal ill and the quality of life is diminished, we have to get off it," she says. There are many options, so it's never an either/or situation. If one therapy doesn't work, there's always another option to try.

Surgery

Surgery is the most common cancer therapy for pets. "Surgery is sort of a two-edged sword," says Dr. Ehrhart. "It has the potential to cure more cancer than any other therapy that we used, especially single modes of therapy. But at the same time, if it's used improperly it has the potential to harm you." She strongly urges owners to seek the advice of a cancer specialist before beginning treatment.

Tumors can be removed with advanced techniques such as lasers and noninvasive arthroscopic technology. Cancer is nearly impossible to cure using surgery alone, though. Surgery often disturbs and may distribute cancer cells to other locations. Also, leaving behind even a single cancer cell could allow the tumor to return. In most situations where surgery is used, it is followed by chemotherapy, radiation, or other therapies.

Radiation

Surgery isn't the best choice when a tumor is near vital organs or nerves that also may be damaged, or on the face, where little extra tissue is available. For these tumors, radiation therapy often is used.

Intense X rays are shot into the malignancy to kill the cells. Conventional beam radiation can't tell the difference between the cancer and normal tissue, and can damage these areas as well. Human cancers treated with radiation therapy tend to be near other sensitive tissues such as the lungs or intestines. That's why human cancer patients treated with radiation often suffer severe side effects, such as nausea and hair loss. These side effects are rare in cats because the pet's tumors typically are on the head or neck, far from sensitive organs. Occasionally cats temporarily lose their appetite or shed whiskers. Radiation cures up to 80 percent of some kinds of cancers. It works extremely well on skin and bone-marrow cancers.

A concern with radiation is that cats must be anesthetized so the X ray can be aimed to the right target. Repeated treatments are necessary—often twice a week for six to eight weeks—so repeatedly giving anesthesia to senior cats is a potential problem. New kinds of linear accelerators (radiation machines) have been designed to better target the tumor while sparing normal tissue. They may incorporate CT scanners to help "see" the tumor in three dimensions and better plan the treatment, such as the ones available at Washington State University and Tufts University.

University of Florida veterinarians and scientists recently have offered a new stereotactic radiosurgery technique using a specially designed medical linear accelerator in conjunction with a three-dimensional ultrasound guidance system. This treatment can pinpoint radiation beams at tumors and avoid damaging normal tissue. Instead of the conventional repeated therapy, it uses a onetime extremely high radiation dose instead of repeated sessions over a period of weeks. That means cats need anesthesia only one time rather than several.

So far, of the more than twenty animals treated, some tumors have completely disappeared, says Nola Lester. In other cases the procedure has not been as effective. Dr. Lester says they're still trying to determine the most effective procedure. It costs roughly the same amount as traditional veterinary radiation therapy.

Chemotherapy

Chemotherapy drugs are designed to poison cancer cells that have spread throughout the body. Chemotherapeutics may be given as pills or injected intravenously. They are often used after surgery to kill any stray cells left behind.

Most chemotherapy drugs come from the human arsenal. There's no standard treatment for a given cancer, says Dr. Kitchell, and different oncologists may have their own favorites. Drugs may be used alone or in combinations, and prices range from expensive to very reasonable.

Since chemotherapy drugs are usually dosed by the animal's weight, the small size of the cat makes this form of treatment pretty economical. But if the first drug you try doesn't work, it's not the end of the world. "Chemotherapy is not like jumping off a cliff," says Dr. Ehrhart. "You can do a reduced dose the next time or change drugs. There are many choices."

Anesthesia isn't a concern with chemotherapy, but there are other risks involved. Cell-poisoning drugs must be metabolized and eliminated via the liver and kidneys, and old cats may not have the necessary capacity to deal with the strain. "We have to be especially careful with geriatric patients when we try to treat them," says Dr. Kitchell. "When you treat with cancer drugs, there are risks. You can't predict who's going to be supersensitive. But if you're going to cure with chemo, you do it and they never come out of remission. They stay in remission forever."

BOTTOM LINE

- Radiation therapy series costs about $2,200.
- Chemotherapy cost varies, from very expensive drugs to quite reasonable ones, and depends on the dose required as well as other variables. Most cats weigh less than twenty pounds, so the small dose needed (often measured in milligrams per pound of body weight) tends to limit the cost. For example:
  - o Ifosfamide (IFEX) used against soft-tissue sarcomas in cats, costs about 30 cents per milligram (wholesale).
  - o Carboplatin (Paraplatin), an analog of cisplatin, is widely used in cats, and an average wholesale cost is $1.80 per milligram.
  - o Doxorubicin (Doxil) is a type of antibiotic that also has activity against certain cancers. Average wholesale cost is approximately $2.30 per milligram.

OTHER OPTIONS

Various cancers respond better to therapies such as cryosurgery, which freezes and destroys localized, shallow tumors using (usually) liquid nitrogen. Cryosurgery ideally treats skin cancers of the face. Cats with white faces are most prone to sun-induced cancers of the nose and ears, and especially benefit from this form of therapy.

A unique new treatment, photodynamic therapy (PDT), employs sensitizing agents that act like chlorophyll, which cancer cells preferentially absorb. Once the agent has been absorbed, the cancer is treated with laser light. That causes energy to be released inside the sensitized cells, killing the tumor but leaving normal tissue intact. PDT particularly helps fight certain skin cancers, oral tumors, and bladder tumors. For example, cats are quite prone to squamous-cell carcinoma, a type of skin cancer, which can be affected with PDT. The availability of PDT is limited to a small number of veterinary teaching universities, including University of California—Davis.

The opposite of cryosurgery is heat therapy (hyperthermia). Basically, the treatment cooks the cancer to kill it, using sound waves that penetrate the body at specific depths and dimensions. Ongoing studies in hyperthermia cancer applications are being done at University of Illinois and North Carolina State University—Raleigh.

Gene therapy remains experimental but is the latest innovation in veterinary cancer treatments. For example, studies on genetically engineered tumor vaccines designed to target mouth cancers are being conducted by internist E. Gregory MacEwen, VMD, and his team at the University of Wisconsin.

Nutrition

Researchers have been examining how cancer changes the way the body uses food. Cats suffering from cancer often lose weight even when they maintain a good appetite—this is called cachexia. "There are metabolic changes you can detect in cancer patients that suggest they're not able to use nutrition as effectively," says Dr. Ehrhart. "This was first noticed in people, and then Dr. Ogilvie did his study looking at how a specific spectrum of nutrients might be able to prevent the weight loss associated with cancer." Better nutrition means their immune system will have a better chance to fight the cancer.

In conjunction with Hill's Pet Nutrition, Dr. Gregory Ogilvie at Colorado State worked to create a commercial canine diet designed to counter the metabolic changes caused by cancer. Studies are under way to develop a cancer diet for cats that works as well as Prescription Diet n/d (for dogs), which is relatively low in simple carbohydrates, and relatively high in DHA, a polyunsaturated fatty acid thought to prevent the growth and spread of tumors.

Dr. Ehrhart has launched a similar study in cats at the University of Illinois to determine how diet might affect cancer therapy. "Cats are very different because they're obligate carnivores, while dogs are omnivores—we can extract human data and apply to the dog and vice versa, but cats are totally different creatures. The way cats assimilate nutrients is very different." She seeks feline cancer patients to participate in the study—contact Dr. Ehrhardt at the University of Illinois for further information about enrolling your cat. Patients admitted to the program receive free food and rechecks, but owners fund the cancer treatments themselves. "It would be people who have chosen to do the cancer treatment already, and also elect to participate in the study," says Dr. Ehrhart.

Feeding the cancer patient well offers important support and goes hand in hand with other therapies such as chemo or surgery, says Dr. Wynn. "We think homemade diets really help them feel better. Sometimes putting them on a homemade diet gives them kind of a boost—whether it's phytochemicals, whether it's a change in the amount of fats and starches, we don't really know." Cats fed homemade diets seem to enjoy a better quality of life, says Dr. Wynn, but adds, "This is something that I wouldn't do without veterinary supervision." Do-it-yourself or fad diets, without the help of a veterinary nutritionist, risk making the cat even sicker.

The website www.petdiets.com is run by veterinary nutritionists who can help you and your veterinarian design an appropriate recipe. "I recommend one that's about 70 percent meat, 30 percent veggies, plus appropriate vitamins and minerals," says Dr. Wynn. In addition, she includes fish oils for their antioxidant properties, as well as turmeric and garlic. "That's not for flavor. Turmeric (*Curcuma longa*) inhibits tumor growth and metastasis, reduces side effects of chemotherapy, and increases action of some chemotherapy agents."

Alternative Therapies

Combination therapies that provide herbs and supplements may help counteract or diminish side effects of cancer treatments, or boost the action of radiation or chemotherapy, says Dr. Beebe. Holistic practitioners often recommend an integrated approach to dealing with cancer. For example, you can use Traditional Chinese Medicine to improve the blood-cell count, which has a tendency to drop as a side effect of the strong radiation or chemotherapy.

Another holistic treatment that may help your cat is called IP6, found in grains such as barley. "Inositolhexaphosphoric acid, or phytate, is available as the extract called IP6 from health-food stores," says Dr. Wynn. Studies indicate IP6 may increase natural killer cell activity, genes that act naturally to suppress tumor growth, and help control the spread of tumors. Dr. Wynn says many of these functions are involved very early in cancer formation, and so IP6 may have a preventive role in addition to helping as an antioxidant.

Various mushrooms and even green tea have anticancer properties that holistic veterinarians often recommend. Green tea may inhibit tumor growth, angiogenesis (mutation from normal to cancer), and the spread of tumors. Although cats may not willingly drink a cup of tea, Dr. Wynn suggests adding a bit of the dried herb in the tea bag to the cat's regular food. Reishi, shiitake, and maitake mushrooms are also known to stimulate the immune system and have antitumor activity, says Dr. Wynn. Most are available only as dried products or extracts from holistic veterinary sources.

Cats are extraordinarily difficult to medicate, so even when herbs, supplements, and drugs are "good for them," the stress of poking multiple items down the throat may counter any benefits. This can become a quality-of-life issue, when your cat begins to fear and avoid you at the very time in her life she needs you most. Dr. Wynn suggests creating a first, second, and third tier of treatment options, so your cat benefits from the most important or helpful ones first. "My first tier is a natural diet, with antioxidants and fish oil," she says. After that, if your cat will accept more, a second tier might consist of IP6 and mushrooms.

PROGNOSIS

Prognosis depends on the individual cat, kind of cancer, and type of treatment. "There are so many of them that do well," says Dr. Garret. Cures are possible. "When you treat cancer, you see miracles all the time. You see responses you'd never in a million years predict were possible," says Dr. Kitchell.

But a cancer relapse means the chance for a cure is gone and your cat is losing the war. Tougher treatments are certainly possible, to buy more time, maintain comfort, and try to get the disease back under control. Throughout the treatment, though, Dr. Kitchell emphasizes that you are free to say *enough is enough*—at any time.

Treatment not only offers help, comfort, and hope to you and your cat; it also gives you, your family, and the veterinarian the necessary time to adjust to the eventual outcome, says Dr. Kitchell. "You go through the ups and downs of everything that happens together, so you're walking the road with them," she says. "Cancer clients are the best, just the best people! Clients that seek cancer care are very openhearted; they have that kind of special relationship with an animal, and not everybody can. So that makes them very special, very wonderful people."

As with any chronic illness, quality of life comes first. Nothing lasts forever, and an old cat with cancer has only a limited time left to spend with you. "You want to make every day that animal has a good day, a golden day."

AGE-DEFYING TIPS

There is no foolproof way to prevent cancer, but you can take certain steps to reduce risk factors for your cat.

- Spaying and neutering cats at an early age decreases the risk of mammary cancer in females, and prostate cancer in males.
- Cats with white faces and ears are at risk for sun-induced cancer. Protect them from sunburn with sunscreen, or prevent outside exposure during the brightest time of the day.
- Secondhand smoke in the air and chlorine in drinking water increase the risk of bladder cancer. Protect your cat from exposure to these carcinogens.
- Obesity increases the risk of cancer. Keep cats thin.

Golden Moments: Casey's Miracle

Casey, a mostly black cat with white "tuxedo" markings, reminded Bonnie Cheak of one of her first cats. "He's a crazy cat," she says. "He goes to extremes." Casey alternates between being very sweet and rubbing against you for attention, then getting cranky. "He's also very determined," she says. That determination may have helped save his life.

Casey was very healthy until Christmas a few years ago, when he was nine. "He'd been eating a lot, then suddenly seemed like he'd lost a lot of weight," says Bonnie. "There wasn't any real warning. It was very sudden."

The same day she noticed the change, she took him for a checkup. "He'd already lost three pounds." Further tests, including a biopsy, determined Casey had a life-threatening form of cancer—intestinal lymphoma. Bonnie was told it was extremely aggressive, didn't respond well to chemotherapy, and that most cats succumbed to the disease within six months.

Casey was referred to an internal medicine specialist who treated him for a few months. "But he didn't really respond to any of the original chemo that normal cats start out on," says Bonnie. Experimental drugs were ordered,

Diagnosed with cancer at age nine, Casey's cancer treatment has kept him healthy and allowed him to recently celebrate his thirteenth birthday. *(Photo Credit: Courtesy of Bonnie Cheak)*

which cost $1,600 for the treatment, and they kept the cancer under control for a few months.

"By that point he'd lost almost ten pounds—he weighed almost twenty before this started," says Bonnie. "They talked to me about putting him to sleep." Casey was essentially starving to death. Despite his eating both normally by mouth and being fed with a tube placed into his stomach, his body wasn't using the nutrition. "I was feeding [Hill's Prescription Diet a/d] a/d, dumping Nutrical [a vitamin supplement] in him; I tried herbal stuff, and he got acupuncture, too." Eventually the internist said he had nothing more to offer.

Bonnie wasn't ready to give up as long as Casey seemed determined to hang on. She took the cat for another opinion. Veterinary oncologist Lisa Fulton in Gaithersburg, Maryland, explained that at this point in the disease Casey was unlikely to respond to other chemotherapy, but that they could certainly try. Bonnie felt they had nothing to lose.

They began rotating various types of chemo drugs once every three or four weeks—sometimes intravenous, other times oral or subcutaneous—in much stronger doses than what he'd received before. "He almost immediately started responding," says Bonnie. Within six months, Casey's cancer was under control.

Casey received chemo for two years and seven months with Dr. Fulton. "I was really impressed by the lack of sickness at all," says Bonnie. Casey vomited a couple of times, and one day after chemo his whiskers fell out. That was all.

Because of the aggressive nature of Casey's cancer, they planned to keep the cat on a maintenance dose indefinitely. Then his red blood cell count dropped a bit, and so Casey is taking a break from the medicine to give his body a rest.

Since Casey has been off chemo, he's gained weight and is back up to over fourteen pounds. Bonnie can't say enough good things about Dr. Fulton. They both agree Casey is a miracle.

He celebrated his thirteenth birthday this past July. "He's doing great; he bounces off the walls," says Bonnie. That just goes to show what determination can accomplish.

Cataracts

Cataracts in cats most frequently develop as a result of other diseases such as feline immunodeficiency or feline leukemia that prompt eye inflammation. Cataracts may develop at any age, or later in life. But unlike with dogs, cataracts are not considered a common "old cat" problem.

The inflammation causes the clear lens of the eye to turn cloudy and opaque. A cataract may affect only a small part of the lens, and the cat can compensate and see "around" the problem. In other cases the entire lens turns white, and the cat loses vision until eventually she becomes blind. The longer these cataracts "mature," the more difficult it becomes to treat them successfully.

Cataracts may be diagnosed by general practice veterinarians, but veterinary ophthalmologists need to treat the condition. "Surgery is the only way to treat cataracts," says Harriet Davidson, DVM.

"Cataract surgery in the cats is much more infrequent than in dogs but almost always has a good success rate," says Paul A. Gerding, Jr., DVM. "They just have much less inflammation following the surgery than the dog, and the surgery turns out very well."

TREATMENT

Advanced age is not a reason to forgo the surgery, says Dr. Davidson. "As veterinary ophthalmologists, we do cataract surgery on elderly patients

---

SENIOR SYMPTOMS

Signs of cataracts develop slowly and may not be obvious until suddenly you notice the cat can't see. Watch for:

- Cloudy lens within the eye
- Impaired vision characterized by reduced activity or cautious movements, especially in strange surroundings

---

all the time." Extra care must be taken if the anesthesia would affect other health complications your cat has, but otherwise healthy older cats tend to do well.

Because cataracts typically cause inflammation in the eye, that may need to be treated before surgery can take place. Your own vet can prescribe the drops, which can be either steroidal drugs or nonsteroidal, depending on the cat's situation. "Once the inflammation checks out fine, we schedule the surgery," says Dr. Gerding.

Cat surgery is the same as human cataract surgery. The process is called phacoemulsification, which is ultrasonic fragmenting of the lens by sound waves, followed by removal of the lens. A hollow needle inserted into the eye sends vibrations into the lens. The pieces are vacuumed out through the needle. Removing the cloudy lens restores sight, but it typically leaves the cat farsighted unless artificial lenses are placed.

Although the cat won't ever return to the same visual acuity she had as a youngster, cataract surgery does improve the quality of life. "They do get their vision back so they can play and navigate their area and not run into things," says Dr. Davidson.

Often both eyes are involved. "We highly recommend doing both eyes at once," says Dr. Gerding. That also means the cat undergoes anesthesia only once, and that can reduce the cost of the procedure. Recovery time

---

BOTTOM LINE

Cataract surgery typically costs about $1,000 per eye, says Dr. Gerding. "It's highly recommended to replace their lens with artificial implants, but sometimes you can't get them in," he says. "The implants run about $200 each, so if not used, it would be that much less per eye."

varies, but most cats remain in the hospital overnight and go home the next morning.

Dr. Davidson cautions that the surgery is not inexpensive, and especially when cats have other health issues, it can have risks. "Cataract surgery is considered an elective surgery. If the owner chooses not to have cataract surgery, it's not unkind to let the animal live blind."

Blind cats are still wonderful pets. By your making accommodations to keep her safe, your cat can do very well. Routine eye checks on cats with cataracts should be continued, though. Cataracts can lead to other conditions such as inflammation of the eye (uveitis), which can lead to painful glaucoma.

Constipation

Constipation is the infrequent passage of hard, dry feces. Although straining often is a hallmark of the condition, straining in the litter box can also point to urinary tract blockage or inflammation, and care must be taken not to confuse the two. Watch for "evidence" in the litter box to figure out what's really happening with your cat.

The colon is designed to contain and eliminate stool, and to pull moisture out of the waste. When stool stays in the colon for more than two or three days, the feces becomes so dry and hard, it is difficult and painful to pass. That makes the cat even more prone to delay defecation, and the waste turns into a fecal ball that continues to grow bigger, harder, and drier.

Cats can develop constipation at any age, often as a result of hair balls. But older pets are more prone to develop problems because they may have weakened abdominal muscles, and often delay bowel movements due to a reduction in exercise, difficulty accessing the litter box, or obesity that makes it difficult to move. Most cases of constipation are uncomfortable for the cat, but not particularly dangerous unless they go on for several days, or the cat has repeated problems.

Severe constipation, referred to as obstipation, lasts many days at a time. The large mass of hard waste that collects stretches the rectum to gigantic proportions. This condition is called megacolon. "This is a degeneration of the muscle in the colon such that it is no longer able to contract and move things along, whereas the part of the colon that is responsible for sucking water out still works," says Dr. Burrows. "The stool in the colon just stays

SENIOR SYMPTOMS

Occasional constipation in older cats isn't considered a serious problem. Prolonged or repeated episodes can point to a more dangerous condition called obstipation. Signs of constipation include:

- Absence of stool in the litter box
- Straining in the litter box without passing stool
- Passing hard, dry stools accompanied by dark brown liquid
- Painful, swollen abdomen
- Failure to defecate for two or more days, accompanied by vomiting and/or anorexia

AGE-DEFYING TIPS

Using basic common sense will keep your cat regular for all his life. Begin these steps during kittenhood, and adjust as the cat matures.

- Groom your cat regularly. Hair you comb or brush off won't end up swallowed by the cat, and that will reduce the chance for hair balls—the number one cause of constipation.
- If your cat has repeated problems with hair balls despite good grooming practices, consider feeding him a commercial hair ball diet. These typically include added fiber that helps move hair out of the system.
- Infrequent problems with hair balls can be managed with home remedies. Mix one-half to one teaspoonful of unflavored Metamucil in canned food to add extra fiber.
- Many cats relish canned pumpkin as a treat, and this natural high-fiber food is a great laxative. Garnish the regular diet once or twice a week with one to two teaspoons.
- At age seven or thereabouts, make the transition to a "senior stage" diet formulation. These tend to have a bit more fiber to take care of the older cat's tendency toward irregularity.
- Encourage the cat to stay active all his life. That helps keep him a healthy weight, and exercise is a natural laxative that keeps his insides moving properly.
- "Lots of times a simple case of constipation is because an animal didn't have access to water," says Dr. Abood. Cats tend to be finicky about water, so watch the cat for a cue about what he likes—fresh or standing water, bowl or dribbling faucet.

there and gets harder and drier and bigger and bigger until it's impossible to eliminate."

TREATMENT

Mild cases of constipation can be treated with a commercial cat laxative such as Laxatone from a pet products store. "I would not generally recommend the hair ball medicine for cats unless there was an actual documented problem," says Sarah K. Abood, DVM. The stimulant laxatives can interfere with normal bowel function if overused, so don't make a habit of relying on these products.

You can instead use one teaspoonful mineral oil for each five pounds your pet weighs, or a half to two tablespoons of nonmedicated petroleum jelly, such as Vaseline. Mix the oil or jelly into the food—most pets relish the oily taste, and it lubricates everything on the inside and helps it move through because it won't be digested. If the cat won't eat the doctored diet, try spreading the oil or jelly on his paw so he swallows it when he licks himself. The laxative should work within twenty-four hours.

Dr. Abood believes preventing constipation is much better than treating it once the condition develops. One simple solution is addressing environmental issues. "Make sure that water and food are accessible on a regular basis, animals don't have to go through a maze to get it, and don't have to wait an extra eight to twelve hours," she says. "It comes down to good animal husbandry habits—regular exercise and regular meals." Avoid missing or delaying meals, and stick to a regular schedule.

FEEDING FOR HEALTH

Regular exercise, lots of water, daily grooming, and the proper diet go a long way toward controlling hair balls that cause constipation. Some commercial foods are designed to reduce hair balls, and if your cat has chronic problems, one of these may be a good option. Hair ball formulas include:

- Eukanuba Adult Hairball Relief Formula
- Science Diet Hairball Control Formula
- Nutro Max Cat Hairball Management

Cases of obstipation and megacolon must be diagnosed by the veterinarian, and generally they cannot be treated at home, says Dr. Burrows. "They need help. They need medication, enemas, and laxatives." Some cats need to be sedated in order to remove a fecal ball that's grown too large to pass through the pelvis. These cats will need medical management for the rest of their lives.

A drug called cisapride (Propulsid) helps the colon to better contract. It has been removed from the human market due to health risks, but these do not apply to cats. "We still use it if we can get hold of it," says Dr. Burrows. Compounding pharmacies are currently the best source for obtaining cisapride. Lactulose also is often prescribed to help soften stools, and is particularly helpful because it not only promotes intestinal contractions but also draws water into the large intestine.

When using drugs, laxatives, and diet isn't effective, some cats require surgery. The malfunctioning colon is removed in a procedure called a subtotal colectomy. "You cut it out and join the [farthest] part of the small intestine to the rectum, and that part of the small intestine then takes over the storage function. Cats tolerate that very well," says Dr. Burrows.

The surgery is used mostly as a last resort but can restore the cat to near-normal function. The feces usually will stay soft with a cow-pie consistency for the rest of the cat's life.

NURSE ALERT!

When the laxative doesn't work in twenty-four hours, an impaction requires an enema. If your cat has chronic constipation or obstipation problems, your veterinarian may suggest you learn how to do this at home. However, cats that struggle during the enema may be injured by the applicator if mishandled. You know your cat best, and if he'll object, you should make a trip to the veterinarian. **Warning:** Human enemas typically contain phosphates and are deadly to cats. Use only preparations recommended to you by your veterinarian. Warm tap water (about 105 degrees or so), one ounce per pound, is the safest option and very effective.

- Put the cat on an absorbent towel, or in the bathtub—in case the enema works very quickly.
- Any standard enema applicator works for most pets. Veterinarians often use red rubber tubing with a large syringe at one end to inject the fluid. But a turkey baster or empty contact lens solution bottle will also work.
- Lubricate the tip with Vaseline or K-Y jelly, and gently insert it into the rectum one to two inches.
- Then depress the syringe, or squeeze the bottle applicator or the bulb of the turkey baster to infuse the liquid into the rectum.

Deafness

In simplest terms, deafness means the cat doesn't recognize or respond to sound stimuli. Hearing connects cats to their world, including their owners, and deafness causes a constellation of behavior changes, says George Strain, DVM. "It may be a gradual change so the owner may be unaware of that for some time."

Cats may be born deaf, or lose their hearing earlier in life. Some cats, especially white cats with blue eyes, are born with a condition that causes the cochlea, deep inside the inner ear, to degenerate and results in deafness at an early age. Chronic ear infections such as ear mite infestation can damage the hearing organs and cause deafness.

Drugs such as gentamicin sulfate (an antibiotic) can produce hearing loss because they're toxic to the nerve cells of the ear, says Dr. Strain. There are almost two hundred medications that can be toxic to hearing. "Those drugs usually have to be given systemically [swallowed or injected] rather than topically as eardrops to produce this effect," says Dr. Strain. He says drops are normally not a problem.

Age-related hearing loss, called presbycusis, is the most common form and is a progressive condition that affects all cats to some degree as they age. It can develop rapidly or be slow and gradual. Basically, the tiny bones of the middle ear tend to lose their mobility and ability to vibrate and transmit sound. Also, the nerves of the cochlea degenerate over time. The cochlea is a fluid-filled tube coiled like a snail shell deep inside the ear where hearing actually takes place. Toxic reactions and sound trauma can also increase the rate of the normal process of presbycusis.

SENIOR SYMPTOMS

Behavior changes are the most common symptoms of hearing loss, including:

- Increased sleeping
- Increased meowing or yowling
- Voice that sounds strident or "odd"
- Cat is more easily startled
- Increased biting or hissing

ACCOMMODATION

Hearing aids have been developed experimentally for dogs but to date have not been offered to any extent in cats. A more economical and effective option is simply making environmental accommodations for the deaf cat, which will help maintain the bond you share.

"The increased reliance on other sensory modalities will offset that loss a little bit," says Dr. Strain. Deaf cats typically depend more on sight and can learn to respond to visual signals. For example, cats often learn to respond to the porch light flashing on and off rather than being called to come in. You can use a flashlight rather than your voice to get your deaf cat's attention. Although they can't hear, deaf cats can still feel vibration, so a slammed door or stomped foot may also work as a signal. It's particularly important to give the deaf pets some sort of warning of your presence to avoid a startle/bite reflex. "If they're startled, sometimes they'll reflexively bite before they have time to recognize that this is not really a threat," says Dr. Strain.

Some cats lose hearing only in certain ranges. Certain felines will still detect high-pitched "dog whistles." In homes that have multiple pets, animals with hearing loss often cue off the behavior of other animals in the household. "If one animal suddenly gets up and starts barking, the deaf one will get up and move around, too," says Dr. Strain.

Besides quality-of-life concerns, deafness becomes a safety issue for cats. If they don't hear the car coming, for example, they aren't able to avoid the danger. It's safest for deaf cats to stay inside.

COMFORT ZONE

- Getting the attention of a deaf cat can be done by stamping your foot, or by tossing a soft stuffed toy or beanbag into their line of sight. Many cats enjoy playing with the red dot of a laser light and can learn to respond to these signals.
- Remote-control vibrating collars may be helpful. The cat learns to respond to the vibration to come inside or run for the dinner instead of the sound of the can opener. Commercial products cost about $115 from Doctors Foster and Smith pet supply. Instructions to make a homemade vibrating collar using a Radio Shack remote-control car are available on Dr. Strain's Web site at: www.lsu.edu/deafness/deaf.htm.
- The Cat Locator is helpful when your cat can't hear you, and you can't find him. A collar has a pendant that emits a tone (pulsing beep or click) and a red light when the handheld transmitter is activated. Some deaf cats may "feel" the sound vibration, too, and the product is helpful for training purposes. That helps locate the cat whenever he goes out of sight—it has a hundred-yard range. The Cat Locator costs about $80 and is available at www.uniquedistributors.com.

Dental Disease

Unlike people, cats don't rely on chewing to process their food. They are more likely to bite off or pick up mouth-size portions and swallow them whole. That means they don't benefit from the scrubbing or detergent action of chewing food the way people do. Also, wet diets stick to the teeth more readily than dry foods.

Cats develop dental disease no matter what form of food they are fed. In fact, all animals commonly suffer from periodontal disease, or problems of the mouth, teeth, and gums. Three-quarters of all cats develop some form of the disease by the time they reach two years old, says Dr. Gengler.

Periodontal disease is a group of disorders that affect the teeth, oral bones, and the gums. Bacterium grows on the tooth surface, which creates plaque and bad breath. When plaque isn't removed, it mineralizes into tartar, which forms hard yellow or brown deposits. The bacteria releases enzymes that attack the cat's gums and cause gingivitis (inflammation of the gums), gum recession, loose or lost teeth, and pain.

Cats can develop a severe inflammation of the gingival tissues, called gingival stomatitis. Maine Coons are prone to the condition, but it appears to be more common in Oriental-type cats such as Siamese, Burmese, and Abyssinians.

Cats are also prone to a type of cavity called feline odontoclastic resorptive lesions (FORLs)—also known as cervical line lesions or neck lesions. Defects develop at the gum line, or "neck" of the tooth, and form a tiny entry hole (or may start from the inside) to ultimately erode the tooth from the inside out. That leaves literally a hollow, fragile shell of tooth that can easily fracture, and cause severe dental pain. Lesions occur with a frequency of up to two-thirds of cats seen for dental problems.

SENIOR SYMPTOMS

Teeth often are ignored because cats are so stoic, owners may not notice their pet is having any problems. "Usually in the early stages, anyway, animals will eat through the pain because the self-preservation instinct is so strong," says Bill Gengler, DVM. What you will see includes:

- Redness of the gums
- Receding gum line
- Strong, offensive odor
- Bleeding on toothbrush
- Broken, loose, or missing teeth

"People think that because an animal has been eating well, a broken tooth doesn't bother them," says Dr. Gengler, but that's not the case. Painful teeth can affect your cat's behavior in subtle ways. For instance, your cat may become irritable, refuse petting, and stop cheek rubbing when the teeth hurt. Typically, though, behavior changes are so gradual owners don't attribute them to a painful mouth. "Just like us, a broken tooth doesn't ache all the time," says Dr. Gengler. When there's a flare-up the cat may simply hide under the bed.

Cats do their best to hide discomfort and usually eat through the pain. "In the later stages, when the teeth start to get mobile, there's pain. That's usually what makes them stop eating," says Dr. Gengler. People tend to think behavior changes are just due to normal aging, and are surprised when treatment returns the cat to the normal behaviors and activities of a much younger cat.

TREATMENT

Dental disease isn't limited to the mouth, though. Mouth bacteria from diseased teeth and gums can spill into the bloodstream and damage organs in the body. One of the best ways to keep your cat healthy is to keep the teeth healthy. When problems have already begun, a professional dentistry by your veterinarian is the best choice.

COMFORT ZONE

A variety of products can help control plaque:

- Chlorhexidine and zinc ascorbate are available in topical gels or rinses.
- Cats rarely indulge in recreational chewing the way dogs do, but some treat products are designed to benefit dental health. For example, the Wysong Dentatreat is helpful. Also, C.E.T. Chews for Cats, made from freeze-dried catfish, are soft chewing treats with enzymes added to help stop plaque from forming. They also include a natural abrasion that cleans teeth as the cat chews. C.E.T. products are available from veterinarians or pet products outlets: www.healthypets.com/cetchewforca.html.
- Some cats benefit from being offered a small piece of very lean cooked beef or other firm meat once or twice a week. The size and flavor induces them to chew, especially on the rear molars, which helps naturally abrade these teeth clean. Check with your veterinarian first to be sure this will not upset the cat's normal diet.

Cats won't hold still for dentistry. "Everything must be done under anesthesia," says Steven E. Holmstrom, DVM, a dentist in San Carlos, California. "They won't say 'Ah.'" Geriatric cats should be screened to make sure the safest anesthesia is used. For cats that also have heart problems, for example, special care needs to be taken, says Dr. Holmstrom. A screening profile checks blood chemistry, electrolytes, liver and kidney function, blood cells and platelet status, and urinalysis. A heart test such as an electrocardiogram (ECG or EKG) may even be run. These preanesthetic evaluations not only help the veterinarian choose the best tools to do the job; they may also identify hidden problems.

Most veterinarians offer routine dental care, such as cleaning and extractions when necessary. Veterinary dentists have the benefit of additional training and more specialized equipment. "As a veterinary dentist I probably do at least one root canal a day," says Dr. Gengler. "We also do crowns, and orthodontia not for cosmetic purposes, but for medical reasons." For example, teeth that are misaligned may cause damage as the pet chews, and need to be realigned to prevent serious injury.

Those practicing at specialty practices or teaching hospitals have an added advantage of having access to veterinary anesthesiologists. Typically, once the cat is cleared for dentistry, an anesthetic such as isofluorine or sebofluorine is administered. With older patients, Dr. Holmstrom says fluids are also helpful to counteract potential hypotension (low blood pressure) that may result from the anesthetic.

"The next step is evaluating all the teeth with a periodontal probe. Dental X rays are extremely beneficial to detect lesions below the gum line, and getting an idea of bone loss," says Dr. Holmstrom. Sometimes tartar is all that holds bad teeth in place. Once the teeth are cleaned, those with severe damage almost fall out on their own.

"There are five classes of resorptive lesions," says Dr. Holmstrom. "Class one can be filled." Class two is borderline, he says, and "Classes three and four and five are usually past doing anything for them other than extraction."

"Active periodontal disease probably cannot be cured in one treatment," says Dr. Gengler. Antibiotics often are required following a dentistry to fight any infection and counteract new problems that may develop from the open wounds (pockets).

For cases of chronic gingival stomatitis in which antibiotics don't help, removal of all the teeth will be necessary. "Fortunately, we don't have to do it often," says Dr. Gengler. This condition probably results from an upper respiratory infection (calicivirus) and prompts a malfunction of the immune system, which attacks the gums and teeth. "Sixty to 80 percent of cats do much better if we remove all their teeth," says Dr. Gengler. The pain is removed, and because cats don't tend to chew food much anyway, they typically do very well. "They're pretty amazing. They kind of gum it down and swallow it. A lot of times they don't even have to have a special diet."

Whenever possible, Dr. Holmstrom tries to keep the canines (fang teeth) and carnassial teeth (big molars), which do most of the chewing. "The lower canine teeth act as a guide for the tongue, and the upper ones keep the lip away from the gum tissue," he says. Without these teeth, the cat may have trouble keeping his tongue in his mouth.

BOTTOM LINE

Cost for professional dental care for cats varies, but the anesthetic, antibiotics, and basic cleaning combined usually starts at $80.

PREVENTION

Some cats have more problems with tartar than others. "There's certainly a genetic predisposition with animals," says Dr. Gengler. Young cats may get away with a yearly professional veterinary cleaning, but more frequent attention usually is required as the cat ages. "Once the animal loses its natural defense mechanism and pockets are formed and bone is lost, that is not regained. It doesn't heal naturally," says Dr. Gengler. "That animal is going to be a much higher-maintenance animal."

Brushing the cat's teeth every day is the best possible answer. Starting when the pet is a baby is ideal, but you can begin brushing at any age. Start slowly, find a toothpaste flavor the cat likes, and use it like a treat, suggests Dr. Holmstrom. "Avoid human toothpaste. They often don't like the flavor, and also there's detergents in it that shouldn't be swallowed," he says. Cats can't spit; and the foam makes them mad, and can upset the stomach if swallowed.

Commercial cat toothpastes in seafood, poultry, and malt flavors are safe for animals to swallow. These pastes may include the enzymes glucose oxidase and lactoperoxidase, which have antimicrobial activity and aid in plaque control. Kitty toothbrushes are also available, or choose a preschool-size human toothbrush with the softest bristles. Some cats more readily accept the finger toothbrushes that slip over your finger.

AGE-DEFYING TIPS

Proper dental care throughout your cat's life provides a positive impact on his total health, improves quality of life as he ages, and may prolong longevity. In addition to your brushing your cat's teeth, a dental diet may help prevent dental disease.

- Look for sodium hexametaphosphate (sodium HMP) listed in the food. This helps to prevent plaque from attaching to the tooth surface. More and more "regular" pet diets contain sodium HMP as a part of the formula. Some diets with dental claims include polyphosphate crystals to help prevent the mineralization of plaque into calculus.
- Some diets have unique fibers that offer a scrubbing action to clean the tooth as the cat chews.
- Look for the "Veterinary Oral Health Council (VOHC) Seal of Acceptance." That means the product has passed a rigorous and objective review of effectiveness from representatives from the fields of veterinary dentistry and dental science along with representatives of the American Dental Association, American Veterinary Medical Association, and American Animal Hospital Association.

Golden Moments: Baby Kitty's Toothache

Sandi Maltese of Pueblo West, Colorado, has always loved black cats. She knew that adopting Baby Kitty (BK for short) would save his life. He returned the favor at age thirteen when he alerted her to a fire in the basement. "I was working in the kitchen last year and he started meowing at me," says Sandi. "I thought he was hungry. His food was downstairs and usually he leads me downstairs. This time he stopped halfway down."

Smoke was everywhere, and she found a cigarette butt smoldering in the wastebasket that could have grown into a tragic fire. "I was done for the day and wouldn't have found it otherwise," she says.

BK is skittish around strangers and even hides from the doorbell. But he enjoys being an indoor/outdoor cat and loves keeping Sandi and her husband, John, company in their home offices when they work. "He's very loving with us, and a terrific pet." She trained the ten-pound cat to come inside from his hunting expeditions with a special voice call, and bribes of cocktail shrimp.

The next year, she noticed the fourteen-year-old cat wasn't feeling well. "He was drinking way too much. I used to hardly ever see him drink," says

After his toothache was cured, Baby Kitty's appetite returned. *(Photo Credit: Sandra J. Maltese)*

Sandi. She decided to take him to the Best Friends Animal Hospital for a checkup.

"He was running a temperature of a hundred and three," she says. Other tests, including an X ray and blood screening, indicated BK was in kidney failure. "I lost it there in the vet's office." She knew the condition was very serious.

The first recommendation was to slowly switch his food to a therapeutic kidney diet. "He hated it, wouldn't eat it," says Sandi. She worked hard to change BK's mind for over two weeks. But when he began to stay under the bed all day and even ignored his wicker sleeping "cat house," she took him back to the vet.

"I left him overnight, they sedated him, and found three teeth so bad they needed to come out," says Sandi. They started him on antibiotics immediately and planned dental surgery for that weekend to remove the decayed teeth and clean up the abscesses. Sandi would need to give him antibiotic pills twice a day for a couple of weeks after the surgery as well. "The cat must have been in horrible pain," says Sandi. "The vet said the infection was so bad it had to start months ago. Intellectually, I know he hid it from me, but I still feel guilty."

The recovery from the surgery has been a slow, rough process. "My three vets—Dr. Cynthia Lopez, Dr. Roger Mauer, and Dr. Cantchaola—have been absolutely wonderful," she says. "The surgery cost about $525, but I've been in there four or five times since then and they've not charged me."

She's noticed a big improvement in BK in just the past two or three days. "He's feeling better, drinking better, and he's already eating good." She knew he was on the road to recovery when he began demanding his shrimp bribe each morning and reminding her if she was late.

Dr. Mauer explained that dental disease sometimes leads to kidney

---

FEEDING FOR HEALTH

Although these diets can help with dental care, be sure the diet itself is appropriate for your cat's total health requirements. The need for a therapeutic kidney diet may override dental concerns, for example.

- Eukanuba Dental Defense System (added to all adult Eukanuba foods)
- Friskies Dental Diet
- Hill's Science Diet Oral Care
- Hill's Prescription Diet Feline t/d (available only from veterinarian)

problems, and BK's kidney test might have been a false reading due to his tooth problems. Sandi hopes so. She plans to have another kidney evaluation once he's fully recovered.

"He always gets a yearly checkup. And they always checked his teeth," says Sandi. "He gets better care than me, but he's my baby. And from now on, he's going in every six months for checkups."

Diabetes Mellitus

When your cat eats, her body processes the food into glucose (sugar). A hormone called insulin moves glucose from the blood into the cells of the body, where it is used as fuel. The pancreas, located near the liver, manufactures insulin and digestive enzymes. "In cats we see what's called amyloid deposition in the pancreas, where you essentially have gradual depletion of functional pancreatic tissue because it's being covered up by this amyloid deposition," says Dr. Davenport.

Diabetes mellitus is a metabolic disorder in which not enough insulin is produced by the pancreas (type I, insulin-dependent), or the body is unable to use the insulin that's present (type II, non-insulin-dependent). Diabetes renders the cat unable to use glucose for energy, in effect starving the body. Diabetes is one of the common endocrine (hormone) diseases in cats, affecting one in every two to three hundred seen by veterinarians, says Sharon Center, DVM, an internist at Cornell University.

"About 20 percent of them have an in-and-out phase of diabetes," says Richard Nelson, DVM, an internist at the University of California—Davis. He notes that transient diabetes is most commonly associated with pancreatitis. "Those cats are ones that are amenable to just diet sometimes, or diet and oral medicine."

Another common cause is obesity. Fat suppresses the insulin function so that even though the pancreas is making insulin, the body can't use it effectively. Diabetic cats are very often overweight.

SENIOR SYMPTOMS

Various signs of diabetes can be similar to symptoms of other serious illnesses, such as kidney disease. They often include:

- Increased thirst
- Increased urination
- Sticky, "sugary" urine
- Missing the litter box
- Increased appetite
- Weight loss
- Bad breath that smells sweetish, like nail polish
- "Plantigrade" stance—walking on her heels

Because cats are true carnivores and have evolved to best use a diet consisting primarily of animal flesh, they've lost the need for dietary carbohydrates. Some experts suspect, therefore, that carbohydrate-based commercial dry cat foods may be one part of the puzzle that causes some cats to develop diabetes and obesity. The jury is out until studies can show definitive proof.

The unused glucose is eliminated via the bladder, turning urine into a sugary liquid that pulls additional fluid out of the body. Losing so much water prompts the cat to drink more water, which creates a vicious circle when she then needs to urinate more frequently. Often, the first sign you'll notice is the cat urinating outside the litter box when she's not able to get to the facilities in time.

A small percentage of diabetic cats develop diabetic neuropathy, which causes a rear-leg plantigrade stance. Instead of walking normally on her toes, her stance drops until she's on her "heels." This neurologic disorder can be reversed once the diabetes is under good control, says Lisa Klopp, DVM. "Diabetes is a very dynamic disease; it's not static," she says, and that can make it difficult to treat effectively. The combination of symptoms point to the disease, and diagnosis is confirmed by testing the blood and urine.

"It's an old animal diagnosis," says Dr. Nelson. Most cats are diagnosed at age ten or older, and average survival time after diagnosis is three years. "I've had diabetics that have had it for eight or nine years," he says. The key is getting the cat regulated and maintaining them.

NURSE ALERT!

- In most cases, a diabetic cat will require insulin injections. Typically these are given with tiny needles that the cat tolerates quite well. Most owners find that giving injections is easier on all concerned than trying to pill the cat—little restraint is required. Try rewarding each injection with a treat so she associates the medication with something pleasant.
- How much your cat eats or exercises influences glucose levels. Maintaining a regular routine is important.
- Too much insulin or too little can have devastating consequences. Diabetic coma may result if the cat gets the wrong amount of insulin, the insulin is too old, she doesn't eat on schedule, or she over-exercises. The cat loses consciousness and can't be awakened. This is a life-threatening emergency that requires immediate veterinary help.
- Too much insulin causes hypoglycemia—an insulin reaction. The cat acts disoriented or drunk, drools, shakes, acts weak, and may develop a head tilt. Giving her a glucose source such as honey or Karo syrup should reverse these signs in five to fifteen minutes. Without intervention, the condition progresses to convulsions, coma, and death.

TREATMENT

Diabetic cats don't tend to have the same severe complications as diabetic people, says Dr. Nelson. A rigid control of the human disease is required because people live for decades and complications tend to develop twenty or more years after diagnosis. Of course, cats don't live that long. The goal is to keep cats happy, active, and interactive with the owners. "It's a quality-of-life issue," says Dr. Nelson.

In the last few years researchers have begun taking a closer look at the practice of feeding cats complete and balanced commercial diets that are largely carbohydrate-source ingredients. "Dietary feeding practices in the cat are kind of mirrored after the dog, and in the dog they've been mirrored after a person. But a cat is a pure carnivore, and the dog is an omnivore just like a person," says Dr. Nelson. "One of the theories is that we would be better off feeding cats a real high-protein, low-carbohydrate type of a diet rather than the more standard omnivore diet that dogs tend to get. DM diet by Purina goes after that approach."

DM-Formula (diabetes management formula), a Purina Veterinary

Diet, comes in dry or canned forms and combines extremely high protein with low carbohydrates. A percentage of type II diabetic cats may be able to live normal lives without insulin injections when fed this or a similar diet. "Cats fed the high protein/low carbohydrate diets are ten times more likely to lose their dependency on insulin injections," says Dr. Center.

FEEDING FOR HEALTH

A high-fiber diet not only helps reduce overweight but also helps regulate the rate at which food is digested and glucose released into the cat's system. Other therapeutic diets increase the protein and reduce the carbohydrates. A number of diets may be appropriate, including:

- Eukanuba Veterinary Diets, Nutritional Weight Loss Formulas, Restricted-Calorie/Feline
- Eukanuba Adult Weight Control Formula
- Max Cat Lite
- IVD Select Care Feline Hifactor Formula
- IVD Select Care Feline Mature Formula
- IVD Select Care Feline Weight Formula
- Nutro Complete Care Weight Management
- Precise Feline Light Formula
- Purina Veterinary Diets, DM Diabetes Management Formula
- Waltham Feline Calorie Control Diet

When the diabetic cat is fat, losing weight is an important part of treatment. "If you can correct that, a lot of times the diabetes will go away," says Rhonda L. Schulman, DVM. A weight-loss diet combined with veterinary supervision and exercise—encouraging the cat to play—is most effective. She says about a third of all diabetic cats can be managed with the diet, but that they typically need some sort of oral medication as well.

"Twenty-five to 30 percent can be treated with oral medication," says Dr. Nelson. Glipizide (Glucotrol) boosts the production of insulin in the pancreas. Some of these cats do well on oral medication for a long time. Other times, this works for only a few months and they end up having to go on insulin.

"About 50 to 60 percent of cats have an absolute requirement for insulin at the time diagnosis is made," says Dr. Nelson. They'll need insulin injections, usually twice a day. Various types of insulin are available, and different ones may work better for individual cats. "The two best are recombinant human lente and PZI insulin," he says. There are other kinds as well, but they may have different durations of effect and require more frequent injections. The amount and frequency of insulin injections varies from cat to cat and depends on activity level and metabolism. Usually it takes time and experimentation to find the right dose, best insulin, and ideal schedule. Most owners become quite adept at giving insulin injections.

BOTTOM LINE

The initial testing and regulating is the most expensive part and may run a couple hundred dollars because typically the cat must be hospitalized for several days. Once that's done, though, managing diabetes with special food, oral medicines, and/or insulin can be quite reasonable. The cost varies in different parts of the country but usually is well under $20 a month.

TESTING

Usually, blood tests are monitored for blood sugar levels, and the amount and frequency of insulin shots are adjusted accordingly. "There's a trend toward clients actually measuring blood sugars at home," says Dr. Nelson. An instrument called a glucometer tests the blood, and a sample is obtained by performing an ear prick. "In the kitty, you heat the ear with a warm washcloth," says Dr. Nelson. Put a damp washcloth in a plastic bag, warm it in the microwave for about five to ten seconds, and then massage the damp, warm cloth against the ear for about thirty seconds. "That brings the circulation to the ear, and then you use the lancet to prick a drop of blood just as a human diabetic does on their fingertip. I have ten or twelve clients now that routinely do blood sugar measurements and send me the information," he says. Home monitoring can be a big advantage because stress can affect the reading, and bringing the cat to the hospital may mean the tests aren't as accurate as when done by the owner.

A newer in-hospital monitoring test examines the blood for levels of fructosamine. "It's a marker of average blood sugars over a period of two to three weeks, and it's not affected by stress," says Dr. Nelson.

COMFORT ZONE

- Many owners of diabetic cats like the Bayer product called Glucometer Elite XL because it requires a very small amount of blood to monitor the glucose level. The care system is available at most pharmacies. You can read about it at www.glucometerelitexl.com.
- A new cat box additive can turn conventional litter into a glucose-monitoring system. Glucotest Feline Urinary Glucose System (Purina Veterinary Diagnostics) is thoroughly mixed with the cat's usual cat box filler and reacts to urine with distinct color changes to indicate the level of glucose in the urine. The test is not intended for home diagnosis of diabetes, but only for monitoring purposes. The Glucotest packets are available from your veterinarian.

Golden Moments: A Second Kittenhood

When Jennifer Schilling's baby brother was born, it was decided that Jennifer needed a baby, too, and a kitten was the answer. She was seven years old when she first met the hissing, scratching ball of calico fluff. "I just grabbed and I caught her," says Jennifer. "I held on for dear life."

Today, Jennifer works as a lab specialist at Virginia Tech in Blacksburg, Virginia, where she does cancer research. Momma Kitty, a mostly white cat with a stylish checkerboard brown-and-black face, has been her constant companion for nearly two decades. The cat acquired her name as you'd imagine—"She started having kittens, and the name just stuck." She was spayed many years ago, though. Last year, Momma Kitty celebrated her eighteenth birthday in August.

"My whole childhood was involved with Momma Kitty and dressing her this way and that," says Jennifer. "If I was going to ballet class where I wore tights, she wore tights, too." The pair grew up together, and when Jennifer had to live in the dormitory her freshman year in college, it nearly killed them both. "That's the only time I've ever been apart from her," says Jennifer. "I would go home on the weekends and she would eat. And she would not eat again until I came home the next weekend." When school began for her sophomore year, Jennifer took Momma Kitty with her. "She's been with me ever since."

As she grew more mature, Momma Kitty gained more confidence, and expected visitors to the house to acknowledge and pet her. When Jennifer and

Wes got married two years ago, Momma Kitty welcomed him to the family. A three-year-old orange cat came as part of the package, and the older cat took Fezzik in stride.

Lately, Wes and Jennifer noticed she'd slowed down, and seemed much more mellow than Fezzik. "We adjusted furniture so she never has to jump more than a foot and a half," says Jennifer. "She can jump on the kitchen counters if she really wants to, but I don't try to force that out of her."

Then her behavior completely changed. "It was like a switch went off," says Jennifer. Momma Kitty began sleeping twenty to twenty-two hours a day, and developed a lot of hind-leg weakness. She'd always had a weight problem, and Jennifer had been careful about feeding her a controlled amount twice a day. "She became ravenous, wanting to eat nonstop. If you sat down to eat, she'd get in your lap to try and eat from your plate," says Jennifer. "She started losing weight dramatically and peeing nonstop. She'd go through a quart water bowl a day."

Dr. Alonzo Jones at Blacksburg Animal Hospital confirmed his suspicions

Momma Kitty has been around nearly two decades. She'd started to slow down when a sweet cure turned back the clock. *(Photo Credit: Jennifer Schilling)*

of the cat's symptoms with a blood test. Momma Kitty was diabetic. "It really hit me hard because I just couldn't imagine her not being perfect," says Jennifer. "My husband and I treat our cats like children and members of our family. I thought it was a death sentence. I felt devastated."

Dr. Jones reassured her that with insulin injections twice a day, diabetes could be managed, especially if Momma Kitty was otherwise healthy. Other tests showed the cat's kidney function was 100 percent, liver function was 100 percent and she had no heart murmur. "I was very happy to hear that," says Jennifer. "I never even thought about not treating her."

One bottle of insulin, available from the pharmacist by prescription, lasts almost sixty days and costs about $22. "We use a needle a day, little TB syringes. Some people use a new needle every injection," says Jennifer. She and Wes have worked out a system so they don't overdose the cat accidentally. If the morning shot has been given, the syringe is with the insulin in the refrigerator, and if it hasn't been given there's no syringe there. "And in the evenings it's vice versa," says Jennifer.

In addition to twice-daily insulin injections, the cat's eating habits and diet had to be adjusted. Food was made available for all-day nibbling but that was low enough in calories that it wouldn't produce a giant rush of glucose after eating each meal. The food also had to be appropriate for Fezzik to eat. A reduced-calorie premium brand available in grocery stores has worked well.

Jennifer learned if they decide to travel, special arrangements must be made for somebody qualified to give the insulin injections. "You can't just leave the food out and go for the weekend anymore." Jennifer and Wes trained both Momma Kitty and Fezzik to walk on a harness and leash. "They just travel along with us," she says. "You'd be amazed at the attention you get when you walk off an elevator with two cats on leashes."

Once Momma Kitty was regulated, she got her strength back and cut back on sleep to the normal sixteen hours a day. "The rest of the time she's playing. She'll attack toes under the covers again. She can run and leap and dance and play and all the things she used to do."

Jennifer hasn't wanted to think about eventually losing Momma Kitty, but she has talked about the eventuality with Dr. Jones. "If she were to become incapacitated it wouldn't be fair to make her live that way just because I don't want to deal with her loss."

She believes accommodations are important for aging cats, "But never treat them like they're old. Expect them to play and be active. When you sit down on the couch and they're not there, go find them," she says. Keep

---

AGE-DEFYING TIP

"The single best thing an individual could do in terms of trying to minimize the potential development of diabetes is weight control, and trying to avoid obesity," says Dr. Nelson. "That causes insulin resistance and has been shown to be a definite cause-and-effect factor in dogs and cats both."

---

them engaged in life and the world around them to help them feel as good as they possibly can.

Jennifer has no doubt Momma Kitty enjoys her life. "When I wake up, she's sitting in front of my face, and as soon as I open my eyes she bursts out with purrs that have just been boiling inside to come out. Now, that's a happy cat!" says Jennifer. "She's got her kittenhood back."

Glaucoma

Glaucoma usually strikes cats older than seven years old. The disease causes intense pain when pressure increases inside the eyeball and pushes the internal structures out of position. It can cause sudden blindness in as little as twenty-four hours, or may take weeks to months depending on the pressure. Without treatment, cats go blind.

The internal components of the eye are held in the right position by a fluid called aqueous humor that fills the front part of the eye. Normally, the level of this liquid stays the same, as the amount that's produced is also drained away. You could compare the system to a sink where the water drains away as fast as the faucet replenishes it. Glaucoma develops if not enough fluid drains away, and the eyeball swells with the pressure.

"Glaucoma can be found in older cats, especially in animals where a cataract is not treated," says Dr. Gerding. Secondary glaucoma develops as a result of disease such as feline leukemia or feline immunodeficiency virus, which scars the inside of the eye and prevents drainage of the fluid. "Uveitis [inflammation] is sort of a low, smoldering condition, and can lead to glaucoma," says Harriet Davidson, DVM. Injury to the eye can also interfere with this natural flow of fluid. Extremely high blood pressure can also prompt glaucoma and retinal detachment. Glaucoma causes the cat to keep his painful eye away from you.

An instrument such as a Schiotz tonometer or TonoPen measures the pressure inside the eyeball to diagnose the condition. The tonometer is

---

SENIOR SYMPTOMS

Glaucoma is a progressive, relatively slow disease in people, but is very aggressive in cats and can lead to blindness. The primary symptom is excruciating pain. Signs to watch for include:

- Excessive tearing
- Cloudy or bloodshot eye
- Squinting or pawing at the painful eye
- Tipping head to relieve pressure from the aggravated side
- Keeping eyelid closed, or pulling away from touch
- Dilated and unresponsive pupil
- Enlarged eyeball

---

gently balanced on the cornea (after drops numb the area), and a scale on the instrument indicates the pressure. The TonoPen is much smaller and contains a computer microchip that registers a reading when it's merely tapped on the surface of the eye.

NURSE ALERT!

- Once glaucoma is diagnosed, the cat needs eyedrops several times a day, perhaps for the rest of his life.
- Should he require surgery to remove the eyeball, watching the area and keeping the socket clean with warm water on a cotton ball will guard against infection. You may also need to apply ointment until the area is fully healed.
- A collar restraint may be necessary to prevent the cat from pawing at and damaging his sore eye. Cats often refuse to eat while wearing an E-collar, so remove it during meals and supervise his activity.

TREATMENT

"Glaucoma is an emergency. You need to have an animal evaluated by the veterinarian and treated immediately," says Dr. Davidson. It takes only a few days for permanent damage to occur.

The condition is treated very aggressively. Eyedrops usually are prescribed but don't tend to work in cats nearly as well as they do in dogs. Beta-blockers such as timolol and metipranolol, and carbonic anhydrase inhibitors such as dorzalamide may be more helpful when combined with

---

BOTTOM LINE

- Costs to treat glaucoma vary from $300 to $1,000, depending on the type and severity of glaucoma and the size of the cat, says Dr. Davidson.
- The cost to implant the prosthetic generally runs about $600 per eye, says Dr. Gerding.

---

other therapies rather than used alone. These medicines help to relieve the pain, contract the pupil, and reduce the inflammation. Some treatments help move the fluid and water inside the eye, says Dr. Gerding.

When medication doesn't control the condition, sometimes surgery is necessary, says Dr. Davidson. Surgery is available from ophthalmologists. Ask for a referral to an eye center.

Options include tiny shunts implanted inside the eyeball to drain excess fluid and control the pressure. Cryosurgery may be used to freeze the fluid-producing cells. One of the most recent and successful innovations uses an ophthalmic-size laser to perform a procedure called laser ciliary body ablation. It selectively destroys fluid-producing tissues in the eye, and so reduces fluid production, says Dr. Gerding. However, the expensive equipment necessary for this procedure is limited to only a handful of veterinary ophthalmic centers in the country.

The cat's pupil will no longer respond to light when the disease has progressed to blindness. If medication can't control the pain, then several surgical options are available. A schleral prosthesis—a silicon ball—is often placed inside the damaged eyeball after the painful internal structures have been removed. This is also a good cosmetic procedure, in which the cat keeps his eye, and the eyeball will still move, but he'll have no vision.

Another possibility is to remove the eyeball altogether, in a procedure called enucleation. If enucleation is performed, a prosthetic implant may be placed, or sometimes the socket is left empty, and the eyelid is sewn shut.

Cats with vision loss in one or both eyes tend to adjust quickly and do very well. Removing the eye offers such great pain relief that the cat becomes even more active after the vision loss.

Heart Disease

Heart disease tends to strike young to middle-age cats. One of its forms, cardiomyopathy, is a disease that affects the muscles of the heart in various ways. The hypertrophic form is most common, and results when the muscle wall of the heart thickens. That reduces the size of the internal heart chambers until they can't fill with enough blood. Heart failure results when the damaged muscle is no longer able to move blood throughout the body properly.

Some breeds seem predisposed to the disease. Researchers suspect that certain families of Maine Coon cats, for example, carry a genetic mutation. Heart disease can also be associated with feline hyperthyroidism.

Some cats may tolerate mild forms of the disease for five years or longer

---

SENIOR SYMPTOMS

Most cats first show difficulty breathing from fluid-filled lungs or fluid in the chest. When the heart can't pump oxygen-rich blood adequately, the cat becomes depressed. Other signs include:

- Tires easily
- Weakness
- Bluish tinge to the skin from lack of oxygen
- Labored breathing
- Loss of appetite
- Hind-limb paralysis and pain

Some cats suffering from heart disease develop rear-end paralysis. A wheelchair designed for paralyzed cats returns them to mobility. *(Photo Credit: © K-9 Cart Company)*

with few to no signs. About half of the cats that show signs of hypertrophic cardiomyopathy die within three months. Irregular blood flow leads to blood clots that typically form and lodge in the lower part of the aorta, the main artery supplying blood to the cat's hind legs. When the blood supply is cut off, acute pain develops from muscle spasms in the hind leg muscles and the legs become paralyzed.

Heart disease has a cascading effect on the whole body, and can lead to damage of other organs such as the kidneys, liver, and lungs. Fluids collect when the body tries to compensate for reduced heart efficiency. Sodium and fluid are retained to increase blood volume, and blood vessels are constricted to increase blood pressure. Treating the high blood pressure can reverse heart-muscle damage.

When the left side of the heart fails, fluid collects in the lungs (pulmonary edema) and makes it hard to breathe. "Breathing problems and coughing can be a distinct and most significant clue, but they tend to be later findings," says Rhonda L. Schulman, DVM. When the right side of the heart fails, fluid fills the chest cavity (pleural effusion). Cats suffering from cardiomyopathy often have a heart murmur.

BOTTOM LINE

Costs for diagnostic tests vary in different parts of the country, and the treatment depends on the specific requirements. Usually the medication itself is quite reasonable once the problem is diagnosed.

- An echocardiogram costs in the $300 range
- X rays typically start at $50 to $75 and go up from there

DIAGNOSIS

Simply listening with a stethoscope may detect a murmur or excessive fluid in the lungs, says Dr. Schulman. X rays usually show an enlarged heart— the hypertrophic heart typically is shaped like a valentine. "You might see changes in the lungs consistent with fluid," she says. Most veterinarians have X-ray machines in their offices and can make a general diagnosis.

An echocardiogram, or ultrasound of the heart, is the ideal way to diagnose heart disease. That requires specialized equipment veterinarians usually won't have. Your veterinarian may refer you to a veterinary cardiologist or internist.

The echocardiogram tells the veterinarian a great deal, says Sheila McCullough, DVM, including how strongly the heart is able to contract. "It gives you a better idea of the heart chamber size, the thickness or thinness of the walls." Thorough testing helps determine which medications will work best. "We often do re-echos after they've been put on the medication to see if they're actually improving," she says.

FEEDING FOR HEALTH

Your veterinarian may suggest a number of therapeutic diets designed to help cats with heart disease, including:

- Hill's Prescription Diet Feline h/d
- IVD Select Care Feline Mature Formula
- Purina Veterinary Diets, CV CardioVascular Formula

TREATMENT

Cats with cardiomyopathy can be helped with drugs that improve the heart's performance and reduce fluid accumulation. "There are some medications that are very similar to what people take with heart disease," says Dr. Schulman. "Certain drugs work on how the heart cells communicate with one another," she says. For example, calcium channel blockers or beta-blockers can help slow the heart rate to give the heart more time to adequately fill. Heart patients can develop hypertension, says Susan Little DVM, and that is treated with medications such as Norvasc (amlodipine). Vasodilator drugs help keep constricted blood vessels open. That controls congestion and makes it easier for the cat to breathe.

Cats that develop blood clots may benefit from clot-reducing or blood-thinning drugs that reduce the "stickiness" of the blood and decrease the chance of new clots forming. Even without these drugs, about 40 percent of cats with rear-limb paralysis will regain use of their legs within a week.

A diuretic drug forces the kidneys to eliminate excess salt and water. Drugs such as spironolactone increase the kidney's ability to absorb sodium. Specially designed therapeutic diets low in sodium also help the cat compensate for the potassium, chloride, and magnesium lost due to increased fluid loss, and help prevent fluid retention. A variety of brands are available, so choose one that not only will be good for your cat, but also that she'll readily eat.

NURSING ALERT!

Heart medications usually come in the form of pills, but sometimes as liquids. You'll need to administer heart medicine for the rest of the cat's life.

- "If the animal can tolerate any variation in their diet, I will have the owner put the pill in a tiny bit of low-fat cream cheese or peanut butter or cheese," says Dr. Schulman.
- If a therapeutic diet is necessary, make the switch gradually. Mix with the "regular" diet for the first several days to slowly introduce the change, and then increase the percentage of therapeutic diet day by day.

Treatment for cardiomyopathy won't cure the heart, but can eliminate some of the symptoms. When caught early, some heart damage can be reversed. With proper medication and monitoring, cats with hypertrophic cardiomyopathy and congestive heart failure can live months to years, says Dr. Hoskins.

Hyperthyroidism

Hyperthyroidism, though unrecognized in cats until 1979, has since become the most commonly diagnosed disease of the endocrine (hormonal) system in cats. "We see it in middle-aged to older cats," says Rhonda L. Schulman, DVM. "It's definitely one of the most common problems in older cats."

The cause remains unknown, but Dr. Duncan Ferguson, a veterinary scientist at the University of Georgia College of Veterinary Medicine, says the disease affects one in three hundred cats older than seven. Risk factors for the disease include being fed a predominantly canned food diet, especially those containing giblets (two- to threefold risk) and exposure to cat litter (threefold risk). Researchers don't yet know what this means—if eating the canned food leads to the disease or the dry food helps protect from developing it.

Hyperthyroidism is the overactivity of the thyroid gland, which is a double-lobed gland located in the base of the cat's neck. The gland manufactures and secretes the hormones thyroxine and triiodothyronine, which help regulate the body's metabolism—the rate at which food and oxygen are burned for energy. For unknown reasons, one or both lobes of the thyroids of many elderly cats become enlarged and create a toxic nodular goiter that causes an overproduction of hormones. Basically, hyperthyroidism speeds up the metabolism, resulting in a variety of behavior and physical changes.

"Many hyperthyroid cats also have high blood pressure, and they may also have kidney insufficiency," says Susan Little, DVM. A study indicated that 87 percent of hyperthyroid cats had elevated blood pressure. "We think of those diseases as a group, a triple play. So if a patient has one, we're looking for the others."

SENIOR SYMPTOMS

Behavior changes are the most common symptoms of hyperthyroidism. Cats with concurrent diseases such as heart or kidney problems may have overlapping signs:

- Increased appetite
- Weight loss
- Increased drinking and urination
- Hyperactivity, pacing, short temper
- Howling or yowling
- Oily coat, hair loss, and/or rapid claw growth
- Diarrhea or vomiting
- Seeks cool place to rest

Diagnosis and treatment of feline hyperthyroidism have made great strides over the years. "It used to be these kitties would come in as a rack of bones," says David Hager, DVM, a radiologist in Rancho Santa Fe, California. Today, veterinarians tend to catch the disease much earlier. "The earlier we catch a disease process, the more likely we are of having a good outcome."

Dr. Hager considers feline hyperthyroidism highly treatable. "It's one of my favorite parts of the practice because first of all, I'm a cat person. Second, there are few things where the kitty comes in with something that's relatively bad, and we send them home with a really high probability of curing them. We're about to treat a twenty-two-year-old kitty. That's very satisfying."

DIAGNOSIS

Most commercial laboratories measure thyroid levels as a routine part of blood tests in cats, says Richard Nelson, DVM. "That allows you to identify when those numbers start to go up." However, the thyroid level can be artificially suppressed by other health conditions, says Dr. Hager. "That's where the scintigraphy confirms and defines the problem."

Also called a thyroid scan, scintigraphy employs a radioactive particle that seeks out and attaches to thyroid tissue, which is then revealed on a gamma camera. "It tells you if all the thyroid tissue is only in the neck right at the thyroid site, or other places," says Dr. McCullough. Scintigraphy defines the extent of the disease, and helps the veterinarian choose the best treatment options. For instance, if the scan shows the thyroid tissue is limited to the glands in the neck, surgery to remove affected tissue may be a good option.

Dr. Hager says scintigraphy is currently the best method to confirm a diagnosis of hyperthyroid disease, and to figure out how much of the thyroid gland is involved, where the thyroid is located, and also whether the enlargement is due to a cancer or a benign adenoma (tumor). A tiny dose of a mildly radioactive but inert metal called technesium is injected into the cat's vein, travels throughout the body, and within about twenty minutes is preferentially taken up by thyroid tissue, salivary tissue, and the gastric mucosa.

"Technesium is the most commonly used imaging agent for nuclear medicine," says Dr. Hager. "It has a very short half-life so it's very safe, and it has a nice imageable photon that emits so we can pick up on the gamma camera." After twenty minutes, the cat is gently placed on the flat-faced camera, and the inch-thick crystal inside the camera picks up the X rays emitted from the cat's body and glows in response. "That information goes to a computer that forms an image that tells us where most of the counts come from," says Dr. Hager. "It gives us the anatomic definition. With cancer the radioactivity is scattered all up and down the neck, versus a localized benign process that's sharp and well defined and in one spot in the neck."

Hyperthyroid disease in cats can be treated three ways. "One is medical, two is to cut it out surgically, and three is to do the iodine-131 [I-131 or radioactive] therapy," says Dr. McCullough.

SURGERY

When a benign adenoma is localized to the neck, surgery can be a permanent fix. But because most cats develop hyperthyroidism during their senior years, the risk of anesthesia and other health considerations are a concern.

"There are two thyroid glands, so sometimes it's a big issue: do you take out just the abnormal one?" says Dr. Schulman. Over time, she says the normal lobe that is left behind in the surgery often also becomes abnormal, and begins causing symptoms all over again. The surgery can also be tricky. "The parathyroid gland sits right next to the thyroid, so if you take out both thyroid glands you run the risk of taking out all the parathyroid glands as well. Then you have a whole different problem!" The parathyroid glands produce parathyroid hormone (PTH), which maintains a normal blood calcium level in the body.

If both thyroid lobes are surgically removed, Dr. Schulman says most cats do very well and bounce back pretty quickly. Interestingly, although a few need thyroid supplements, most do not need further medication at all.

MEDICAL TREATMENT

"The drug methimazole (Tapazole) is the most common medical management for hyperthyroidism," says Steven L. Marks, BVSc.

Depending on its severity and the size of the cat, the dose ranges from about 2.5 to 7.5 milligrams twice a day. The drug only suppresses the thyroid hormone production, so it must be given every day for the rest of the cat's life. Some cats are given Tapazole on a temporary basis until other treatment can be scheduled.

Dr. Hager warns that up to a fifth of the cats treated with Tapazole will have an adverse reaction. "They become terribly ill with problems with their liver. It can affect their blood, cause itchy face. They can have lots of problems," he says. Also, because the drug is not a cure and little adenomas continue to grow, he says the cat needs more and more Tapazole as time goes on.

"Kitties have an aversion to being pilled," he cautions, which can interfere with the bond you share with your pet. Repeated unpleasant associations with medicating can cause the cat to hide when he sees you. Another option is transdermal application of the medicine. Tapazole is compounded into a cream or gel that is able to carry the medicine through the skin when smeared on the inside of the ear.

Transdermal medication has been successfully used for years in human medicine, and has been used for some time in veterinary medicine, especially for pain control (fentanyl patches) and in hyperthyroid cats. Research by Dr. Marks and others looks at the benefits of transdermal application of several products, including methimazole in cats. "Pets don't like to receive pills if they don't have to," says Dr. Marks. The struggle and stress of medicating cats can make them even sicker, so ask your veterinarian about less stressful medication options. More transdermal medications should become available when results of these studies are published.

When a hyperthyroid cat has other health concerns, those may also require medical treatment. For instance, Dr. Little says that hypertension is very common but highly manageable with the proper medication. "The most commonly used one is Norvasc (amlodipine). It's a human heart drug but it's the best drug for hypertension in cats." She says controlling high blood pressure makes a clear difference to their quality of life day to day.

RADIOACTIVE IODINE

The third option for feline hyperthyroidism is radioactive iodine treatment, I-131. "That's a one-time-only deal, but it has limited availability, typically in veterinary universities," says Dr. Schulman. A commercial enterprise, called Radiocat, has established a chain of clinics throughout the United States that are mostly in large metropolitan areas. "We have a private radio iodine clinic in our area that one of the local veterinarians set up," says Dr. Little. "They're increasingly common. The vet should know where the nearest radioactive iodine clinic is."

No anesthesia is involved. Treatment consists of a subcutaneous (beneath the skin) injection of radioactive iodine, usually at the back of the neck. "You could inject it anywhere, because it circulates everywhere in the body in the bloodstream," says Dr. Hager. As thyroid tissue absorbs the radioactive iodine, it is subsequently destroyed.

This treatment is ideal, especially if the disease is caused by a cancer and has spread to other places in the body. "The prognosis is pretty good. The nice thing about radio-iodine is that it will kill just the tumor cells and leave the healthy cells, even the cancer cells that have moved elsewhere." The cancers are treated with a high dose of radio-iodine, and the benign disease is given a lower dose.

"Our dose for the radio-iodine is between 2 and 6 millicuries [measure of radioactivity]," says Dr. Hager. The dose depends on the size of the cat, as well as size of the thyroid glands—smaller glands get a smaller dose. Dosage is also based on the cat's thyroid hormone (T4) levels. "Also, if kitties have kidney disease, then I'll give them a lower dose. Kitties that are frail and have been hyperthyroid for a long time, we give them a lower dose because they have less reserves." He says using scintigraphy has helped take away much of the guesswork.

This treatment option has a 98 percent cure rate for cats. The government regulates the use of radioactive iodine, and requires that a treated cat be quarantined for a period of one to four weeks and have his urine and feces monitored for radioactivity before being released. Dr. Hager says these restrictions are the biggest drawback to the treatment. "The kitty has to stay with us for five days—that varies between states."

Quarantine can be hard on the owners and on the cats. "Mom and Dad are worried about having them gone, and what their kitty will do. Cats are creatures of habit. They love their routine. And the minute you take them out of their routine, then they become upset," says Dr. Hager.

For that reason, the centers where he works include a viewing room for people to come in and see the cat, and for the cat to see them. Although about half the owners are reluctant to visit, fearing they'll just upset the pet, Dr. Hager says he's not noticed any cat becoming really upset over that.

A small percentage of treated cats become hypothyroid afterward—that is, require thyroid hormone supplements, but that's rare, says Dr. Hager. Because most treated cats are older, he advises they be monitored for kidney function. "This is going to be the best thing for the overall health of your kitty in the long run. People are extremely happy. The kitties go home and they live a good quality of life."

BOTTOM LINE

- Cost of the scintigraphy varies across the country. "With us it's between $200 to $250," says Dr. Hager.
- Radioactive iodine treatment also varies from place to place. Dr. Hager estimates on average it costs between $600 to $700 for the iodine treatment alone. With the scintigraphy included, the treatment costs $1,000 to $1,100.
- Medication at first look will seem much less expensive. However, daily Tapazole for the lifetime of the cat also requires the cost of regular blood tests to monitor the thyroid levels and make sure the liver isn't damaged. Compounded medication will be easier on the cat—you'll avoid the trauma of twice-daily pilling—but will be more expensive. Price varies from practice to practice.

Golden Moments: Blanche's Thirst for Life

Eight years ago, when she lived in Jersey City, New Jersey, Karen Allison adopted a pair of three-year-old cats that needed a new home. One was a petite Siamese she named Stella. "The other was a very chubby Russian Blue with incredible green eyes," says Karen. She named the unusual blue fourteen-pound cat Blanche. "Russian Blues are usually very svelte. But not Miss Blanche."

Blanche quickly became accustomed to the house and loved her life. She got along well with Stella, and remained healthy and retained her portly figure and outgoing personality. Blanche was a bit upset when another feline interloper, Stanley, joined the family. Now, at the mature age of twelve years old, Blanche is best friends with Stanley.

Last year, Karen noticed that the blue cat was drinking more water. Although there was no increase in urination, Blanche had also lost weight. "That concerned me, and I thought it must be time for the first geriatric blood screen anyway," says Karen. She took the cat to see Dr. Cindy Bressler at Symphony Veterinary Center on the Upper West Side of New York City, and had a blood test run. "The vet got back to me and said yes, something's wrong. She's hyperthyroid."

Karen was concerned, but immediately knew what was involved. She'd learned about hyperthyroidism by reading an account of the condition, diagnosis, and treatment on the CompuServe CatsForum. "I knew she would have radioactive iodine treatment."

She began looking for a facility to have Blanche treated. The facility Dr. Bressler recommended was moving, though, and Karen was also making plans to relocate to Las Vegas. Stella would stay behind with a friend, since

When Blanche began drinking too much water her owner realized that something was wrong. *(Photo Credit: Karen R. Allison)*

she wouldn't easily tolerate the move. The timing for Blanche's treatment just wasn't right.

Until a facility could be found, Blanche was given the drug Tapazol to suppress the action of her overactive thyroid gland. "She's not that hard to pill, but I hate to inflict that on a cat every day, so I asked if it could be compounded." Karen, who expected a flavored oral medicine, was surprised and pleased at the form of application. "You put it in the ear for transdermal absorption," she says. The medicine is the texture of Vaseline and is measured onto a finger, then placed in the ear. "For Blanche it was something that irritated her ear for a second. For me it was easy as pie."

Karen searched the Internet to locate a veterinarian and facility for Blanche's treatment. "Dr. Hager was surprised beyond measure that I found him, because he's a California doctor who comes in once a month to do procedures in Las Vegas," she says. "He sat with me the better part of half an hour, going through the procedure with me, telling what would happen, what to expect, telling me about the disease, what the findings were on Blanche. Dr. Hager has a great bedside manner—and all the time he was holding and petting Blanche."

Blanche had more blood tests done before the procedure, and Karen was told to stop treating with the Tapazole a week before the radioactive iodine treatment. Then the cat was checked into the hospital. "The vet was just wonderful with her," says Karen. After the dosage was figured out, based on Blanche's history, the beneath-the-skin injection was given. "They kept her for five days, which is the government minimum [for quarantine]," says Karen. Radioactive emissions have to be under a certain level before treated cats are released.

The cat's body is radioactive for a period of time following treatment even once she comes home from the hospital. "I was told to think about her as a little flashlight, radiating this radioactivity," says Karen. Although Blanche posed no risk to other pets, Karen was cautioned to avoid close contact for another week because the emissions could damage her own thyroid gland.

Karen had just moved to Las Vegas, so when Blanche came home from the hospital, both Stanley and Blanche started life in the new house in the guest bedroom suite. They stayed there until Blanche was no longer radioactive.

"I was under instructions to take away her feces every day, and not have her on my lap. They said don't touch her too much and don't let her touch her face to yours," says Karen. "Blanche is a big lap cat, and she loves head bumps. That was a week I didn't like very much, but she got through it okay," says Karen. "Stanley certainly wasn't under orders to stay away from her, so she had some companionship."

A month following the radioactive iodine treatment, Blanche's thyroid levels were tested. "She was perfect," says Karen.

Today Blanche is fully recovered. "She has been active, and obviously happier," says Karen. "She still is quite thin, and went from thirteen to about nine pounds. She's gotten comfortable with the lesser weight and doesn't seem to be putting too much back on."

Blanche and Stanley love their new home in Las Vegas, especially the eighteen-foot-high ceilings with tall platforms over the tops of closets and shelves halfway up the walls, all just made for feline climbing. "That's definitely a cat arrangement, not a person arrangement," says Karen. "Stanley keeps Blanche very active by chasing her around." Karen visits Stella regularly on trips back to New York.

The lost weight seems to have increased her agility and triggered a new trick. "This is a cat that never hopped onto anything except my bed, and that was a big struggle," says Karen. Ever since coming home from the treatment, Blanche hops into the bathroom double sink every night for an evening drink of water before she goes to sleep. "It's become a ritual," says Karen.

Paying attention to Blanche's behavior is more than a ritual for Karen; it's a kind of health insurance. "Cats don't ever tell you when they're sick. You just have to figure it out for yourself."

Kidney Failure

The cat's kidneys have several functions, including the manufacture of hormones such as erythropoietin, which controls the production of red blood cells and blood pressure. In addition, kidneys regulate the nutrients carried in the bloodstream and the fluid content of the body, and they also screen toxins and waste from the bloodstream and eliminate them in the urine.

Renal, or kidney, failure is not necessarily caused by age, but it is extremely common in aging cats, says Dan Carey, DVM. A recent survey by the veterinary teaching hospital at the University of Minnesota indicates that kidney disease is one of the top six reasons cats begin veterinary treatment. When the kidneys fail to screen out toxins the way they're supposed to, the poisons build up in the blood—a condition called uremia. "That's what causes the animal to feel bad," says Dr. Carey.

The acute form of the disease happens suddenly, often as a result of ingesting a poison such as antifreeze. In old cats, though, kidneys fail a little at a time, perhaps from simple wear and tear over the years. Chronic disease creeps up on the cat. "Kidney disease is either the number one or number two cause of death in cats and dogs in every study that's been done," says Debbie Davenport, DVM. "About 30 percent of cats in the senior population have renal disease, and the owners may or may not be aware of it." That's because the cat's kidneys are able to compensate and work well even when a large percentage of their function is gone.

Individual structures inside the kidneys, called nephrons, form the

SENIOR SYMPTOMS

Typical signs of kidney failure begin gradually, and increase with the progression of the disease.

- Increased urination, missing the litter box
- Increased thirst
- Lethargy
- Loss of appetite, weight loss
- Dehydration
- Vomiting, diarrhea, or constipation
- Mouth sores, foul ammonia breath
- Yowling

urine. As kidneys age, nephrons die and are not replaced, and when enough are lost, the cat begins showing signs of kidney failure. "Typically when 75 percent or more of the nephrons are lost, that's when we begin to see the real critical problems," says Blake Hawley, DVM.

Symptoms are similar to diseases such as diabetes. Blood and urine tests are necessary to diagnose kidney disease. By checking blood urea nitrogen (BUN) and creatinine levels, and comparing them to specific urine gravity, veterinarians can get a good idea about kidney function. "You begin to see an inability for the animal to concentrate its urine," says Dr. Hawley. "And you may see a persistent low urine specific gravity." Further screening of the kidneys by X rays or ultrasound may be necessary.

"Kidney disease very often is intertwined with high blood pressure and thyroid disease," says Susan Little, DVM. Hypertension in cats, though only recently recognized, is quite manageable. "Cats with kidney insufficiency have a derangement of the physiological system that helps monitor blood pressure, and it can get out of whack, and they get high blood pressure from it." Many cats have kidney disease, hypertension, and hyperthyroidism at the same time.

About one in four cats with chronic renal failure or hyperthyroidism also develops hypertension. "We don't wait until they're ill. We do blood-pressure checks routinely on any older cat with a blood-pressure cuff," says Dr. Little. The Doppler blood-pressure monitor is currently considered the most accurate machine for use on cats. An inflatable cuff is placed on the cat's foreleg, and a transducer reads reflected ultrasound signals bouncing off moving red blood cells.

Getting an accurate reading can be tough, though. Normal systolic blood pressure (during heart contraction) is about 110 to 125. Stress from going to the hospital can make the cat's blood pressure go higher and cause an inaccurate reading. Sedation also interferes with accuracy. Often, multiple readings over several days must be averaged to get the best picture of the cat's situation. "When their high blood pressure is controlled, they often feel better and do better with their kidney failure. So they're intertwined; it's hard to separate them," says Dr. Little.

DIET THERAPY

Chronic renal failure will get worse, regardless of what you do, says Dr. Carey. "Our objective is to slow the progression." Medications help normalize the blood, and special therapeutic diets are prescribed that reduce the workload of the kidneys.

Many of the "regular" senior diets for cats offer a nutrient profile that reduces the risk factors associated with kidney disease, says Dr. Davenport. Dietary phosphorus, sodium, protein, and essential fatty acids are of particular importance, as well as ensuring the diet does *not* acidify the urine. The point is emphasized because regular feline maintenance diets often do acidify the urine to reduce the risk of certain kinds of crystals, called struvite. Older cats, however, are more prone to calcium oxalate crystal formation, and an acidic diet promotes this.

Usually the first step is a special diet designed to minimize the amount of stress placed on the kidneys, says John F. McAnulty, DVM, an associate professor of surgery at the University of Wisconsin. "I've seen cats that were not doing well that start to gain weight, and really seem to be a lot more energetic on the diets."

Nearly all the major pet food companies offer therapeutic diets for kidney disease, and most also have one for "early stage" and another for a more advanced stage of the disease. Most restrict phosphorus and sodium, and provide a low to moderate level of highly digestible protein to help relieve the burden on the organs. "Protein and phosphorus are linked together, so when you try to control dietary phosphorus, you also reduce dietary protein," says Dr. Davenport.

Adding the right type of fiber to the diet also reduces the workload of the kidneys, says Dr. Carey. Here's how it works. Failing kidneys leave behind nitrogen waste in the blood. Certain kinds of bacteria trap this nitrogen in the intestine. Feeding a fermentable fiber to the cat maintains the health of these beneficial bacteria. "You can shift the excretion of nitrogen from the kidney to the intestine enough to help the body," says Dr. Carey.

Most cats with renal failure lose their appetite, and most of these diets are not tremendously palatable, says Dr. McAnulty. Some cats refuse to eat the therapeutic diet. If so, you can offer other brands and try to find a kidney diet your cat will accept. In many cases, though, you must give in to the cat's preferences. "You have to cut your losses; you are better off feeding a suboptimal diet than you are starving it."

FEEDING FOR HEALTH

Cats can suffer different degrees of kidney failure, and may prefer one food over another. Some of the more common therapeutic diets available from your veterinarian for kidney disease include:

- Eukanuba Nutritional Kidney Formula Multi-Stage Renal/Feline
- Hill's Prescription Diet Feline g/d (early stage)
- Hill's Prescription Diet Feline k/d (moderate stage)
- IVD Select Care Feline Modified Formula
- Purina Veterinary Diets, NF Kidney Function Formula
- Waltham Feline Renal Support

FLUID THERAPY AND MEDICATIONS

Once the disease progresses to the point that diet alone isn't enough, additional medications along with fluid therapy are the next step. Kidney failure often causes severe dehydration. Fluid therapy not only improves your cat's physical status but also makes a difference in quality of life. "If the animal needs fluids, there is no single thing you can do for them that's greater than rehydrating them," says Dr. Wynn.

Initially, once or twice weekly administration of fluids at the veterinarian's office may be sufficient. But it's more comfortable and less stressful for your cat to have you give them at home. Once the disease progresses to the point that fluid therapy several times a week is required, the cost may be prohibitive unless you learn to give subcutaneous (under the skin) fluids.

Most owners are more concerned about the needle than the cat is. A needleless option is the implantation of a beneath-the-skin catheter. The fluids are then administered by attaching the IV line to an external port that feeds fluids beneath the cat's skin. You'll find further details about administering fluids in Chapter 5.

Dr. McAnulty says that often by the time your cat requires fluids, she'll also need drugs to control symptoms of the renal failure. For instance, medications such as cimetidine (Tagamet or Zantac) or famotidine help to control stomach acidity, and other medicine helps reduce the amount of phosphorus. "A cat that's on home fluid therapy can get potassium supplements in their fluid, so they may not need an oral form," says Dr. Little.

Since the kidneys are responsible for producing the hormone that stimulates the production of red blood cells, kidney failure can result in anemia. Commercial replacements of erythropoietin such as Epogen are helpful in these cases, says Dr. Little.

Hypertension as a result of kidney failure can cause a stroke at worst,

---

AGE-DEFYING TIPS

Researchers would love to be able to predict which cats will develop kidney disease, as well as figure out how to prevent the condition. Recently Dr. Michael R. Lappin, a professor in the clinical sciences department at Colorado State University, along with other scientists investigated the unexpected role certain vaccines may play in feline health. The investigation was presented in an abstract at the twentieth Annual American College of Veterinary Internal Medicine Forum in June 2002.

The report indicates that FVRCP (a combination of three protective vaccines) given as a SubQ injection can induce antibody response to feline kidney tissues. In other words, this vaccine can stimulate the immune system to become sensitive and react to certain cells of the cat's kidneys. The same study reported that the intranasal form of the FVRCP vaccine (nose drops instead of injection) did not produce antibodies to kidney tissue.

Why should cat owners care? Until recently, virtually all cats were vaccinated every year with FVRCP to protect them against potentially deadly diseases. There's no question that these vaccinations save cat lives, but current research by Dr. Lappin and many others indicates the protection lasts beyond a single year.

Today, many feline experts agree that less frequent vaccinations are equally effective at preventing common cat illnesses. The news that SubQ injections of FVRCP can induce antibodies against feline renal tissue further supports the notion that you should discuss alternatives to annual vaccination with your cat's veterinarian.

The vaccine-and-CRF investigation is too new for researchers to offer an opinion or conclusion about any potential cause-and-effect (or lack thereof). "Further research will be needed to define the role of these autoantibodies in the development of chronic renal failure in cats," says Dr. Lappin.

and erratic behavior and yowling at night at best. In fact, increased blood pressure is one of the major factors causing the disease to progress. Some diets increase omega-3 fatty acids to help reduce hypertension, and if they don't, you should supplement the food with fish oil, says Susan G. Wynn, DVM. Hypertension can also be treated with a number of drugs, says Dr. Little. She says one of the best choices for cats is a human heart drug called Norvasc (amlodipine). "That can make an amazing difference to their quality of life."

Dr. Wynn is a great believer in natural therapies, if the cat will tolerate additional medications. "There are some herbs that are pretty amazing. A Chinese herbal formula called *Liu Wei Di Huang Wan* really does seem to help some of these animals live longer, feel better, and it just seems to be the little extra something that some of them need." The herbal combination also is known by the brand names Six Flavor Tea Pills or Rehmannia Six. These prescription medications are available only through a holistic veterinarian.

Golden Moments: Tending Daffy

Last July, Chris Jevitz of Chicago noticed that her fifteen-year-old tortoiseshell cat, Daffy, just wasn't herself. "She's a fairly outgoing cat," says Chris, but she seemed to be losing weight and not eating as much. "She spent a lot of time under the bed, and I also noticed she was dehydrated. Daffy was more lethargic than normal."

Daffy always had an annual geriatric screening, and everything had checked out fine in January. "But a change in behavior is an indication that something must be going on," says Chris. Over the years she'd loved, cared for, and lost other geriatric cats to kidney disease, hyperthyroidism, diabetes, and heart problems, and she had learned to get help quickly.

A new blood test for Daffy came back okay except for the kidney values. In less than seven months, the cat's BUN (blood urea nitrogen value) jumped from normal to 51, and creatinine to 3.4—well over the normal range. "Things can change very quickly with cats, and overnight something will crop up," she says.

The veterinarian suggested dietary changes, and gave Daffy beneath-the-skin fluids for her dehydration. "They asked me to bring her back in two days for more fluids," says Chris, an experienced home-care owner. She compares performing home nursing care to addressing the needs of any aging family member, and she had no hesitation about giving Daffy 100 milliliters of fluids every other day.

When she returned for a follow-up visit, Chris shared her concern that Daffy had started throwing up her food, and was still lethargic. Blood values were reduced, though, and an X ray showed nothing unusual. Once Daffy had eaten the special diet for a couple of days and received additional fluids, she began to improve. A week later, Daffy's blood test revealed how well the special diet and fluid therapy were working when BUN and creatinine values dropped into the normal range. "I'm continuing to give her fluids every other day."

Several years ago, when she had been first faced with giving subcutaneous fluids to a cat, Chris had a lot of hesitation. She wondered if being poked with a needle would be bad for the quality of her cat's life. "But I see the difference when they have those fluids, and how much better they feel," says Chris. "There's no question in my mind that this is good for them. If I can alleviate their discomfort, that's what I'll do, even if makes my life difficult for a while." She accepts that as part of the responsibility of loving pets.

Being in the home environment reduces their stress level and can be therapeutic. Chris established a routine that makes the operation comfortable for the cat and the people involved. "This is the third cat I've done this to. I've learned it's easier if someone holds and talks to the cat." So Daffy has a treatment team—Chris and her twelve-year-old daughter, Michelle.

Daffy is holding her own, with the help of at-home fluid therapy from her owners. *(Photo Credit: Chris Jevitz)*

"Michelle really does a great job. She holds her front end while I kind of sit behind Daffy, pull the skin up to make a little tent, and insert the needle at the base of the tent, parallel to the body. Then I let it relax and turn on the fluids," says Chris.

In the meantime, Daffy's doing well. Chris considers the process of home care to be a loving way to cherish every moment with the aged cat. "Treating Daffy has given my daughter an opportunity to feel like she's doing something to help," says Chris. "With all of my animals I truly feel blessed that they were a part of my life. Maybe that sounds corny," she says, "but they just bring us so much and ask for so little."

HEMODIALYSIS

In human renal failure, the standard medical treatment is dialysis, in which a machine takes the place of the damaged kidneys, and cleanses the blood of the toxins. The first program for pets was launched in 1998 at University of California—Davis. "We use neonatal equipment, and we can accommodate dogs and cats as small as two kilograms," says Larry Cowgill, DVM, founder of the program.

Hemodialysis is used primarily for acute kidney failure, designed to give the organs the time to heal the damage. "Usually an animal will die of acute kidney failure in four to five days, but it may take weeks or even months for the kidney to get resolved," says Dr. Cowgill. Cats with chronic kidney failure usually are not good candidates for dialysis, because the process is so expensive, and they would need treatment for the rest of their lives.

Hemodialysis is often used before, during, and/or after a feline kidney transplant until the new organ starts to work. "Many pet owners today are willing to use their discretionary money to bear that cost if in fact there's some expectation the animal's going to recover," says Dr. Cowgill. "We probably dialyze 50 percent of the animals we transplant." The school handles up to four hundred treatments each year.

Hemodialysis units for pets are available in only a handful of places. The University of California—Davis, in a joint venture with the University of California—San Diego Veterinary Medical Center, also provides dialysis services in a facility at the Helen Woodward Animal Center in Rancho Santa Fe. "There are other programs at the Animal Medical Center in New York, and Tufts University also has a program," says Dr. Cowgill.

BOTTOM LINE

- "The typical cost for hemodialysis here is about $300 to $400 per treatment," says Dr. Cowgill. During the course of treatment that can easily run to $5,000 to $7,000.
- Kidney transplant costs between $6,000 to $8,000 at the University of Wisconsin, and antirejection medicines following surgery typically cost about $1,500 per year for maintenance, says Dr. McAnulty. Costs vary at other programs.

TRANSPLANTS

Dr. McAnulty began transplanting pet kidneys in 1995. "We're doing about a dozen a year now, and we've done thirty-five transplants at this point," he says.

Cats are fortunate in that their bodies will accept the healthy kidney of any other cat with few rejection problems. Different transplant programs obtain donor cats from different sources. Dr. McAnulty gets donor cats from commercial laboratories and from a private local shelter.

Since healthy cats need only one kidney to live long, healthy lives, no cat is sacrificed so another can live. In fact, the owner of the recipient cat adopts the donor cat. That means a happy ending for all concerned. "The owners who do this are true cat lovers," says Dr. McAnulty. "Everyone has been very happy with the donor cats in their household."

Candidates for a kidney transplant must be otherwise healthy to be considered for the program. "But we don't discriminate based on age," he says. Most are in the seven- to nine-year-old range, but the oldest cat to date has been sixteen, and one was less than a year old. "If they're old and look fairly robust, and they're healthy, then it's a reasonable thing to do."

Antirejection drugs such as cyclosporine work well in cats. However, surgery is expensive, and antirejection medication will be needed for the rest of the cat's life. "I've found our clients are very good at it," says Dr. McAnulty. But if the struggle of forcing pills into your cat destroys his quality of life, a kidney transplant may not be worthwhile for him.

Kidney transplants are available at only a handful of veterinary centers around the country. University of California—Davis began the first program, and another established program is at the University of Pennsylvania.

Liver Disease

The liver has multiple functions, from screening out toxins and metaboliz-ing drugs to creating necessary nutrients and enzymes. Liver disease can be any condition that interferes with one or more of these processes, and it may develop at any age.

Fortunately, the liver has quite a bit of built-in redundancy, and only a small portion of the organ needs to function to maintain the cat's health. "After some insults, it's fully capable of regenerating to its original size," says Cynthia R. Leveille-Webster, DVM. A lifetime of exposure to toxins, stress, and damage means old cats are more prone to liver problems. Some diseases damage the liver so badly it isn't able to recover.

Hepatic lipidosis is the most common liver disease of cats, and cholan-giohepatitis is the second most common, says Dr. Davenport. "Occasionally you see cats that have both diseases simultaneously."

Dr. Schulman says it's a myth that only obese cats get hepatic lipidosis. Once the cat stops eating, fat is released into the blood as a source of nutri-tion. Because the liver cells store fat, they quickly become overwhelmed and are no longer able to function. "About ten years ago, the disease was invariably fatal because doctors did not know how to treat it. These days, most cases survive," says Dr. Schulman.

There are also three forms of inflammatory liver disease (hepatitis) that affect cats. The acute form is usually caused by bacterial infection, says Dr. Webster. The two others are so similar they can be told apart only by exam-ining cells under the microscope. One tends to be a disease of young to middle-aged cats. Lipacidic hepatitis, or lipacidic cholangiohepatitis, most commonly affects aged cats, says Dr. Webster. Some studies indicate that even when they don't become sick from it, many old cats have this mild to moderate inflammation in their livers. "My own cat has it," she says. "It's rare that it requires intervention and therapy."

Signs can be confusing because liver disease mimics other illnesses, and often the sick cat has problems in other body systems at the same time, with symptoms that overlap. "Cats that have liver disease can actually get concurrent diseases of their intestinal tract and pancreas," says Dr. Webster. "It's called triaditis, and means all three are inflamed at once."

SENIOR SYMPTOMS

Signs of liver problems are similar and quite vague, whatever the type of disease:

- Jaundice—yellowish tinge to gums, whites of eyes, or inside of ears
- Refusal to eat
- Vomiting
- Weight loss
- Increased drinking and urination
- Lethargy
- Neurological signs including confusion or dullness

DIAGNOSIS

Signs of liver disease are so vague it requires sophisticated tests to diagnose. "The owners sometimes notice they turn yellow," says Dr. Webster, but that happens most often with advanced cases. Bile produced by the liver aids in the digestion of fat, and it can turn the cat's skin yellow when it backs up in the blood circulation.

Also, increased pressure on the veins entering the liver can prompt an accumulation of fluid (ascites), causing the abdomen to swell, but that's a rare finding in cats and much more common in dogs. Another rare consequence of liver disease is hepatic encephalopathy that affects the brain. "Toxins build up in the blood that the liver normally removes. It can go to the brain and cause confusion—they just look out of it," says Dr. Webster. "Occasionally they can have seizures."

A biochemical profile of the blood is the first step toward diagnosis. Liver enzymes may be elevated for a number of reasons, though, and elevated

enzyme values do not automatically mean the cat has liver disease. "Probably the number one reason for a high liver enzyme in an old cat is thyroid
disease," says Dr. Webster. "You have to go further into diagnostic testing.
Sometimes you get a picture of the liver with the ultrasound, then get a
biopsy."

Blood tests, imaging techniques, and symptoms can point to liver disease. But a definitive diagnosis can be made only by examining tissue beneath the microscope. An ultrasound-guided needle allows cells to be
collected through the abdominal wall, often without invasive surgery.

TREATMENT

Treatment depends on the cause of the problem and how early it's
caught. Once the inflammation scars the liver, the damage is hard to reverse. Inflammation of the liver—the various hepatitis diseases—is treated
with drugs to suppress the inflammation. "If I diagnose lipacidic hepatitis
in an older cat, I tend to use prednisone," says Dr. Webster. This is not a
cure, but cats do improve with this therapy and they don't have a lot of side
effects from prednisone the way dogs do. A rare complication of using
prednisone would be development of diabetes.

Dr. Webster also likes to use SAMe in cats. "I've had a couple cats using
these long-term. My cat has been on those medications now for four
and a half years, and she's doing pretty well." The nutraceutical SAMe
(S-Adenosylmethionine) increases antioxidant levels in liver cells to protect
them from toxins and death. This oral medication, brand name Actigall or
Ursodiol, is a naturally occurring bile acid that can help protect the liver
from further damage.

For cats that are acutely ill and refuse to eat for days and even weeks, a
feeding tube may be placed to allow the cat to be fed a soft diet, either
while in the hospital or after going home. It may take weeks of tube feeding before the cat's appetite returns to normal. Cats tolerate these tubes
quite well, though, and most owners become adept at feeding the cat in
this way.

Once the cat's appetite returns, the right diet helps them recover. "Cats
have some very peculiar amino acid requirements, and these are particularly important in liver disease," says Dr. Davenport. Arginine, taurine, and
carnitine are critical. "Carnitine is really more of an amino vitamin than an
amino acid, but it's integral to the shunting of fat in and out of the components of the cell where fat is metabolized." She says that an inadequate
amount of carnitine is thought to be one of the mechanisms by which fat is

believed to accumulate in cats with hepatic lipidosis. Therefore, Hill's Pet Nutrition therapeutic diet called Prescription Diet Feline l/d for cats with liver disease is supplemented with carnitine, taurine, and arginine. Depending on your cat's specific needs, other therapeutic diets may be appropriate as well.

NURSE ALERT!

Liver disease in aging cats often requires long-term care to help the cat maintain a good level of quality of life.

- Cats with liver disease often refuse to eat for days to weeks at a time. A feeding tube placed surgically into the stomach through the body wall provides the conduit for temporary nutrition. A soft, semiliquid diet given by syringe through the tube maintains nutrition until the appetite returns. Owners may be required to tube-feed the convalescing cat.
- A number of oral medications, usually pills, are often needed to relieve the symptoms of liver disease. When you must tube-feed the cat, these medications can be added to the food. Other times, compounding the medicines may be helpful in helping the cat accept medication.

Golden Moments: A Royal Treatment

Aztec was a surprise. Andrea Dorn, a research associate at Iowa State College of Veterinary Medicine, had set out to capture an adult feral cat, but she discovered the six- to eight-week-old baby. It took Aztec only a couple of days to learn to love Andrea, and the feeling soon became mutual. "I had just lost my first cat, seventeen-year-old Gabriel, so I was pretty needy at the time," says Andrea.

The little brown-and-white tabby baby was soon acting the part of princess among the other cats in the household. Aztec grew into a petite, seven-pound kitty, and the bond between Andrea and the special cat grew stronger year by year.

Then several months ago, just before her seventh birthday, Aztec began to have mysterious health problems. "She's always been extremely thin, and is not a big eater," says Andrea, "but I noticed she slowly stopped eating. She started vomiting maybe once a week, but then it got more frequent. We weren't sure what was going on." Andrea immediately took the cat for a veterinary exam. "I practiced as a veterinary technician for fifteen years before I got to Iowa State, and I don't put up with a cat not eating for very long."

Because of her background, Andrea was aware that these vague symptoms could be caused by a wide range of problems. But she immediately suspected liver problems. When an X ray and ultrasound seemed to substantiate her fears, a liver biopsy was scheduled.

Often a liver biopsy can be done with a tiny incision through the abdomen to take the necessary tissue sample. But Aztec's liver was too small. Instead, an exploratory laparoscopy was performed, using a specialized endoscope to also take a look at the abdominal cavity and organs inside of the body. The tests determined that Aztec had cholangiohepatitis.

"It's an autoimmune-type problem. There's something that makes the liver react to itself," says Andrea. The cause remains unknown. The cat's liver was so severely inflamed that it was having trouble functioning normally. Drugs such as steroids are commonly prescribed to help counteract the inflammation.

"Usually you're not going to cure it. It's never going to go away, so she'll have to be treated the rest of her life," says Andrea. She's researched the condition since Aztec was diagnosed and is heartened to learn some cats have lived with cholangiohepatitis for as long as seven years.

Treatment is tricky and must be tailored for each individual cat's tolerance level and situation. Because liver disease often is associated with other body systems such as the intestines or pancreas, some medicines are designed to treat these problems, too.

With special home care and dedicated veterinarians, Aztec's liver disease is coming under control. *(Photo Credit: Andrea Dorn)*

Prednisone, a steroid, is the most common and easiest treatment, but a host of other medicines are often required. Aztec also takes metronidazole [Flagyl] to control inflammation in the intestines. "That's one she'll probably be on the rest of her life," says Andrea. She's also given a drug that boosts the effects of the steroid drug, and gets Ursodiol, a naturally occurring bile acid that helps protect her liver from further damage."

Multiple drugs can have side effects. "She stopped eating—that's her barometer," says Andrea, and tests showed Aztec had developed diabetes. Besides all the pills being poked down her throat, Aztec also was given insulin injections twice a day. Switching to a different steroid medication cured the diabetes, though, so Aztec doesn't need insulin shots anymore.

The struggle to first diagnose and then treat and maintain Aztec's disease began to affect the cat's quality of life. After being force-fed pill after pill, soon she began avoiding Andrea altogether. "It's so hard when you deal with something like this because you want to take care of your cats, but at the same time they start hating you," says Andrea. "It's just very emotional."

The struggle continued until Aztec recently stopped eating again. This time the veterinarian placed a stomach tube so that she could be fed a puddinglike high-calorie food, called Prescription Diet a/d. "I have to mix it with water to get it through the tube," says Andrea. Aztec should weigh six or seven pounds, and her weight has dropped to about five pounds, so she needs all the calories she can get. Andrea feeds tiny amounts three times a day. An added advantage is that Aztec's meds are administered at the same time—no more pilling.

Now the cat feels a whole lot better about Andrea and being medicated. "I don't have to stick things down her throat all the time. Now she sits on my lap

---

FEEDING FOR HEALTH

Foods designed to be highly palatable and digestible are appropriate for cats suffering from liver disease.

- Eukanuba Veterinary Diets, Nutritional Stress/Weight Gain Formula, Maximum-Calorie/Feline
- Hill's Prescription Diet Feline a/d (recovery)
- Hill's Prescription Diet Feline l/d (liver diet)
- IVD Select Care Feline Mature Formula
- IVD Select Care Feline Development Formula
- Purina Veterinary Diets, EN Gastroenteric Formula
- Waltham Feline Convalescence Support Diets

and purrs while I'm watching TV, and it takes about a half hour to get every-thing down," she says. "I'm a big fan of stomach tubes; it's a lifesaver!"

To date, Andrea has spent over $3,000 on Aztec's diagnosis, care, and medications. She's also had to deal with the rest of her feline household. "It's pretty common for cats to reject a cat after it's been in a clinic, because it has different smells about it," she says. "That can be a real problem. But Aztec is a very strong personality; she's very independent." She says the other cats can yell and scream all they want, and "Princess" Aztec doesn't care.

Andrea says it's vital for people to know what's normal for their cat while they're healthy, so they know when to get them help. "Be sensitive to them. That's what helps me."

Obesity

Obesity, defined as an excess of body fat 20 percent beyond the normal, more often affects middle-aged and older cats. Obesity is their most common nutritional disorder. A recent survey of veterinarians indicates that half of the adult cats seen are overweight or obese. "In the six- to twelve-year-old group as many as 40 percent of the cats are overweight or obese," says Debbie Davenport, DVM.

Aging cats tend to gain weight as they age because their activity level decreases, their metabolism slows, and cat diets are designed to be very tasty. Free feeding of dry food can lead to obesity, and canned or semimoist foods are so delicious, cats tend to overeat. "Studies show that a partial reduction in the sense of smell seems to prompt the cat to eat more food," says Dr. Myers. "Perhaps this is one reason aging cats are more prone to obesity."

Although excess weight may not directly cause other health problems, overweight old cats are also prone to them. "Obesity definitely doubles, triples, or quadruples risk for diabetes," says Dottie LaFlamme, DVM. It is also an aggravating factor in heart problems, arthritis, and skin problems. "Pancreatitis is linked to obesity, and to increased incidence of lower urinary tract disease in cats. Feline hepatic lipidosis, fatty liver in cats, is very strongly linked to obesity," says Dr. LaFlamme.

Long-term studies indicate that fat dogs don't live as long as thin ones. One study of overweight cats reported an increased risk for dying in middle age, says Sharon Center, DVM. Researchers suspect fat cats don't live as long as thin ones, so obesity becomes a longevity and quality-of-life issue.

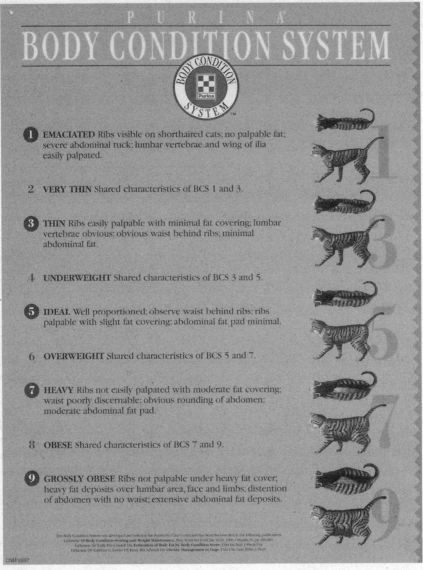

PURINA
BODY CONDITION SYSTEM

BODY CONDITION SYSTEM — Purina ™

1   EMACIATED Ribs visible on shorthaired cats; no palpable fat; severe abdominal tuck; lumbar vertebrae and wing of ilia easily palpated.

2   VERY THIN Shared characteristics of BCS 1 and 3.

3   THIN Ribs easily palpable with minimal fat covering; lumbar vertebrae obvious; obvious waist behind ribs; minimal abdominal fat.

4   UNDERWEIGHT Shared characteristics of BCS 3 and 5.

5   IDEAL Well proportioned; observe waist behind ribs; ribs palpable with slight fat covering; abdominal fat pad minimal.

6   OVERWEIGHT Shared characteristics of BCS 5 and 7.

7   HEAVY Ribs not easily palpated with moderate fat covering; waist poorly discernable; obvious rounding of abdomen; moderate abdominal fat pad.

8   OBESE Shared characteristics of BCS 7 and 9.

9   GROSSLY OBESE Ribs not palpable under heavy fat cover; heavy fat deposits over lumbar area, face and limbs; distention of abdomen with no waist; extensive abdominal fat deposits.

This Body Condition System was developed and refined in the Purina Pet Care Center and has been documented in the following publications: LaFlamme DP. Body Condition Scoring and Weight Maintenance, Proc. N Am Vet Conf. Jan 16-21, 1993, Orlando, FL, pp 290-291. LaFlamme DP, Kealy RD, Schmidt DA. Estimation of Body Fat by Body Condition Score. J Vet Int Med 1994;8:154. LaFlamme DP, Kuhlman G, Lawler DF, Kealy RD, Schmidt DA. Obesity Management in Dogs. J Vet Clin Nutr 1994;1:59-65.

CNM 2897

(Reprinted by permission)

DIAGNOSIS

The normal weight range doesn't vary much from cat to cat or from breed to breed. The breed extremes are represented by the Singapura, with a normal weight range of four to six pounds, and the Maine Coon and Ragdoll breeds, which can tip the scale at twenty pounds or more. For most

---

AGE-DEFYING TIPS

Keeping your cat thin and svelte from kittenhood on will prevent health problems, help her live longer, and increase her enjoyment of life.

- Make twice-daily play therapy part of your routine. This not only provides good exercise but also is a powerful bonding tool that brings you closer.
- Reward with attention, not treats.
- Choose an age- and activity-appropriate diet. Pets that sleep on the sofa all day do not need the equivalent of rocket fuel.
- Feed measured amounts of food two to three times a day instead of simply keeping the bowl full all the time.

---

cats, though (pedigreed or not), the average weight is seven to twelve pounds, with males typically on the higher end of the scale.

A scale by itself isn't the best way to evaluate whether or not your cat is overweight. A much better measure is a hands-on approach that checks the cat's profile and palpates, or feels, the body composition. Weight gain can happen very gradually, and the owner of a fluffy cat can be surprised to discover she's fat. Most people simply aren't aware the cat falls outside healthy weight parameters.

Some breeds call for slightly different conformations—for instance, the Oriental-type breeds, such as Siamese and Oriental Shorthair cats, tend to have longer, thinner bodies than the cobby-type Persian breeds. In all cats, though, generally you should be able to feel the ribs but not see them. From above, you should see a decided break at the waist, beginning at the back of the ribs to just before the hips.

In profile, cats should have a distinct tummy tuck beginning just behind the last ribs and going up into the hind legs. Many adult overweight cats tend to carry a "pouch" of fat low in the tummy, but seem of average size otherwise. If you can't feel the cat's ribs, and/or she carries a pouch on her tummy, the cat is overweight. To evaluate your cat's condition, compare her appearance to the illustrations in the Body Condition System chart. Remember to account for fur, which can hide pounds.

Crash diets for cats can be deadly. Overweight felines in particular are prone to liver problems, called hepatic lipidosis, and so care must be taken to ensure your cat loses weight in a safe, gradual way. Before beginning a diet, your veterinarian should examine the cat to rule out potential health complications. The veterinarian will calculate how much weight should be lost, and suggest a diet and exercise plan appropriate to your individual pet. Usually, the target is to lose about 1 to 1½ percent of her starting weight per week.

NURSE ALERT!

Obese cats very often have a difficult time grooming themselves. Until the cat has lost the necessary weight, be sure her fur is kept in good condition with combing and/or brushing. Pay particular attention to the anal region, which may capture waste and cause urine scald or attract flies or maggots. Perfect Coat Bath Wipes (www.eightinonepet.com) offers a premoistened towelette that's convenient for keeping pets clean.

SLIMMING THE CAT

Exercise is vitally important not only to maintain weight or prevent weight gain, but also to take off the extra pounds. Cats should get about twenty minutes of aerobic exercise every day to stay healthy. Keep in mind that obese animals can't maintain activity for extended periods. Any exercise program should begin slowly and be adjusted to the cat's ability level. Interactive play is the best way to engage your cat in exercise. Feather toys or fishing-pole lures that the cat will chase are ideal, says Rhonda L. Schulman, DVM. "If you just spend some time, some cats will learn to play fetch," she says. Try using tiny wads of paper and flipping them across the room or down the stairs. "My cats really like the laser light. They will chase that all over the house."

Cats enjoy watching the world, so setting up a bird feeder outside a couple of windows may engage them enough to move. "Something they can watch that would actually force them to pace a bit, that's great," says Dr. LaFlamme. For cats that are blind, try tying a bell or rattle toy on the end of a string, and let sound help you exercise the cat.

Controlled leash walking is great if your cat will put up with a halter and leash. "There's no reason cats can't be taught to walk on a leash," says Dr. LaFlamme. Cats won't power-walk, but a slow to moderate stroll at the end of the leash once or twice a day around the house or garden will help burn energy.

Very overweight cats may be reluctant to move at all. "Make the animals work a little bit for their food," suggests Sarah K. Abood, DVM. "Your animal can't handle a flight of stairs, so how about a ramp up to a chair so they're expending a few calories. For pets that are more ambulatory, put the food at the top or bottom of the staircase so the animal always has to go up and down to get her food." Even setting the food bowl at the opposite end of the house far from the cat's favorite couch will get her moving.

Controlling calories is easier than getting the cat to exercise. "Avoid the tendency to ad lib feeding," says Richard Nelson, DVM. "That's a major factor in causing obesity." In other words, instead of just setting out the full bowl of food for the cat to nibble all day long, switch to meal feeding of controlled portions.

Moderately overweight cats may shed pounds simply by cutting out the treats and increasing play sessions. Senior diets typically have fewer calories, and switching the cat to a more age-specific formula can help. "Lite" formula diet cat foods are available, but they aren't magical. In fact, pets often gain weight on lite diets if they're fed ad lib, or if the brand of food is different from the cat's former diet. That's because the lite designation means only that the food is lower in calories than the same-brand "regular" food—it's a comparison within the same family of foods.

Divide the food into four or even five small meals a day to help keep her from feeling deprived. Multiple small meals also tend to increase the body's metabolic rate, so she burns more calories faster and consequently loses

At one point, Pooh's weight ballooned up to twenty-six pounds (shown here). An innovative diet plan slimmed the tubby tabby down to sixteen pounds, and improved his overall health along the way. *(Photo Credit: Michelle West)*

the excess weight. Once she's reached the target weight, serving meals twice daily will maintain her health.

When cats are obese, medical supervision by the veterinarian, and often a special therapeutic weight-loss diet, is necessary. Several are available from different pet food manufacturers, and each offers innovative formulations that help the cat safely lose weight.

COMFORT ZONE

- **Treat Balls**: When put on a diet, cats often pester owners endlessly, meowing for more food. "If the cat is interested in playing at all, you can put food inside these little balls," says Dr. LaFlamme. Most cats must be taught how to use the commercial treat balls. Once the cat realizes there's food inside, and play makes it come out, you've solved portion control, exercise, and the pester factor all in one. "You can put a good portion of all their food in there, make them work for it, and it slows down their food intake. I think that is a great little trick." There are several treat-dispensing balls for cats available in pet products stores, including the "Talk to Me Treatball" (www.talktometreatball.com), which records your voice message to entice your cat to play.
- **Kitty Café**: This is a handy trick for dealing with multicat households where a fat cat and skinny cat need to be fed separately. Basically, a box is fitted with a tiny door that only the thin cat can get through. The thin cat is fed inside the box, and the fat cat can't get inside to swipe anything and must be satisfied with the diet food available on the outside of the box. "Until the fat cat gets skinny enough to fit in there, he can't have any," says Dr. LaFlamme. You can make your own box, or purchase a commercial one at www.kittycafe.net. This product also works well to keep dogs out of the cat's food.

Golden Moments: Pooh Shapes Up

Pooh Bear, a blue spotted tabby Domestic Shorthair, was diagnosed with diabetes when he was nine-and-a-half years old. "I found some sticky stuff on the side of the tub where the cats go to the bathroom," says Michelle West of Toronto. Pooh was in the hospital for four days, and came home perfectly regulated on 4 units of Humulin U insulin once a day. "Then I had to diet him down—he weighed twenty-six pounds."

He had always been a big boy, says Michelle, but she hadn't really noticed how bad he'd gotten. "Then one day I looked at him, and was horrified that I'd let that happen to him. I'm sure that if he hadn't gained so much weight, he never would have become diabetic. I could just kick myself for letting it happen."

She decided to put him on a strict but careful diet, hoping to gradually slim him down and also help with his diabetes. She knew that trying to force weight loss too quickly could create fatal liver problems.

She tried some of the commercial "lite" reducing diets, but the high fiber caused serious constipation problems. "There were a couple times I thought poor Pooh was going to have a heart attack just trying to go to the bathroom," says Michelle. High-fiber foods counteract diarrhea and constipation by normalizing the bowel movement, but fiber works a bit differently in individual cats.

Michelle settled on a combination of three different brands: 50 percent Waltham Calorie Control, and 25 percent each of Hill's Science Diet Senior and Meow Mix. "Without the Meow Mix, he gets seriously constipated from all the fiber in the other two," says Michelle. She says it took a long time to work out the perfect mixture for Pooh—and what works for him might not work for others. "It might take a couple of months to work out the right mix for your overweight cat," she says.

As a breeder of Scottish Folds, Michelle had two other cats in the household that needed a different diet: Toni, a breeding female, and an aging retired girl named Punkin with arthritis problems. "I needed three different foods for my cats," she says. "The minute I knew Pooh had to go on a diet, that was the end of free feeding in my house." Before, they didn't like each other's food anyway, so leaving it out all the time wasn't a problem. But once he was on a diet, Pooh wanted to eat anything that didn't move faster than he did.

Once the diet started, Michelle locked up all the food in one-pound cottage cheese containers, labeled them for Toni, Punkin, or Pooh, and kept a set for each cat by the living room chair, by the couch, and by her bed next to the desk where she works. "Wherever I am, I am close to food," says Michelle. "For the girls, it was easy to teach them to come to the containers when they wanted to eat. I'd just open the right one when they'd rub against or sit by the container." She says they get as much food as they want, every time they ask, so it's still very similar to the free-feeding schedule from before.

To begin his diet, Pooh was given one cup of his mixed dry foods spread out over a twenty-four-hour period. This amount was slowly reduced. "Now he's holding at about half a cup mixed dry foods a day," says Michelle. "He is always hungry and always begging for food. He has the biggest gold eyes, and he looks at me so sadly. But I had to learn to be strong."

Pooh is fed on a strict schedule around the clock, to keep his blood sugar

---

FEEDING FOR HEALTH

Some cats are able to lose weight simply by reducing the amount of their regular diet and increasing exercise. Most cats, though, need the extra help of a reduced-calorie food. Some "lite" products are available in grocery stores, but obese cats usually do best on a therapeutic diet dispensed from the veterinarian. Products designed for feline reducing diets include:

- Eukanuba Veterinary Diets Nutritional Weight Loss Formulas Restricted-Calorie/Feline
- Eukanuba Adult Weight Control Formula
- Hill's Prescription Diet Feline r/d
- Hill's Prescription Diet Feline w/d
- IVD Select Care Feline Hifactor Formula
- IVD Select Care Feline Weight Formula
- Nutro Complete Care Weight Management
- Max Cat Lite
- Precise Feline Light Formula
- Purina Veterinary Diets, OM Overweight Management Formula
- Waltham Feline Calorie Control Diet

---

as stable as possible, which has ensured a lack of complications from the diabetes. Each morning Pooh's daily ration of half a cup is measured into a cottage cheese container, and his meals are doled out every two-and-a-half hours throughout the day until the tub is empty.

"I give him these dry-food meals spread out in a large fifteen-inch round tray. It takes him longer to eat because he has to hunt all the pieces down," she says. She'll give him ten pieces or so as a snack if he paw-pats her head to wake her during the night for a snack. "Then I fall right back asleep," says Michelle. "Pooh is so used to his schedule, his little tummy-clock keeps perfect time."

For times when she must be out of the house, Michelle bought an automatic Cat Mate Feeder ($40 from Drs. Foster & Smith). Its two food compartments are on a timer and open only at prescribed intervals. "He always tries to break into it when I'm gone," says Michelle. "I've even found it in a different room from him pushing it. Even if he did get in, he would get no more than his usual next tablespoon a little early."

Michelle's method for locking up all the food works best for someone who works at home, or for people able to come home at lunchtime. "My girls ask for food at least eight to ten times a day each," says Michelle. "If you are home at mealtimes, this container system makes feeding different foods a breeze. It's so much easier than feeding multiple cats in different rooms, some on the counter and some on the floor. That's very difficult."

The system simplifies giving Pooh his insulin shot. "He's so hungry that when he's eating at eleven A.M., I give the shot and he never even notices!"

Pooh's diabetes has been well regulated for four years. Michelle's diet system enabled him to lose ten pounds in one year—he's thirteen-and-a-half years old and stable at sixteen pounds—and to reduce his insulin needs to one unit once a day. "I know I'm probably going overboard in my care for Pooh, but I love him so much and want him to be with me as long as possible," says Michelle. "He's in perfect health now, and is more alert and lively than when he was younger. I hope he will be with me another thirteen years."

Pancreatitis

The pancreas, a small organ situated near the liver, provides digestive enzymes for the small intestines, and insulin that aids in glucose metabolism. Inflammation of the organ, called pancreatitis, disrupts the function and spills enzymes into the bloodstream and abdominal cavity. That causes an array of subtle to severe symptoms.

Pancreatitis has been recognized in cats only in the last decade. Most often chronic pancreatitis affects middle-aged and older cats. "Pancreatitis is a very frustrating disease in cats," says Debbie Davenport, DVM. The disease is hard to diagnose and difficult to treat, and there are no good answers about what causes the condition. Since the organ is linked to the intestines and also to the liver, cats suffering from pancreatitis may have concurrent liver or inflammatory bowel disease. "It's possible that an inflammation can actually move from one organ to the other," says Dr. Davenport. That makes the disease even more difficult to diagnose and treat.

In dogs, feeding fatty table scraps, obesity, and injury are commonly incriminated. Fatty diets and obesity don't seem to play a role in the feline disease, although the list of potential causes includes trauma, parasites, and toxins, says Susan Little, DVM.

Despite these puzzles, more cases are being recognized than ever before. "Part of that is we're looking for it, and part of it is the advent of abdominal ultrasound," says Richard Nelson, DVM. "Part of it is that I think for some reason, something has shifted, and it's causing an increase in the prevalence of pancreatitis in cats. It's become a significant problem."

DIAGNOSIS

Tests that diagnose pancreatitis very well in dogs and people don't work with cats because the disease reacts differently in the feline body. For example, humans with pancreatitis have certain enzyme levels in the blood that consistently go up. "That doesn't happen in cats," says Cynthia R. Leveille-Webster, DVM.

Even the symptoms and test results are frustrating. "They're just tremendously varied. It's really hard to hang your hat on anything," says Dr.

Susan Little. "The blood work can be highly variable. The signs of illness can be highly variable."

One of the more recent and promising tests is the feline trypsinlike immunoreactivity (TLI), but most times diagnosis is based on an ultrasound of the cat's pancreas. Even then the diagnosis may not be definitive, says Dr. Webster. "Chronic pancreatitis is an old-cat disease that's really hard to get a handle on without doing surgery and a biopsy of the pancreas."

TREATMENT

Currently there is no consensus on the best way to treat feline pancreatitis once it's diagnosed. Dogs usually have acute disease and are supported with fluid therapy to counteract the dehydration, pain-relieving drugs, medicine to control vomiting, and fasting—withholding food for three or four days. Food stimulates the pancreas to continue releasing enzymes, so fasting helps break the cycle.

But cats with chronic disease have symptoms that come and go. They rarely vomit, and fasting can cause life-threatening hepatic lipidosis. "It's very difficult to safely fast a cat," says Dr. Davenport. "Most people feed in the face of pancreatitis." Other supportive care, such as fluid therapy, or drugs to control vomiting, is offered as needed.

Cats that have a mild form of chronic pancreatitis often benefit from a daily dose of pancreatic enzyme, says Johnny D. Hoskins, DVM. A teaspoon of dried powdered extracts of beef or pig pancreas (Pancrezyme, or Viokase-V) can be mixed in the food, given twice daily. If the cat refuses the treated food, the veterinarian may have other alternatives, such as raw beef pancreas or a fish-based liquid supplement.

Dr. Webster treats cats on a case-by-case basis. "If the cat's vomiting every two hours, I'm not going to shove food down the throat," she says. "You can give it some parenteral nutrition through the vein for a couple of days until it calms down a little bit."

Parenteral nutrition—intravenous nutrition—does not stimulate the pancreas as much, agrees Dr. Davenport, but it requires constant monitoring. "If you overfeed calories—in particular, fat—to cats intravenously, you can predispose lipidosis, so you're back to making the situation worse."

In most cases, she says veterinarians will place a tube device either down the throat or directly into the stomach through the cat's side. That is combined with fluid therapy to keep the cat well hydrated. "Sometimes it just becomes a wait-it-out phenomenon," she says. "You just have to keep the cat supported long enough for the pancreatic inflammation to subside."

Senility

As they age, cats can develop signs of senility, or cognitive dysfunction syndrome (CDS). "CDS basically represents a loss of memory and learning, or a reduction in learning memory," says Benjamin Hart, DVM. The syndrome has long been recognized in elderly dogs, and cats also are affected. "Cats age much more gracefully than dogs," says Dr. Hart, and because they live much longer, the age when they develop symptoms is therefore much later.

SENIOR SYMPTOMS

Signs of feline cognitive dysfunction can be vague and confusing, and mimic other disease conditions. Look for:

- Disorientation: wanders aimlessly, acts lost and confused, may not recognize family members or other familiar people or places, gets "stuck" in corners or lost in the house
- Interaction changes: no longer greets family members, dislikes or avoids petting, not as interested in getting attention, interaction changes with other pets
- Sleep changes: is awake and active at night, sleep cycles are disrupted or reversed
- Housetraining is forgotten
- Anxiety or compulsive behaviors: tremors, yowling and crying, repetitive pacing, floor or object licking

---

"You're more likely to see it in fifteen-year-old and older cats," says Gary Landsberg, DVM. He authored one of the first research papers on cats that concluded, in part, that as many as 80 percent of cats he sees that are over the age of sixteen show signs of senility. "Some of the brain changes in [these cats] are similar to those seen in the early stages of human Alzheimer's," he says. Like the affected humans, cats with cognitive dysfunction also have deposits of amyloid material in the brain.

In the past, these symptoms would have been brushed off as a normal part of feline aging, says Susan Little, DVM. Today, there are treatments available that can help. "It actually should be recognized as a specific health issue of a geriatric cat." Affected cats typically seem to forget how to do normal cat activities. For example, they are unable to find the litter box, or simply sit in the middle of the room and cry.

Often, dog studies have been based on tests used to help diagnose human Alzheimer's patients. Fewer studies have been conducted in cats, and these studies, in turn, often have been based on the canine studies, says Kelly Moffat, DVM. She conducted one of the first studies in cats that included full blood panel examinations and neurological workups. So far, over the two-year study period, she's examined 155 cats, aged eleven to twenty-one years old. She evaluated whether the cat's relationship with the owner or other animals changed—perhaps a decrease in tolerance to being handled or being left alone, for example, or failure to recognize familiar people or places. "We asked if these cats were waking up the owner at night, or excessively vocalizing at night; if they're wandering, pacing, or any type of repetitive or compulsive type behaviors; and we looked at anxiety, fear, and irritations to see if cats seemed to be more irritable than when they were younger." The last question covered memory and learning—if the cat still used the litter box, for example. "We definitely had a lot of cats that didn't have any medical conditions [to account for] showing signs," she says, with cats older than fifteen vocalizing much more at night.

Melissa Bain, DVM, also is researching feline cognitive disorder. She began by conducting phone interviews to screen the owners of cats aged eleven to nineteen that were patients at the Cal-Davis Veterinary Medical Teaching Hospital. Basic questions were asked to identify and eliminate cats from the study that did have physical causes for suspect behavior changes. They ended up with 130 cats for the study. These were then further identified as being positive or negative for a behavior change due to potential cognitive dysfunction in these four categories: disorientation, interaction with owner, housetraining, sleep-awake cycle. "We asked them three to four questions in each category. For disorientation, we asked if the cat got lost in the house or the yard, or stuck in corners or behind furniture, for example." Owners were asked to answer with *increase, decrease, the same,* or *absent.* They were also asked to compare the aged cat's behavior to when they were middle-aged at seven to eight years old.

"They were all spayed females and castrated males," says Dr. Bain, "and the cat had to be positive for two or more signs in a category to be considered positive for that category. We haven't done the statistics on it, but there doesn't appear there's any difference between the sexes." She says many of the cats showed increased vocalizing for no reason. "We didn't know what category to put it in. The cat would just meow and act confused. It seemed to happen at night."

The acronym D.I.S.H. (disorientation, interaction, sleep changes, housebreaking) was created to help identify cognitive disorders in dogs, and because the drug Anipryl was licensed for use in those specific categories, says Dr. Landsberg. However, the acronym doesn't account for anxiety or compulsive behaviors such as howling and repetitive pacing that tend to be quite common in both older dogs and older cats. "Broader categories are probably a bit better. That's what we were looking for in cats, because you don't look at learning and memory tests in exactly the same way," he says.

So far Dr. Bain's cat study indicates that 20 percent of eleven- to twelve-year-old cats were positive for one or more categories. "We considered one category mild impairment," says Dr. Bain. "Only 3 percent were positive for two or more categories—a very small amount."

As the cat's age increased, so did the prevalence. The percentage of

---

AGE-DEFYING TIPS

Researchers agree that mental stimulation drastically improved the cognitive function of aging cats.

- Keep your cat both physically active and mentally engaged throughout her life to keep her brain young and potentially prevent or slow the progression of aging changes. Teach her to walk on a leash; teach her tricks; offer brain-stimulating viewing entertainment such as bird feeders outside windows.
- Offer puzzle toys that reward the cat's interest by dispensing treats. This can mimic feline hunting behaviors and keep the cat entertained and mentally sharp.

thirteen- to fourteen-year-olds positive for one or more categories was 33 percent, but only 8 percent were positive for more than two categories. Forty-two percent of the fifteen- to sixteen-year-olds were positive for one or more categories; 16 percent of this group was positive for two or more categories. Sixty-one percent of the final group of cats, aged seventeen to nineteen years old, were positive for one or more categories. "Forty-three percent were positive for two or more," says Dr. Bain.

TREATMENT

It's vital that the condition be diagnosed correctly. A single behavior change in an old cat could potentially have several causes. For example, a break in housetraining might be due to arthritis, which makes getting in and out of the litter box painful. It could also be caused by kidney disease or diabetes, which prompts increased urination. Personality changes could be caused by a brain tumor, hyperthyroidism, or pain from dental disease. Wailing at night sometimes is a sign of high blood pressure.

Without the proper screening tests to rule out other causes, it can be very difficult to definitively diagnose this condition. A large percentage of geriatric cats displaying these objectionable behaviors are simply put to sleep. Today, medical help can reverse the condition in a percentage of affected cats.

Once properly diagnosed, the human medicine selegiline hydrochloride (Anipryl) has been FDA approved in the United States to treat canine cognitive disorder. "Anipryl can be used in cats now in Canada," says Dr. Little, and it has been used with success off-label in the United States. Bill Fortney, DVM, says the drug may work to prevent the ongoing damage to the brain. "It acts on one of the neurotransmitters in the brain responsible for nerve-to-nerve communication, and slows the natural destruction of the chemical compound dopamine in the brain."

Cognitive dysfunction is a progressive disease, and medication can slow or reverse these behavior changes, but not on a permanent basis. "The medicine is not a magical elixir or fountain of youth," says Nicholas Dodman, BVMS. Time will catch up with the cat, and there will be an eventual decline. But selegiline can buy time and improve the cat's quality of life for perhaps a year or more. And when your cat is seventeen or eighteen years old, another year or two is golden. Generally the cat will need to be on the drug for about four weeks before any results can be expected.

COMFORT ZONE

Cats suffering from senility often forget to use the litter box. Keeping the cat's bedding and your carpet and upholstery clean and odor-free helps maintain quality of life for you both.

- Nature's Fresh spray (made by Nature's Sunshine) contains natural proteins derived from vegetable sources and fruit acids to neutralize organic odors due to urine, feces, and vomit, and helps prevent or remove stains. It is safe to spray into the air or on any material not harmed by water (shoes, clothing, bed linens, upholstery, carpet, auto interiors, etc). Nature's Fresh with sprayer costs about $9 and is available at www.vir-chew-all.com.
- Tuff Oxi (Tuff Products for Pets) is an enzymatic cleaner that "digests" the smell and organic particles to eliminate odor, and is available from info@tuffcleaningproducts.com.

NEW FRONTIERS

A number of other studies of dogs using selegiline have shown promising results regarding increased longevity. The newest treatment, a therapeutic diet for canine cognitive disorder, was made available in 2002, but researchers say that work on a comparable feline diet has not made significant strides.

"There are a couple of other drugs available in Europe, Canada, and Australia," says Dr. Fortney. One is called Fitergol (nicergoline), made by Rhone Merieux in France. "They end up increasing the blood flow to the brain, and therefore delivering more oxygen to the brain so that the memory is supposed to work better. There are newer drugs on the horizon that

---

COMFORT ZONE

A natural component of some foods, called phospholipids, can help reverse some signs of cognitive disorders by helping brain cells send and receive nerve impulses more effectively. Choline and phosphatidylcholine, two common message-sending compounds, are found in a dietary supplement called Cholodin FEL, which is a less expensive alternative to Anipryl. The product is available through veterinarians, and comes in a pill form or powder flavored to appeal to cats, to be mixed into the food. More information is available at www.mvplabs.com.

perhaps can better treat this particular problem, or treat those that don't seem to respond as well to the Anipryl."

A wide range of various antioxidant, neuroprotective nutraceuticals, supplements, vitamins, and diet can be adjusted to enhance the cognitive function in the older animal, says Dr. Lansberg. "But what's proven to be effective or not is hard to say."

Although many therapies may hold promise for the future, cat owners today can't afford to wait years for them to become available. Dr. Kelly Moffat says environmental enrichment is easy, costs nothing, and your cat can benefit today. Studies by Dr. Norton William Milgram, a professor at the University of Toronto, in dogs proved that enrichment greatly improved canine cognition. "That's definitely been proven in people, too," says Dr. Moffat, and it applies just as well to cats. "Use it or lose it, definitely. If they work the brain on a regular basis, the memory ability is preserved longer." She suggests you offer your cat lots of play sessions to keep her mind as healthy and well toned as her body. This can also help wear her out in a nice way, especially prior to bedtime, to help curb unwanted nighttime activity and vocalizations.

BOTTOM LINE

Anipryl is dosed by weight, and costs about $1.50 a day for a cat.

Golden Moments: Love to the Max

"I've had Max since he was six weeks old," says Elizabeth Jones, a computer graphics specialist in Mesa, Arizona. She chose the white-with-gray Manx baby because he was so playful and affectionate. Throughout their lives together, Max never met a stranger he didn't like. "He'd always come right up, get in your lap, make himself comfortable, and just rub himself on your face," she says.

When Max was five years old, Elizabeth rescued a needy white Persian cat. Tenna and Max had the same golden eyes, and had been born within a month of each other. Although it wasn't love at first sight, the personalities of the sweet, laid-back Tenna and the outgoing, brash Max seemed to complement each other. "The two of them became very close," says Elizabeth.

Max, Tenna, and Elizabeth were a threesome for eight years, until the Persian became progressively ill with cancer. "I had to put her to sleep," she says. "That's when a dramatic change happened with Max. When she left, he was just devastated."

Elizabeth couldn't explain to Max what had happened to his furry companion. The cat was grief stricken, and his meow-wails went on for hours. Finally the thirteen-year-old Manx slipped away from the patio retreat and was gone for two days. "I knew he was looking for Tenna. And he wasn't going to find her," says Elizabeth.

She was relieved when he came home, but he was still crying and very upset. "I tried to comfort him—he was desperately unhappy. I was upset, too," says Elizabeth, her voice shaking at the memory. With time, the pain eased for both of them, but Max was never the same.

His behavior and personality began to change, so slowly that at first Elizabeth couldn't quite put her finger on what was wrong. "He doesn't look fifteen years old to me, but I know he's getting up there," she says. He'd always been food motivated, but now even treats lost their allure. Max began to lose weight, and became reluctant to interact. The gregarious cat she'd always known began to hide. Then last March when she graduated from school and began working, things went downhill fast.

"He'd poop on my bed, or pee right in my spot where I sit on the couch," says Elizabeth. The glazed look in his eyes and his anxious behavior made Elizabeth fear that her beloved cat was losing his mind. Nothing she did seemed to help.

Max either hid from her or wailed for attention. Without warning, he'd climb into bed in the middle of the night, cry to wake her, and make a mess. "I was at the end of my rope," she says. "I had to deal with this ailing kitty that's always been so friendly and wonderful, good company and very loving." She knows not to take it personally, but dealing with middle-of-the-night messes makes it hard. "It hurts so much to see him this way."

Elizabeth became more and more upset as Max's condition deteriorated. "He had this look in his eyes that said, 'Who are you? Where am I? I don't know what's going on! I'm upset, and I don't feel well,' " she says. "If you see an animal suffer like that, I feel it's your responsibility not to prolong it." She loved her cat and was torn by the thought of losing him, but knew she'd ultimately have to put Max to sleep.

The suffering—for them both—had been going on for five months when Elizabeth received a questionnaire from Max's veterinarian, Dr. Kelly Moffat, requesting information for a study about senior-cat patients. Participation in

Max's confusion was helped with an innovative treatment that reversed his Alzheimer's-like symptoms. *(Photo Credit: Elizabeth Jones)*

the study included complete blood work, and physical and neurological exams. Elizabeth jumped at the chance that something would be found that could help Max.

The tests came back normal. For his age, Max was quite healthy and there were no physical problems they could find that would account for his distress and behavior problems. "Dr. Moffat explained that at a certain stage of the game, sometimes cats deteriorate on a cognitive level."

As a last-chance effort, Elizabeth agreed to try an experimental treatment of Anipryl, a drug approved for use in dogs for cognitive dysfunction. Max received half a tablet every morning. Elizabeth noticed a change within only a couple of days. "It was pretty dramatic," she says.

Max seemed to regain his composure overnight. His appetite returned, and he began to beg for food just like old times. "Now he knows where he is, he recognizes me, he knows what's going on," says Elizabeth.

Thoughts of putting Max to sleep have been put on permanent hold, ever since the glazed look in his golden eyes lifted to reveal what was always there, under the confusion.

Max looking back with love.

Stroke

Common causes of human strokes are smoking, primary high blood pressure, and atherosclerosis—deposits of cholesterol-rich plaques within the arteries. Strokes are not nearly as common in cats because they don't have those diseases, says Lisa Klopp, DVM. "Cerebral vascular accident is something we definitely see in pets," she says, but the causes are different. A cerebral vascular accident—called a "stroke" in humans—is a disorder of the blood vessels in the brain that results from interference with the blood supply.

"There is also a specific syndrome called feline ischemic encephalopathy," says Dr. Klopp, and in most cases a cause can't be determined. But

---

SENIOR SYMPTOMS

Not all cats that act dizzy have suffered a stroke. "I can't diagnose a stroke just by looking at an animal," says Dr. Klopp. Symptoms are vague, and will be variable, depending on what part of the brain is affected, and usually very sudden. Often they are severe and initially cause extreme impairment, but then tend to improve.

- Seizure
- Depression
- Circling and/or dizziness
- Incoordination
- Behavior change (anything!) may also be a sign

sometimes it's due to a parasite, cuterebra, when it migrates into the cat's brain by mistake.

More commonly, infectious diseases and endocarditis, an inflammation of the heart tissue, bring about strokes in cats. But by far the major culprit in feline strokes is high blood pressure caused by kidney failure or heart disease. "They can have strokelike events with hypertension. They may go blind, or have bleeding inside the eye," says Susan Little, DVM.

DIAGNOSIS

Diagnosis can be difficult. Even with an MRI, the changes caused by the brain damage may be hard to see. "If the stroke is big enough to see in the brain stem, the animal is probably not alive," says Dr. Klopp. "The brain stem is very sensitive and there's no functional redundancy there, so a very small stroke is going to do a lot of damage."

However, strokes that occur in the forebrain are easier to see on the MRI. "We can have fairly good-size strokes in the forebrain and have animals survive. If I think a stroke is possible, but I'm not seeing signs on the MRI, I try to rule other things out and go from there."

AGE-DEFYING TIPS

Monitoring the cat for hypertension is easy. A blood-pressure cuff designed for felines used by the veterinarian determines if medication such as amlodipine is necessary. A common sign of hypertension in cats is erratic behavior and/or yowling at night, says Dr. Little.

TREATMENT

Not much can be done once the injury has occurred, says Dr. Klopp. "By the time I see it, it's probably as bad as it's ever going to be. If you can treat the primary disease, that's your best bet." In other words, you should figure out what disease caused the stroke—high blood pressure—and treat that.

Cats often seem severely affected but then begin to slowly improve and recover more quickly and easily from strokes than people do. "I've seen very badly affected animals walk out of the hospital," says Dr. Klopp. That's because cats usually suffer strokes in the forebrain, but they rely on their brain stem for their strength and function. If they have a stroke in the forebrain

---

NURSE ALERT!

The aftermath of a stroke may leave your cat very weak, confused, or unable to walk. Recovery time varies, depending on the severity of the damage. But in almost all cases, cats improve. In the meantime, you may need to offer extra TLC:

- Soften food or hand-feed
- Carry her to the litter box or provide absorbent pads in her bed to help deal with accidents
- Rehabilitation exercises may help strengthen weak muscles
- Medicate as indicated to deal with underlying diseases

---

they may initially be very weak. "But they'll usually get up and get going again with only a few subtle deficits," says Dr. Klopp. "They're not going to be paralyzed on one side like the human."

Another reason they recover quickly is they aren't required to function to the high level that people aspire. They are very good at compensating for a weak leg, for example, and don't worry about needing to drive a car or that people might look at them funny if they wobble a bit. "They're much more able to function and deal with their disabilities and adjust," says Dr. Klopp.

PART THREE

Additional Resources

Senior-Care Directory

One of the best ways to find out about care options and receive emotional support is to talk with other cat owners who have experienced similar situations with their pets. A good place to start is at the veterinary schools, which often have resources for pet owners on various senior-cat conditions, as well as grief counseling services. If you have access to the Internet, go to the various Web sites and do a "search" on the topic of your choice.

VETERINARY SCHOOLS AND BEREAVEMENT HOT LINES

Alabama

Auburn University
College of Veterinary Medicine
Auburn University, Alabama 36849
www.vetmed.auburn.edu

Tuskegee University
School of Veterinary Medicine
Tuskegee University College of Veterinary Medicine, Nursing, and Allied Health
Tuskegee, Alabama 36088
http://svmc107.tusk.edu/Tu/svm/svm-toc.html

California

University of California
School of Veterinary Medicine
One Shields Avenue
Davis, California 95616
www.vetmed.ucdavis.edu
Grief Hot Line: 800-565-1526

Colorado

Colorado State University
College of Veterinary Medicine and Biomedical Sciences
Fort Collins, Colorado 80523-1601
www.cvmbs.colostate.edu
Grief Hot Line: 970-491-1242

Florida

University of Florida
College of Veterinary Medicine
P.O. Box 100125
Gainesville, Florida 32610-0125
www.vetmed.ufl.edu
Grief Hot Line: 352-392-4700, ext. 4080

Georgia

University of Georgia
College of Veterinary Medicine
Athens, Georgia 30602
www.vet.uga.edu

Illinois

University of Illinois
College of Veterinary Medicine
2001 South Lincoln
Urbana, Illinois 61802
www.cvm.uiuc.edu
Grief Hot Line: 217-244-2273 or 877-394-2273

Indiana

Purdue University
School of Veterinary Medicine
1240 Lynn Hall
West Lafayette, Indiana 47907-1240
www.vet.purdue.edu

Iowa

Iowa State University
College of Veterinary Medicine
Christensen Drive
Ames, Iowa 50011-1250
www.vetmed.iastate.edu
Grief Hot Line: 888-478-7574

Kansas

Kansas State University
College of Veterinary Medicine
101 Trotter Hall
Manhattan, Kansas 66506-5601
www.vet.ksu.edu

Louisiana

Louisiana State University
School of Veterinary Medicine
Skip Bertman Drive
Baton Rouge, Louisiana 70803
www.vetmed.lsu.edu
Grief Hot Line: 225-578-9547

Massachusetts

Tufts University
School of Veterinary Medicine
200 Westboro Road
North Grafton, Massachusetts 01536
www.tufts.edu/vet
Grief Hot Line: 508-839-7966

Michigan

Michigan State University
College of Veterinary Medicine
6100 Vet Med Center
East Lansing, Michigan 48824-1316
www.cvm.msu.edu
Grief Hot Line: 517-432-2696

Minnesota

The University of Minnesota
College of Veterinary Medicine
410 Veterinary Teaching Hospital
St. Paul, Minnesota 55108
www.cvm.umn.edu

Mississippi

Mississippi State University
College of Veterinary Medicine
Box 9825
Mississippi State, Mississippi 39762-9825
www.cvm.msstate.edu

Missouri

University of Missouri
College of Veterinary Medicine
Columbia, Missouri 65211
www.cvm.missouri.edu

New York

Cornell University
College of Veterinary Medicine
Box 39, Schurman Hall S3-005
Ithaca, New York 14853-6401
www.vet.cornell.edu
Grief Hot Line: 607-253-3932

North Carolina

North Carolina State University
College of Veterinary Medicine
4700 Hillsborough Street
Raleigh, North Carolina 27606
www.cvm.ncsu.edu

Ohio

Ohio State University
College of Veterinary Medicine
1900 Coffey Road
Columbus, Ohio 43210
www.vet.ohio-state.edu
Grief Hot Line: 614-292-1823

Oklahoma

Oklahoma State University
College of Veterinary Medicine
110 McElroy Hall
Stillwater, Oklahoma 74078
www.cvm.okstate.edu

Oregon

Oregon State University
College of Veterinary Medicine
200 Magruder Hall
Corvallis, Oregon 97331-4801
www.vet.orst.edu

Pennsylvania

University of Pennsylvania
School of Veterinary Medicine
3800 Spruce Street
Philadelphia, Pennsylvania 19104
www.vet.upenn.edu
Grief Hot Line: 215-898-4529

Tennessee

University of Tennessee
College of Veterinary Medicine
P.O. Box 1071
Knoxville, Tennessee 37996
www.vet.utk.edu

Texas

Texas A&M University
College of Veterinary Medicine
Suite 101-VMA
College Station, Texas 77843-4461
www.cvm.tamu.edu

Virginia

Virginia Tech and University of Maryland
Virginia–Maryland Regional
College of Veterinary Medicine
Duck Pond Drive
Blacksburg, Virginia 24061-0442
www.vetmed.vt.edu
Grief Hot Line: 540-231-8038

Washington

Washington State University
College of Veterinary Medicine
Pullman, Washington 99164-7010
www.vetmed.wsu.edu
Grief Hot Line: 509-335-5704

Wisconsin

The University of Wisconsin—Madison
School of Veterinary Medicine
2015 Linden Drive
Madison, Wisconsin 53706-1102
www.vetmed.wisc.edu

WEB SITES AND E-MAIL LISTS

The Internet provides enormous resources in terms of informational Web sites, message boards, live "chats," and E-mail discussion groups. A Web search on any subject, such as "pet loss" or "hyperthyroidism," will return a list of helpful resources. It's best to visit the site or read a description before subscribing to an E-mail list or joining in open discussions, to determine if the resource fits your needs. Here are a few to get you started.

General Resources

(Good jumping-off point, search for "cat health" or specific subjects)

www.smartgroups.com
www.topica.com
http://dir.groups.yahoo.com/dir/

Arthritis

Feline Hip Dysplasia
http://users.netropolis.net/kazikat/FelineHD1.htm

Back Problems

AbleDogs
We are primarily for people whose pets are experiencing back problems, recovering from surgery (mostly spinal), paralyzed, in carts, and so forth.
http://groups.yahoo.com/group/abledogs/
www.abledogs.net

Cancer

http://groups.yahoo.com/group/feline_lymphoma
http://groups.yahoo.com/group/feline_cancer/

Diabetes Mellitus

www.felinediabetes.com
www.sugarcats.net/sites/dmstrickland/felinediabetesflyer.htm

PETDIABETES list
Subscribe by E-mailing: majordomo@netwrx1.com with the message:
subscribe PETDIABETES

The Muffin Group (pet diabetes list)
Subscribe with E-mail to: majordomo@netwrx1.com with the message:
subscribe muffin

Diabeticat
Subscribe to: diabeticat-subscribe@yahoogroups.com

Heart Disease

Feline-Heart (heart disease in cats)
http://groups.yahoo.com/group/feline-heart/

General/Geriatric Pets

Vetmed
A moderated discussion list for veterinary medicine and animal health issues. Veterinary professionals and pet owners are equally welcome to join. Subscribe by E-mailing: LISTSERV@IUPUI.EDU with the message: SUB VETMED Yourfirstname Yourlastname
Fanciers Health, a list dedicated to the discussion of feline health issues
http://groups.yahoo.com/group/fanciershealth/

Kidney Disease

Feline Chronic Renal Failure
www.felinecrf.com

PKD List (Polycystic Kidney Disease in cats)
Subscribe with a blank E-mail to: pkd-list-subscribe@topica.com
www.felinepkd.com

Caring-for-CRF-Felines
http://groups.yahoo.com/group/Caring-for-CRF-Felines/

FelineCRF
http://groups.yahoo.com/group/FelineCRF

Feline-CRF-Support (Chronic Renal Failure in Cats)
http://groups.yahoo.com/group/Feline-CRF-Support/
Subscribe with blank E-mail to: Feline-CRF-Support-subscribe@yahoogroups.com

Pet Loss

Pet Loss Grief Support Web site
www.petloss.com

Association for Pet Loss and Bereavement
www.aplb.org

Finding a Pet Cemetery
International Pet Cemetery Association (referrals)
www.iaopc.com/home.htm

FURTHER READING

Bereavement

Coping with Sorrow on the Loss of Your Pet by Moira Allen
Alpine Publishing, 1996

The Loss of a Pet by Wallace Sife
John Wiley & Sons, 1998

For Children

Cat Heaven by Cynthia Rylant
Scholastic Trade, 1997

For Every Cat an Angel by Christine Davis
Lighthearted Press, 2001

Mr. Rogers' First Experience: When a Pet Dies by Fred Rogers
Paper Star, 1998

Health Care Management

Cat Massage by Maryjean Ballner
St. Martin's Griffin, 1997

Natural Health Bible for Dogs and Cats by Shawn Messonnier, DVM
Prima Publishing, 2001

The First-Aid Companion for Dogs and Cats by Amy D. Shojai
Rodale Press, 2001

New Choices in Natural Healing for Dogs and Cats by Amy D. Shojai
Rodale Press, 1999

The Purina Encyclopedia of Cat Care by Amy D. Shojai
Ballantine Books, 1998

Pain Management for the Small Animal Practitioner, by William J. Tranquilli, Kurt A. Grimm, and Leigh A. Lamont.
Teton NewMedia, 2000

INSURANCE AND CARE PLANS

Banfield, the Pet Hospital
"Banfield's Optimum Wellness Plans"
11815 NE Glenn Widing Drive
Portland, OR 97220
Phone: 800-838-6738
Web site: www.vetsmart.com

CareCredit
901 East Cerritos Avenue
Anaheim, CA 92805-6475
Phone: 888-255-4426
Web site: www.carecredit.com

PetAssure
10 South Morris Street
Dover, NJ 07801
Phone: 888-789-7387
Web site: www.petassure.com

PetCare Insurance Programs
P.O. Box 8575
Rolling Meadows, IL 60008-8575
Phone: 866-275-7387
Web site: www.petcareinsurance.com

Pet Plan Insurance
777 Portage Avenue
Winnipeg, MB R3G 0N3
Canada
Phone: 800-268-1169
Web site: www.petplan.com

Veterinary Pet Insurance
3060 Saturn Street
Brea, CA 92821
Phone: 800-872-7387
Web site: www.petinsurance.com

Vetinsurance
#201-557 Southdale Road East
London, ON N6E 1A2
Canada
Phone: 877-838-7387
Web site: www.vetinsurance.com

FOOD FOR SENIORS

Hill's Pet Nutrition
Science Diets and Prescription Diets
www.hillspet.com

Iams Company
Eukanuba, Iams, and Eukanuba Veterinary Diets
www.iams.com

Innovative Veterinary Diets (IVD)
Limited Ingredient Diets, Select Care
www.ivdvetdiets.com

Nestlé Purina PetCare Company
Cat Chow, Purina Veterinary Diets
www.purina.com

Nutro
Natural Choice Complete Care, Max Cat
www.nutroproducts.com

Precise
www.precisepet.com

Steve's Real Food
(Commercial frozen or freeze-dried raw diet)
http://stevesrealfood.com

Waltham
www.waltham.com

Wysong
www.wysong.net

PRODUCT SOURCES FOR SENIORS

Doctors Foster and Smith
2253 Air Park Road
P.O. Box 100
Rhinelander, WI 54501
Phone: 800-381-7179
Web site: www.Drsfostersmith.com

Drinkwell Pet Fountain
Veterinary Ventures
844 Bell Street
Reno, NV 89503
Phone: 800-805-7532
Web site: www.vetventures.com

K-9 Cart Company
656 SE Bayshore Drive, Suite 2
Oak Harbor, WA 98277
Phone: 360-675-1808, 800-578-6960
Web site: www.k9carts.com

Kong Company
(Catnip Spray and Toys)
16191-D Table Mountain Parkway
Golden, CO 80403-1641
Phone: 303-216-2626
Web site: www.kongcompany.com

Me-Ow-Trageous Kitty Cat Creations
4832 Highlands Way, Suite C
Antioch, CA 94509
Phone: 925-778-1517
Fax: 925-778-4246
Phone: 877-778-MEOW (6369)
Web site: www.catfurniture.com

MyEtribute, Inc., provides information and services addressing the
health care and end-of-life needs of senior animals. Features ramps, orthopedic beds and incontinence pads, specialized greeting cards, gifts,
and burial items.
73415 Pinyon Street
Palm Desert, CA 92260-4711
Web site: www.mypettribute.com

Perfect Coat Bath Wipes
Eight in One Pet Products
2100 Pacific Street
Hauppauge, NY 11788
Phone: 800-645-5154
Web site: www.eightinonepet.com

Practivet
Greta Implantable Fluid Tube (GIF-Tube)
2386 Grants Ferry Drive
Biloxi, MS 39531
Phone: 800-535-4057
E-mail: Kristy@practivet.com
Web site: www.practivet.com

Spillnet Protective Barrier
(protection for floors from pet accidents)
Phone: 800-438-7668
Web site: www.stainmaster.com

Talk to Me Treatball
Phone: 877-860-6227
Web site: www.talktometreatball.com

Tuff Products for Pets
(Tuff Oxi)
4035 Wade Street, Suite B
Los Angeles, CA 90066
Phone: 310-574-3252
E-mail: info@tuffcleaningproducts.com

Unique Distributors
(cat locator collar)
5401 S. Siesta Lane
Tempe, AZ 85283
E-mail: Info@uniquedistributors.com
Phone: 800-333-4793
Fax: 480-456-0108
Web site: www.uniquedistributors.com/catlocwittra.html

Vir-Chew-All Enterprizez
Phone: 877-695-3750
E-mail: presh@vir-chew-all.com
Web site: www.vir-chew-all.com

Worldwise Inc.
"Crazy Catnip Bubbles"
Department WS, P.O. Box 3360
San Rafael, CA 94912-3360
Phone: 415-721-7400
Web site: www.worldwise/crazcatbub3.html

APPENDIX B

HOME MEDICINE CHEST

Human medications are often helpful for cats, and you may already have many of the following medications in your medicine chest. However, the dosages vary depending on the size of the pet and other ongoing health issues. It's a good idea to keep these products and/or herbs on hand, but it's best to call the veterinarian for a specific dose and medication recommendation for your individual animal.

Medication	Purpose
A and D Ointment	Antibacterial ointment for scrapes or wounds
Aloe (herb)	Constipation, skin irritation
Artificial Tears	Eye lubricant
Benadryl	Antihistamine, itch relief, sedative properties
Betadine solution	Antiseptic soak for cleansing injuries
Burow's solution	Topical antiseptic
Calendula (herb)	Topical for skin injuries
Chamomile (herb)	Topical skin irritation, tea for stomach problems, stress
Comfrey (herb)	Skin injuries
Dandelion (herb)	Diuretic, for water retention
Desitin	Soothing skin cream
Echinacea (herb)	For infections and inflammation
Eucalyptus (herb)	Nasal congestion
Ginger (herb)	For nausea
Ginkgo (herb)	For mental dullness
Goldenseal (herb)	Infections, bronchial inflammation
Hawthorn (herb)	Heart irregularities
Kaopectate	For diarrhea
Metamucil (unflavored)	For constipation
Milk thistle (herb)	Liver problems
Pedialyte or Gatorade	For dehydration
Pepcid AC	For vomiting
Phillips' Milk of Magnesia	For constipation
Red clover (herb)	Bronchitis
Robitussin Pediatric Cough Formula	Cough suppressant
Slippery elm (herb)	Diarrhea, constipation
Valerian (herb)	Stress, pain
Vicks VapoRub	For congestion

APPENDIX C

GLOSSARY

Acupuncture Therapeutic use of needles to effect reversal or relief of medical conditions

Acute Sudden onset of condition or disease, and/or condition of recent origin

Adrenal Glands Endocrine glands located next to the kidneys that produce, among other things, steroid hormones

Anemia A reduction in the number of circulating red blood cells

Arrhythmias Abnormal heartbeats

Arthritis Inflammation of the joint

Arthroscope An endoscopic tool specific for use within the joints of the body

Arthroscopy Noninvasive joint surgery using a specialized endoscope to see inside the body

Ascites Fluid accumulation inside the abdominal cavity

Atrophy Wasting or shrinking

Benign A tumor that doesn't spread, harmless

Bile Acids Compounds made from cholesterol and produced in the liver, responsible for absorption of fat from the intestine

Biopsy Procedure wherein small samples of tissue are obtained for microscopic examination to diagnose a medical condition

Blood Urea Nitrogen (BUN) A by-product of protein metabolism within the body

Cachexia Wasting syndrome, malnutrition condition that develops despite adequate intake of food, often associated with cancer

Calcium Important mineral for muscle function, heart function, blood clotting, nerve conduction, and integrity of bones

Calcium Channel Blockers Drugs used to treat abnormal heart rates

Catheter A tubelike medical device inserted into blood vessels, body cavities, or passageways (i.e., the urethra) to permit injection or withdrawal of fluid

Central Nervous System (CNS) The brain and spinal cord

Chemotherapy Cytotoxic or cell-poisoning drugs used as systemic (whole body) therapy to attack cancers that have spread throughout the body

Cholesterol A steroid compound made by the liver that is vital to normal cellular structure and function

Chronic Slow or gradual onset of condition or disease, and/or condition of long duration

Compounding Refers to the creation of custom-designed prescriptions made more dose-specific and/or easier to administer

Creatinine A compound made from amino acids and regulated by the kidneys

Cryosurgery Therapeutic treatment using extreme cold (freezing)

CT Scan (computed tomography) A noninvasive diagnostic test that uses multiple X rays of "slices" of the internal structure, and then "reconstructs" that object through computer projections into a three-dimensional image of the patient.

Cyclosporine An immunosuppressive drug used in organ transplants that helps prevent rejection by the body

Dialysis Use of an artificial kidney machine to filter waste from the blood

Echocardiography A noninvasive diagnostic tool that uses reflection of sound waves from the heart muscle and surrounding tissues, specialized processing of the echoed signals, and then display of this information in a visual or auditory format. Doppler echocardiography is the newest form and adds the detection of direction and velocity of blood flow through the heart

Edema Fluid retention usually characterized by swelling in the legs

Electrocardiogram (ECG or EKG) Diagnostic test that records the electrical activity of the heart during muscle contraction and relaxation.

Endoscope A long, flexible tube employing fiber optics or other imaging technology able to be inserted through small incisions to view internal structures of the body, which transmits an image of the area to a video screen during surgical procedures

Enucleation The surgical removal of a painful and/or damaged eye, as in glaucoma

Euthanasia Humane ending of life

Femoral Head Ostectomy Surgical procedure that removes the "ball" portion from the end of the femur (thighbone) to treat hip dysplasia

Gastrotomy Tube A hollow tube passed into the stomach to feed an ill or recovering patient

Gene Therapy Various techniques that manipulate genes to create medicines or treatments designed to interact with the body on the cellular level and promote healing.

Gingivitis Inflammation of the gums

Glucose Sugar that is the primary source of energy in the body

Graft Donor tissue

Hematocrit Also called packed cell volume; the ratio of red blood cells to the total blood volume

Hemoglobin The molecule in red blood cells responsible for transport of oxygen

Hyperthermia Therapy Use of heat to kill cancer cells

Immune System The natural response of the body to fight disease or outside foreign substances. It includes both local (cell mediated) and systemic (antibody/blood system) immune components

Insulin Hormone that regulates the uptake and utilization of glucose within the body

Intravenous (IV) Delivery of therapeutic substances directly into the bloodstream through the veins

Joint Replacement Surgical technique that removes the natural diseased joint and replaces with a metal prosthetic joint, most commonly done in the hip

Ketones Products formed as a result of abnormalities in fat and energy metabolism

Laser Instrument that uses photothermal (heat) energy of various kinds of light to vaporize tissue

Lymphosyntigraphy A diagnostic technique for cancer that injects radioactive tracers that collect in cancer tissues for easier identification

Magnetic Resonance Imaging (MRI) A noninvasive diagnostic technique that records radio frequency signals given off by the tissue, using an external magnetic field, and translates the signals into a two-dimensional image

Malignant A cancer capable of spreading throughout the body beyond the site of origination

Mean corpuscular hemoglobin concentration The ratio of hemoglobin to the hematocrit

Mean Corpuscular Volume The ratio of the hematocrit to the red blood cell count

Metastasis The spread of tumor cells from site of origination

Myelopathy Degenerative disease of nerve fibers

NSAIDs Nonsteroidal anti-inflammatory drugs (such as aspirin), commonly used for pain control

Nutraceutical Nutrients (such as vitamins, minerals, certain amino acids, etc.) used as medicine

Off-label The use of nonapproved drug therapies, also called "extra-label."

Omega-3 Fatty Acids Fatty acids derived from cold-water fish oil

Palliative Treatment that alleviates signs of disease without curing the condition

Phacoemulsification Surgical technique that breaks up and removes the lens from the eye using ultrasonic vibrations; typically used in cataract surgery

Phosphorus Chemical element that helps run metabolic processes of the body

Photodynamic Therapy (PDT) A light-activated chemotherapy using lasers and photosensitizing compounds that target cancer cells

Placebo "Pretend" medicine or drug that has no physiologic effect; used in controlled studies to compare and measure against real therapy

Platelet Specialized blood cell important to clotting mechanism

Pleural Effusion An accumulation of fluid within the chest wall

Presbycusis Age-related hearing loss
Presbyopia Age-related visual changes

Radiation Therapy Use of directional X ray to treat cancer
Radiograph The use of gamma rays to view the internal dense structures of the body, also called X ray
Red Blood Cells Cells that carry oxygen from the lungs to the cells. Red blood cells make up 99 percent of the total blood cells

Schiotz Tonometer A device used to measure pressure inside the eyeball to diagnose glaucoma
Scintigraphy Also called a thyroid scan; this test employs a radioactive particle that seeks out and attaches to thyroid tissue, which is then revealed on a gamma camera. Used in the diagnosis of hyperthyroidism
Sodium Salt important to the fluid balance within the body
Specific Gravity Refers to the amount and weight of substances found in urine
Sub-Q Subcutaneous, or beneath the skin, as in fluid administration

Therapeutic Diet Commercial or homemade diet designed to specifically treat a health condition that typically is prescribed by the veterinarian
Tonopen A pen-sized tool for diagnosing glaucoma by measuring pressure inside the eyeball
Transdermal Delivery Drugs, often for pain, able to penetrate the skin and achieve local or systemic therapeutic effect
Transplant Surgical replacement of diseased organ with donor organ. In pets, most typically the kidney
TRAP (Telomeric Repeat Amplification Protocol) A test for cancer that detects telomerase, an enzyme that helps cancer cells re-create themselves indefinitely

Ulcer An erosion in the lining or surface of an organ, such as the stomach
Ultrasound Noninvasive diagnostic technique that uses reflected sound waves to form an image of internal structures

White Blood Cell Disease-fighting cells of the immune system

X ray The use of gamma rays to view the internal dense structures of the body, also called radiograph

APPENDIX D

EXPERT SOURCES

Sarah K. Abood, DVM, Ph.D., is an assistant professor and a small animal clinical nutritionist at Michigan State University

Melissa Bain, DVM, is a lecturer at University of California at Davis

Signe Beebe, DVM, is a certified veterinary acupuncturist and herbologist practicing at Sacramento Veterinary Surgical Services

Colin Burrows, BvetMed, Ph.D., MRCVS, DACVIM, is a professor of medicine and the head of the department of small animal clinical sciences at the University of Florida

Dan Carey, DVM, is the director of technical communications for the Iams Company

Sharon A. Center, DVM, DACVIM, is an internist and professor of medicine at Cornell University

Michael G. Conzemius, DVM, Ph.D., DACVS, is an associate professor at the veterinary teaching hospital at Iowa State University in Ames

James L. Cook, DVM, Ph.D., DACVS, is a surgeon in the comparative orthopedic laboratory at the University of Missouri

Larry Cowgill, DVM, Ph.D., DACVIM, is an internist and a faculty professor in the department of medicine and epidemiology, chief of small animal medicine, and head of the Companion Animal Hemodialysis Unit at University of California at Davis

Debbie Davenport, DVM, MS, DACVIM, is an internist and the director for special education for Hill's Pet Nutrition

Harriet Davidson, DVM, DACVO, is an ophthalmologist and an associate professor of clinical sciences at Kansas State University

Nicholas Dodman, BVMS, DACVA, ACVB, is a professor, section head, and program director of the animal behavior department of clinical sciences at Tufts University School of Veterinary Medicine

Nicole Ehrhart, VMD, MS, DACVS, is an assistant professor of surgery, and the scientific director of the comparative musculoskeletal tumor laboratory at University of Illinois

Bill Fortney, DVM, is the director of community practice at Kansas State University

Laura Garret, DVM, DACVIM (oncology), is an assistant professor of oncology at Kansas State University

Bill Gengler, DVM, DAVDC, is a veterinary dentist and an associate professor in the department of surgical sciences at University of Wisconsin

Paul A. Gerding, Jr., DVM, MS, DACVO, is an associate professor and chief of the ophthalmology section, department of veterinary clinical medicine at University of Illinois

David Hager, DVM, MD, DACVR, is a veterinary radiologist with Veterinary Specialty Hospital in Rancho Santa Fe, California

Benjamin Hart, DVM, DACVB, is a professor and chief of behavior service at the veterinary medical teaching hospital at University of California at Davis

Blake Hawley, DVM, is the director of E-business for Hill's Pet Nutrition

Steven E. Holmstrom, DVM, DAVDC, is the president of the American Veterinary Dental Society and practices in San Carlos, California

Johnny D. Hoskins, DVM, Ph.D., DACVIM, is an internist and a specialist in small animal pediatrics and geriatrics, and is professor emeritus at the Louisiana State University School of Veterinary Medicine

Jeff Johnson, DVM, is a general practitioner with Four Paws Animal Hospital in Eagle River, Alaska

Barbara Kitchell, DVM, Ph.D., DACVIM (oncology), is an assistant professor of small animal medicine at the University of Illinois

Lisa Klopp, DVM, is an assistant professor of neurology and neurosurgery at University of Illinois

Dottie LaFlamme, DVM, Ph.D., DACVN, works in research and development with Nestlé Purina PetCare Company

Gary Landsberg, DVM, DACVB, is a behaviorist at Doncaster Animal Clinic in Thornhill, Ontario

Michael R. Lappin, DVM, Ph.D., DACVIM, is a professor of small animal medicine in the clinical sciences department at Colorado State University

Nola Valerie Lester, BVMS, is an adjunct clinical instructor in radiology at University of Florida

Cynthia R. Leveille-Webster, DVM, DACVIM, is an associate professor of small animal medicine at Tufts University

Kathleen Linn, DVM, DACVS, is an orthopedic surgeon at University of Wisconsin

Susan Little, DVM, Dipl ABVP (feline), is a veterinarian at Bytown Cat Hospital in Ottawa, Canada

Grace Long, DVM, is a veterinarian and brand manager of Purina Veterinary Diets

Steven L. Marks, BVSc, MS, MRCVS, DACVIM, is an assistant professor of internal medicine, and head of the small animal ICU at the School of Veterinary Medicine at Louisiana State University

Jonathan F. McAnulty, DVM, MS, Ph.D., is an associate professor of surgery at University of Wisconsin

Sheila McCullough, DVM, DACVIM, is an internist at University of Illinois

Mike McLaughlin, DVM, is a general practitioner at the Animal Medical Center in Cumming, Georgia

Norton William Milgram, Ph.D., is a professor in the department of psychology and pharmacology at University of Toronto

Kelly Moffat, DVM, is a general practitioner at Mesa Veterinary Hospital in Mesa, Arizona

Lawrence Myers, DVM, MS, Ph.D., is an associate professor of anatomy, physiology, and pharmacology at the College of Veterinary Medicine at Auburn University

Richard Nelson, DVM, DACVIM, is an internist, professor, and department chair in the department of medicine and epidemiology at University of California at Davis

Nancy E. Rawson, Ph.D., is an Associate Member of the Monel Chemical Senses Center, a nonprofit research institute in Philadelphia dedicated to research in the fields of taste, smell, chemical irritation and nutrition.

William W. Ruehl, VMD, Ph.D., DACVP, is director of clinical pathology for Antech Diagnostics, a veterinary laboratory in northern California

Rhonda L. Schulman, DVM, DACVIM, is an assistant professor of small animal medicine at University of Illinois

Wallace Sife, Ph.D., is a psychologist and president of the Association for Pet Loss and Bereavement

George M. Strain, DVM, Ph.D., is associate vice chancellor of the office of research and graduate studies, and professor of neuroscience in the School of Veterinary Medicine at Louisiana State University

William Tranquilli, DVM, MS, DACVA, is a professor of veterinary clinical medicine at University of Illinois

Alice Wolf, DVM, DACVIM, ABVP, is a professor of small animal medicine and surgery in the College of Veterinary Medicine at Texas A&M University

Susan G. Wynn, DVM, is a certified veterinary acupuncturist, the director of the Wynn Clinic for Therapeutic Alternatives in Marietta, Georgia, and the executive director of the Georgia Holistic Veterinary Medical Association and of the Veterinary Botanical Medicine Association

INDEX

Photo credit: Lavor Quin

Amy D. Shojai is a nationally known authority on pet care and behavior. She is the author of more than a dozen award-winning nonfiction pet books and hundreds of articles and columns. Ms. Shojai addresses a wide range of fun-to-serious issues in her work, covering training, behavior, health care, and medical topics.

Ms. Shojai is a founder and past-president of the Cat Writers' Association, and a member of the Dog Writers' Association of America and Association of Pet Dog Trainers. She frequently speaks to groups on a variety of pet-related issues, lectures at writing conferences, and regularly appears on national radio and television in connection with her work. She and her husband live with assorted critters at Rosemont, their thirteen-acre "spread" in north Texas. Ms. Shojai can be reached through her Web site at www.shojai.com.